VAT and the NHS

a technical guide

Martin Kaney, BA, LLB (Hons)

This second edition published September 2016 by

Spiramus Press Ltd
102 Blandford Street
London W1U 8AG
United Kingdom

www.spiramus.com

© Spiramus Press Ltd

Paperback   ISBN 978 1907444 71 5

Digital   ISBN 978 1910151 22 8

This publication is based upon the law as at 30 June 2016.

First edition published 2012

The right of Martin Kaney to be identified as the author of this work has been asserted by him in accordance with the Copyright, Designs and Patents Act, 1988.

Printed and bound in Great Britain by Grosvenor Group, UK

About the author

Martin Kaney is the founder of the online VAT resource, X-VAT.

He has over 30 years' experience in the tax including eight years with HM Customs & Excise and various senior roles with Liaison, RSM Tenon and latterly, Deloitte. He is a graduate of Edinburgh University, a member of the VAT Practitioners Group, a Council Member of the Gerson Lehrman Group, as well as holding an external law degree from Strathclyde University.

He is also the author of *VAT & Government Departments* (Spiramus 2015) and regularly lectures in VAT, training accountancy and legal professionals, as well as presenting courses for ICAS and CIMA.

Acknowledgements

My thanks are due to my VAT colleague, Malcolm Comrie, for his help and technical comments in preparing this edition of *VAT & the NHS* for publication.

Tables of Authorities

Cases

Statutes

Regulations

Other Authorities

Contents

CONTENTS

CONTENTS

1 VALUE ADDED TAX

Value Added Tax is a transaction tax on the supply of goods or services for the purpose of business charged by businesses to consumers as part of sales income. It is a self-assessed indirect tax on consumption, theoretically a tax borne by the final consumer, that is, a person who cannot claim it back. As a transaction tax it is not a tax on profits and the concept of profit has no meaning in VAT; liability is not calculated on net values (as opposed to determination of the amount due to be paid) but rather on the full value of supplies made or received (although, as always in VAT, there are exceptions to the general rule).

The NHS will be charged VAT on its purchases like any other organisation or individual consumer and insofar as it is deemed to be in business or in competition with the private sector it has to charge VAT where appropriate. NHS organisations can recover some of the VAT they are charged under the normal rules and there are special rules for VAT recovery on certain services. The great majority of NHS activities are non-business for VAT purposes and no VAT is chargeable. Equally, irrecoverable VAT incurred on purchases of goods or equipment is a significant cost to NHS organisations.

VAT was introduced in 1973 when the UK joined the then Common Market and it is the principal funding mechanism of the European Union, as well as being used as a form of taxation in up to 150 countries worldwide, including all of the OECD countries except the USA. The current position (while the UK remains a Member State of the European Union) is that VAT in the UK is ultimately governed by EU law (the *Principal VAT Directive 2006/112/EC*). All Member States enact their own domestic legislation interpreting the Directive to give effect to it in that Member State (known as indirect effect). Where there is a conflict the domestic law of the Member State is subordinate to EU law (although taxpayers are entitled to rely on domestic law until it is changed).

In the UK the primary legislation is the Value Added Tax Act 1994 (VAT Act) although there are various other Statutory Instruments and Regulations (notably the *VAT Regulations 1995 SI 1995/2518*), collectively known as secondary legislation. In addition, some HMRC publications have the force of law (tertiary legislation) and amendments are regularly made via the annual Finance Acts (changes to secondary or tertiary legislation can be made at any time).

1.1   The Scope of VAT

The scope of VAT is defined in VAT Act 1994 s.4:

(1) VAT shall be charged on any supply of goods or services made in the United Kingdom, where it is a taxable supply made by a taxable person in the course or furtherance of any business carried on by him.
(2) A taxable supply is a supply of goods or services made in the United Kingdom other than an exempt supply.

Thus the scope of the tax is very wide and includes all activities in the course of business (or "economic activities" as defined in the Principal VAT Directive).

All supplies of goods or services made in the course or furtherance of business are taxable supplies unless they are specifically excluded such as the reduced-rate supplies listed in VAT Act 1994 Schedule 7A, the zero-rated supplies listed in VAT Act 1994 Schedule 8 and the exempt supplies listed in VAT Act 1994 Schedule 9. Exempt supplies are business activities within the scope of the tax but excluded from the charge to tax in s.4 by Schedule 9 and these include supplies of land or property (though this can also be taxable in certain circumstances), education, financial services, welfare and healthcare. Any person can make a taxable supply but only a taxable person (i.e. a legal person registrable under the Act, for example, any person or group of persons, a sole trader, partnership or corporate body), is required (or indeed, able) to charge VAT when making a taxable supply. All NHS organisations are registered for VAT as "bodies governed by public law" (*Principal VAT Directive*).

The scope of the tax is defined by HMRC as:
(1) a supply of goods or services;
(2) which takes place in the UK;
(3) is made by a taxable person (someone who is, or is required to be registered); and
(4) and is made in the course or furtherance of any business carried on or to be carried on by that person.

All four conditions must be met or the transaction or activity is outside the scope of UK VAT. For the NHS the key condition is whether or not an activity is carried on in the course or furtherance of business or whether it is non-business (i.e. a statutory function or carried on for no consideration).

1.2   General Principles

VAT as a tax may be summed up as a value added charge on:

WHO supplies **WHAT** to **WHOM, WHY, WHEN, WHERE** and for **HOW MUCH**...

- the **WHO** is the person who makes the supply – VAT is only chargeable by taxable persons – even then the status of the person making the supply can determine the VAT liability
- the **WHAT** is what is supplied i.e. goods or services – anything which is not a supply of goods is a supply of services (unless there is a defined exclusion or for services no consideration i.e. nothing received in return)
- the **WHOM** is the person who receives the supply of goods or services – the status of the person who receives a supply can determine the VAT liability
- the **WHY** is the purpose of the supply – is it business or non-business?
- the **WHEN** is when the supply becomes chargeable to tax – this is called the tax point and this determines the VAT period in which it should be accounted for – and whether the supply is out of time
- the **WHERE** is where the supply is made (or deemed to be made) – the liability can be affected either by where the supplier is based or where the recipient is based (or whether the supply is one of goods or services)
- the **HOW MUCH** is the consideration for the supply – whatever is received in return i.e. anything received including barter, not just money (although it must be capable of expression as a monetary value)

All of the above are aspects of supply, the fundamental concept of the tax:

WHO? – the person who makes the supply

WHAT? – the type of supply

WHOM? – the recipient of the supply

WHY? – the purpose of the supply

WHEN? – the time of supply

WHERE? – the place of supply

HOW MUCH? – the value of the supply

The VAT liability of any transaction can be analysed (and therefore understood) in the context of these defining questions. If supply is the fundamental concept of the tax, the charge to tax (output tax) arises as a value added charge on a relevant transaction (i.e. within the scope of the tax and a taxable supply).

Tax which is charged out on business income is called output tax (there are currently three positive rates of tax: standard @ 20%; reduced @ 5%; and zero @ 0%). Tax which is incurred on business expenditure is called input tax. The net amounts of income or expenditure (i.e. the relevant sums exclusive of VAT) are called outputs (business income) and inputs (business expenditure) respectively and the net amount payable or repayable in the VAT Return is the amount of credit for input tax allowable (not all input tax is allowable) deducted from the total output tax payable.

Allowable input tax (*VAT Act 1994 s.26*) means VAT incurred which is attributable:

- to taxable supplies of goods and services made in the UK; or
- to supplies made outside the UK which would be taxable supplies if made in the UK (including within and outside the EU); or
- to exempt supplies within the *de minimis* limits (see **Chapter 7. Partial Exemption**).

Input tax attributable to exempt supplies outside the *de minimis* limits is not allowable (more than £7,500 p.a. or more than 50% of the total input tax incurred).

VAT is unique in having the dual output and input perspective. All other taxes (including other indirect taxes) only have a single focus, but in VAT the output tax and input tax implications of any transaction must always be considered because the scope of the tax is so wide. This fundamental aspect of the tax is often overlooked and it is not unusual to find a transaction which has only been considered from either the output or the input perspective but not both simultaneously. Understanding the duality of the tax is the key to understanding the tax itself and making informed decisions.

1.3   The NHS Context

Why is there VAT in the NHS? It may seem counter-productive to have Treasury funds moving from one budget to another as appears to be the case with the NHS and VAT, but within the EU (and while the UK remains a Member State) the UK Government has no powers to change this (even if there was a political will to do so) because VAT is governed by EU law (with which Member States must comply). Public Sector Bodies (or "bodies governed by public law" in EU terminology) must be registered for VAT where they engage in "economic activities" (i.e. business activities for UK VAT purposes), especially where there is any competition with the private sector (*Principal VAT Directive Article 13*).

NHS VAT has two distinct aspects, the first being the special rules for the NHS and Government Departments under VAT Act 1994 s.41 (the Treasury (Contracting-Out) Directions) known as the Contracted-Out Services or COS rules (in relation to non-business activities), the second being Value Added Tax itself, governed by VAT legislation (in relation to business activities). Section 41 is a public policy compensation scheme which only applies in relation to non-business activities. VAT which is refunded under s.41 is not tax (*VAT in the Public Sector and exemptions in the Public Interest* TAXUD/2009/DE/316), but rather a refund of the amount of the tax charged (specifically, it is not input tax which can only be incurred in relation to business activities).

There is no overlap between the VAT regime and the s.41 special legal regime, these are mutually exclusive (and this is acknowledged in *The National Health Service/A Guide to Value Added Tax* (HMRC 2004) at para 5.1.2 – "the Contracted-Out Services Regulations are an entirely separate issue from the normal VAT rules applicable to business activities, and should be treated as such"). To understand VAT in the context of the NHS it is essential to understand this second fundamental duality in the tax in relation to the NHS. Again, this is often overlooked and because in certain situations VAT can apparently be recovered in both contexts, COS eligibility to recover and input tax entitlement on VAT incurred can be confused. The VAT legislation and input tax entitlement always take precedence over the Treasury (Contracting-Out) Directions and eligibility to recover (because UK law is subordinate to EU law while the UK remains a Member State of the EU). The distinction is important because if the VAT incurred is not correctly characterised it may lead to compliance errors and affect the amount of VAT an NHS organisation is able to claim back overall.

These two aspects of VAT in the NHS context merge into a third in relation to capital expenditure on construction or building works. Capital expenditure may be on new construction, on alterations or extensions, or on the refurbishment or repair of existing buildings. This expenditure has to be considered not only from the distinct perspectives of COS and input tax, but also in relation to potential output tax liabilities depending on the circumstances of the project. Because of this VAT in the NHS will be examined in three main areas: the first being non-business activities and contracted-out services; the second, business activities & partial exemption; and the third, capital expenditure and land & property.

VAT & the NHS is intended to be both a reference manual and a practical guide to managing VAT in the NHS. Several convenient acronyms are used, such as VAT for Value Added Tax and COS for Contracted-Out Services. For reference, there is a Glossary of Terms attached at **Appendix 10**, a list of Definitions at **Appendix 11** and a list of References at **Appendix 12**. Many of the areas covered in the text are complex in themselves and *VAT & the NHS* does not attempt to examine all possibilities in all circumstances or to reproduce the full technical guidance or statute. Rather the objective is to identify all of the issues in the tax relevant to the NHS and in a logical analysis explain these from an NHS compliance perspective and in relation to the organisational activities of the NHS (providing further references where appropriate if more detailed information is required).

To read VAT Notices or other VAT guidance referenced in the text:

www.hmrc.gov.uk/thelibrary/publications

To read the full text of UK Statutes referenced in the text:

www.legislation.gov.uk

As always in VAT there are various areas of uncertainty and unresolved issues and this is in the nature of the tax which is constantly evolving through case law and new legislation. *VAT & the NHS* is based on published HMRC and Treasury guidance and policy and on current case law and legislation in force as at 30 June 2016.

At 30 June 2016 the UK was a Member State of the European Union and *VAT & the NHS* analyses the legal position on that basis.

2 ADMINISTRATION

2.1 An NHS VAT Overview

NHS VAT is administered by the NHS Compliance Team, part of the Public Bodies Group of HM Revenue & Customs. The Treasury determines policy in relation to COS and VAT but NHS taxpayers have no direct contact with the Treasury. All contact is with HMRC which administers COS on behalf of the Treasury and implements policy. VAT policy is determined by HMRC in accordance with VAT legislation. VAT policy applies to the NHS subject to VAT legislation in relation to business activities and partial exemption, that is, in relation to output tax and input tax but not in relation to COS. All NHS organisations are taxable persons and all are thus registered for VAT. All NHS organisations are separate taxable persons but HMRC have created three concessionary Divisional Registrations, one for the NHS in England, Scotland and Wales respectively (in Northern Ireland VAT is refunded on supplies of both goods and services under VAT Act 1994 s.99 – see **2.11 Northern Ireland**). The significance of the concessionary Divisional Registrations is that supplies between NHS organisations within a Divisional Registration are disregarded and treated as outside the scope of VAT although supplies between NHS organisations in different Divisional Registrations are treated as supplies subject to VAT in the normal way (see **2.2 Divisional Registrations**).

Like all taxable persons NHS organisations are required to maintain a VAT Account and the figures from the VAT Account are transferred to the online VAT Return each month. The VAT Account is a summary of all transactions in the source ledgers and accounts e.g. the value of taxable and exempt supplies and corresponding output tax, the value of purchases attributable to business activities both taxable and exempt and input tax and COS claimed etc. In addition, adjustments e.g. journals or other adjustments such as the correction of errors are shown in the VAT Account. Whilst not strictly necessary it is also good practice to include non-business income and non-business expenditure (see **3.1.1 The VAT Account**).

All NHS organisations submit monthly online VAT Returns based on calendar months. The VAT Returns are the same as for any other taxable person but NHS organisations also are required to complete a VAT 21 form (to be completed online with the VAT Return) which identifies both the value of input tax claimed and the value of the refund claimed under each COS Heading (see **3.2.10 The VAT Return**). Output tax should be charged at the appropriate rate (standard, reduced or zero) in relation to business activities (e.g. catering and parking etc) and declared on the relevant VAT Return. Input tax should be deducted where applicable and allowable (e.g. VAT incurred in relation to catering or parking etc and an apportionment of VAT incurred in relation to general overheads known as residual input tax). COS entitlement should be quantified according to each individual Heading and claimed on the online VAT 21 (automatically included in the online VAT Return).

Technically, partial exemption calculations should be completed monthly on a provisional basis with an annual adjustment in Month 12 or 13, the March VAT Return due by 30 April or the April VAT Return due by 31 May (not applicable to the business/non-business apportionment calculations). However, as a concession (to the NHS) HMRC allow these calculations to be completed on the basis of annual submissions in arrears. Because this is technically an error, HMRC require an error correction notification to be submitted for approval before allowable input tax can be reclaimed in a VAT Return (i.e. notification of an error on a VAT Return over £10,000; historically, a voluntary disclosure or VAT 652 claim – see **2.5 Error Correction Notifications**). If the calculations are completed on a monthly basis in the appropriate VAT Return, there is no requirement to submit an ECN to HMRC for prior approval because the tax is intended to be self-assessed and inclusion in the correct VAT Return is fully compliant.

NHS VAT has recently been the subject of an HMRC consultation and review with new draft guidance published in October 2015 and March 2016 with a continuing trend of bringing NHS VAT into line with mainstream VAT procedures (historically, the NHS has been treated as a special case with various departures from the normal rules).

2.2 Divisional Registrations

HMRC have created three concessionary Divisional Registrations, one for the NHS in England, Scotland and Wales respectively. The significance of the concessionary Divisional Registrations is that supplies between NHS organisations within a Divisional Registration are disregarded and treated as outside the scope of VAT although supplies between NHS organisations in different Divisional Registrations are treated as supplies subject to VAT in the normal way. Membership in England is not mandatory but it is mandatory as a matter of NHS policy in Scotland and Wales (HMRC cannot compel an NHS organisation to be part of an NHS Divisional Registration because it is a concessionary arrangement).

A body corporate carrying on its business in divisions may register as a Divisional Registration with the approval of HMRC under VAT Act 1994 s.46 and subject to certain conditions (*VAT Notice 700/2/11 Group & Divisional Registration*). All of the Divisions must be registered and all must submit Returns for the same VAT periods but a Divisional Registration under s.46 is a single taxable person whereas all NHS organisations are separate taxable persons in their own right. Further, the Divisional Registration as a body corporate must be fully taxable i.e. it must be *de minimis* for partial exemption as a whole and the NHS does not qualify in relation to that condition.

2.3   Registration & Deregistration

The NHS Compliance Team also manages the registration and deregistration of NHS taxable persons. Mergers, acquisitions and the creation of new legal entities in the NHS are regular occurrences. The only legal entity defined in the VAT Act 1994 is a taxable person under s.3 and a taxable person can be a legal or natural person or persons, including an individual, partnership, corporate body or trust. As "bodies governed by public law" NHS organisations are all separately registered as taxable persons although HMRC can register a single corporate body as a Divisional Registration under s.46 and groups of companies under s.43 as a Group Registration. Both Divisional Registrations and Group Registrations are single taxable persons unlike the concessionary NHS Divisional Registrations (which comprise multiple taxable persons).

Mergers may result in the creation of a new taxable person in which case the predecessors are deregistered. Alternatively, HMRC may treat the merger as an acquisition by one party and retain the existing VAT registration number and taxable person status of that party and deregister the other. Where there is an acquisition or merger in which one party continues the supply of the business and business assets between NHS organisations is disregarded. There is a provision for this in VAT Act 1994 s.49 (Transfer of a Going Concern) but in any case, the supply would be disregarded within a concessionary Divisional Registration. HMRC have not clarified the position where an NHS organisation is not a member of a concessionary Divisional Registration.

All VAT rights and liabilities are transferred to the new legal entity or acquiring party. Although the right of succession was one of the key issues (now decided) in the resolution of Fleming claims (*Fleming (HL 2008)*), HMRC had never previously raised it as an issue in mergers or changes of legal entity in the NHS. All that was required historically was the production of the relevant Statutory Instrument with the VAT Registration documents and in practice any repayments due to the predecessor organisation either of COS or VAT were made to the successor (the right to COS refunds is transferred as a property right as an asset of the predecessor rather than as a transfer of a tax right).

2.4 Appeals & Reviews

Historically, it was the view of HMRC that the NHS as an emanation of the Crown under UK Law (or alternatively an emanation of the state under EU Law) could not appeal to a VAT Tribunal (but nor could penalties be levied for non-compliance). However, the changes in the legal entities in the NHS (e.g. Foundation Trusts) and those in the Health & Social Care Act 2012 combined with the NHS *Fleming (HL 2008)* appeals currently at Tribunal and the new appeals procedure introduced in 2009 mean that NHS taxable persons now enjoy the same rights of appeal (in relation to VAT rather than COS) as any other taxable person (the corollary being that penalties are also applicable). Ultimately, it is a matter for the Tribunals and the Courts to decide jurisdiction i.e. on what basis (VAT) appeals by NHS organisations are valid (COS is not an appealable matter) but the First Tier Tribunals and Upper Tribunal have not rejected the Fleming appeals and some of these have now been decided. The appeals and reconsideration process will therefore be different depending on whether the decision queried or challenged relates to COS or VAT.

2.4.1 COS Appeals

In relation to COS there is no formal right of appeal because refunds under s.41 are made as a matter of public policy rather than as a matter of law. Therefore, the Treasury or HMRC may take a view on any particular area of refund on the basis of policy or interpretation. The only qualification to that is that they still must act in accordance with the duties at public law which govern the conduct of all civil servants and Government Departments (GDs) i.e. they must be fair, reasonable and consistent, they must be open and transparent, any decision must be proportionate and rational, reasons for the decision must be given, and if there is a change of policy information must be provided to those affected by the change and there must an adequate transitional period before the change is implemented.

If a COS decision is to be queried or challenged it should be raised with the Officer who made the decision in the first instance and another Officer should reconsider the decision. If they uphold the original decision the matter can be raised at a management level within the NHS Compliance Team (internal reviews under VAT Act 1994 s.83A only apply to appealable matters listed in s.83 i.e. not COS). There is no appeal directly to the

Treasury. If still not satisfied with the decision, there is nothing further that can be done if the disputed point is purely technical. However, if there is a procedural element e.g. the HMRC decision is anomalous, inconsistent with other decisions or guidance or otherwise unfair, then it is possible to query the decision indirectly as a complaint or procedural impropriety (but this is only likely to be a viable route where the sums involved are significant and there is an obvious error by HMRC).

2.4.2 VAT Appeals
VAT & Duties Tribunals were abolished in 2009 and replaced by a new system of Tax Tribunals with a First Tier Tribunal and Upper Tribunal. Generally, the Upper Tribunal deals with appeals from the First Tier Tribunal and there is then a further right of appeal to the Court of Appeal and then to the Supreme Court. Where matters of EU law are in point a Tribunal or Court can refer questions to the Court of Justice of the European Union in order to obtain its view on the proper interpretation of the relevant EU law (while the UK remains a Member State of the EU).

At the beginning of the process there is a statutory right of internal review under VAT Act 1994 s.83A. This is optional for the taxable person and the review is carried out by a trained review Officer not previously involved in the decision (the review to be completed within 45 days or other agreed period). If the taxable person does not agree with the reviewing Officer's decision, then an appeal can be made to the Tribunal. The internal review is the recommended route if an NHS organisation disagrees with an HMRC decision on VAT. Tribunals are expensive and time consuming and should only be considered in exceptional circumstances such as *Fleming (HL 2008)* although HMRC have recently introduced an Alternative Dispute Resolution procedure as a different way of resolving tax disputes.

2.5 Error Correction Notifications
ECNs are required where there is an error in a previous VAT Return outside the limits below.

Method 1 – if the net value of errors is less than £10,000 or is between £10,000 and £50,000 but does not exceed 1% of outputs (the value of taxable and exempt supplies net of tax – Box 6 of the VAT Return for the period in which the errors were discovered) then the errors may be corrected directly on the VAT return without the requirement to submit an ECN (correction of an error using this Method does not constitute a disclosure for the purposes of VAT Penalties, this must be made separately, if appropriate).

Method 2 – if the net value of errors is between £10,000 and £50,000 and exceeds 1% of outputs (the value of taxable and exempt supplies net of tax

– Box 6 of the VAT Return for the period in which the errors were discovered) or the net value of the errors is greater than £50,000 or the errors were made deliberately then an ECN is required. This can be made in writing or by submission of form VAT 652 to the NHS Compliance Team.

2.5.1   Submissions & Procedures

Error Correction Notifications or claim submissions require authorisation by the taxable Person. This can either be by letter of authority or by VAT 652 Form and these should be signed by a responsible person from the NHS organisation. Option to tax VAT 1614 forms also require authorisation by the taxable Person and should be signed by a responsible person. Form 64-8 is an HMRC general agent's authorisation and a central record is kept of these. If a Form 64-8 is completed and signed by a responsible person, then the agent (i.e. an adviser) does not require any further authorisation for general communications and correspondence. Form 64-8 can be downloaded from the HMRC website (see **Appendix 12 – References**).

2.5.2   Error Penalties

If an NHS organisation takes reasonable care to complete the VAT Return but makes an error despite this, it will not be liable to a penalty. The definition of 'reasonable care' varies according to circumstances but when taking reasonable care HMRC expect taxpayers to:
- make and keep sufficient records to provide a complete and accurate VAT Return;
- update records regularly; and
- take tax seriously and take care to get it right.

An NHS organisation may be liable to a penalty if:
- the VAT Return is inaccurate and correcting this means tax is unpaid, understated, overclaimed or under-assessed; or
- HMRC are not informed within 30 days that a tax assessment is too low

When assessing a penalty HMRC will explain:
- which error or errors made the NHS organisation liable to a penalty;
- the period the penalty applies to;
- the tax amount liable to a penalty;
- the amount of any reduction allowed;
- the amount of any penalty previously assessed for the period;
- the total amount of the penalty for the period; and
- how and where to pay the penalty.

The penalty rate for an inaccurate VAT Return depends on how the error was made. The more serious the reason, the greater the penalty can be. The penalty is calculated as a percentage of the potential lost revenue i.e. the tax unpaid, understated, overclaimed or under-assessed, as a result of taxpayer errors.

If a penalty is a result of a 'careless' error, HMRC can sometimes suspend it for up to two years. If HMRC can suspend a penalty, they will impose certain conditions that will help to avoid making the same error again. If it is not possible to set and agree these conditions a penalty cannot be suspended. If all of the conditions are met at the end of the suspension period HMRC will cancel the penalty provided the taxpayer does not become liable to another penalty during this period. HMRC cannot suspend a penalty that comes from 'deliberate' or 'deliberate and concealed' errors.

2.6   Universities & Further Education Colleges

NHS organisations are frequently involved in joint working projects with Universities and Further Education Colleges, particularly in relation to the training of doctors, nurses and other medical staff and also in relation to medical research.

The supply of training or education by a University or a FEC is an exempt business activity (as an eligible body), whereas for the NHS the training of medical staff is a statutory duty and intrinsically non-business. This means that NHS funding for training etc. is outside the scope of VAT but any payments made to Universities or FECs may be exempt (from the perspective of the University or FEC – it is important to distinguish between the perspectives of the supplier and the recipient – the liability may well be different).

Joint working arrangements are a significant area of risk and have already given rise to the issues in *University of Glasgow (VTD 19052)* which resulted in the Memorandum of Understanding between HMRC and the Department of Health, NHS Employers, the Universities and Colleges Employers Association, the University and Colleges Union, British Medical Association and British Dental Association. Supplies covered by the Memorandum are outside the scope of VAT, but the Memorandum only applies to staff with honorary contracts engaged in both teaching and/or research as well as the delivery of patient care. Any other supplies of staff between an NHS organisation and a University or FEC (or vice versa) are standard-rated. Secondments can only be treated as outside the scope of VAT in limited circumstances, for example, where the recipient organisation pays the salary of the secondee. Where there is a recharge of salary between an NHS organisation and a University or FEC (or vice versa) this will normally be consideration for a standard-rated supply and output tax should be charged (the only exception being under the Memorandum). Universities and FECs are not covered by the concession which applies between GDs and the NHS nor are they part of an NHS Divisional Registration therefore the normal rules apply.

The normal rules also apply to other types of joint working, for example, the provision of accommodation or shared accommodation or joint research projects. Any supply of goods or services between an NHS organisation and a University or FEC (or vice versa) will be subject to VAT in the normal way (e.g. recharges of utilities, supplies of drugs or equipment, rent of premises). Universities and FECs make predominantly exempt supplies with a minor proportion of non-business activities and taxable supplies. Generally, allowable input tax recovery will be minimal (unless directly attributable to a specific taxable supply). This means that any VAT charged by an NHS organisation to a University or FEC will generally be mostly irrecoverable.

2.7 Local Authorities & Section 33 Bodies

NHS organisations are involved in a range of community partnership ventures with local authorities (and other s.33 bodies such as fire and police authorities). NHS Act 2006 s.82 requires NHS organisations and local authorities to co-operate in the promotion of community health and welfare (such as community partnerships, pooled budgets, joint ventures and NHS LIFT). An example of this the Better Care Fund and projects arising therefrom.

VAT Act 1994 s.33 provides for the refund of VAT to local authorities, police and fire Authorities and certain other organisations on the purchase of goods and services in relation to non-business activities. This is a more advantageous position than under s.41 and where the NHS and local authorities collaborate HMRC generally allow recovery under the regime of the lead partner.

However, care should be exercised in relation to transactions between the partners. Supplies of goods or services (including supplies of staff) are subject to the normal rules. Certain joint property transactions can be very complex and the sequence of transactions can have a significant impact, for example, land transfers from one partner combined with construction services procured by the other may give rise to an irrecoverable VAT charge (but if the sequence of transactions is reversed the VAT charge may be recoverable). The complexity of the tax position reflects both the underlying legal position and the overlap of VAT regimes.

2.8 Charities, Social Enterprises & RSLs

NHS organisations may enter into partnerships with charities, Social Enterprises or Registered Social Landlords (RSLs). Charities other than Trust Charities are separate organisations and therefore no COS entitlement arises. As above, any supplies of goods or services (including supplies of staff) are subject to the normal rules.

Charities often make donations or contributions to specific NHS projects. These are outside the scope of VAT and may relate to building projects or the purchase, letting on hire or repair of relevant goods. Charities generally make predominantly exempt supplies of welfare and care, although there may also be non-business activities. There has been an increasing trend for charities to take on the health and welfare functions of local authorities as part of the strategy to integrate the health and social care provisions of the NHS, local authorities and not-for-profit organisations (for example, palliative care charities). This can give rise to VAT issues because there are three separate VAT regimes in conflict, s.41, s.33 and the normal VAT regime.

Charities qualify for a series of zero-rating reliefs e.g. in relation to the purchase of aids for the handicapped, the purchase of medical and scientific equipment, advertising and the sale of donated goods. Social Enterprises may be defined as businesses that trade for a social purpose but that includes private businesses as well as charities and social firms. A Social Enterprise may not have charitable status and therefore will not qualify for the VAT reliefs available to charities; it may have the same VAT profile as any other private sector business.

NHS organisations may also enter into partnerships or joint ventures with RSLs e.g. sheltered housing for disabled people. An option to tax is disapplied in relation to any grant of land to be used for the construction of dwellings or a relevant residential purpose by a relevant housing association (RSL). Zero-rating applies to the supply of services to a relevant housing association in the course of conversion of a non-residential building (or part thereof) to a dwelling or for a relevant residential purpose (see **Chapter 10. Land & Property**).

However, this does not include the separate supplies of professional services such as architectural or surveying services, or the hire of goods or equipment e.g. scaffolding, nor does it include subcontractors' services (because these are not supplied directly to the relevant housing association). Care should be exercised in relation to property transactions. The complexity of the tax position reflects both the underlying legal position and the overlap of VAT regimes.

2.9 Scotland

The NHS in Scotland is the responsibility of the Scottish Government, accountable to the Scottish Parliament. It is organised into 14 Health Boards (there are no NHS Trusts – these were abolished in 2004) supported by function-based Special Health Boards. In Frameworks Scotland NHS Scotland has a procurement facility process similar to Procure21+ (Frameworks Scotland) but the Scottish Government has created the Scottish Futures Trust (SFT) as an alternative to the Private Finance Initiative to invest in public sector infrastructure in Scotland, including NHS construction and building new NHS hospitals as non-profit distribution projects. The "hub" initiative (loosely modelled on NHS LIFT) is also the responsibility of the SFT and aims to create a series of joint working projects across Scotland involving the NHS, local authorities and community partnerships.

The difference is primarily organisational and structural. VAT Act 1994 s.41 applies in Scotland in the same way as in England and Wales and there is an NHS Scotland Divisional Registration (see **2.2 Divisional Registrations**). Supplies of goods or services between NHS Scotland and NHS England or Wales are liable to VAT in the normal way except where they are intrinsically non-business i.e. NHS healthcare, NHS education and training and the provision of NHS accommodation.

2.10 Wales

The Welsh Assembly Government is responsible for health and social care in Wales, accountable to the Welsh Assembly. NHS Wales comprises seven Health Boards and three NHS Trusts. As with Scotland the difference is primarily organisational and structural. VAT Act 1994 s.41 applies in the same way and there is an NHS Wales Divisional Registration.

2.11 Northern Ireland

In Northern Ireland health services and social care are integrated and are the responsibility of the Department of Health, Social Services and Public Safety (DHSSPS), accountable to the Northern Ireland Assembly. Under VAT Act 1994 s.99 all VAT incurred by the DHSSPS (on both goods and services) in relation to the Non-Business Activities of the Department is refundable. VAT Act 1994 s.41 therefore does not apply and the majority of *VAT & the NHS* is not relevant to Northern Ireland (only the references to supplies of goods and services by an NHS organisation, output tax and partial exemption).

2.12 Cost Sharing Exemption

Following consultation in 2011, Principal VAT Directive Article 132(1)(f) (The VAT Cost Sharing Exemption) was introduced into UK Law via the Finance Act 2012. The exemption can be used by organisations such as the NHS (via a form of shared services agreement), charities, Universities and FECs or RSLs to make efficiency savings by working together to achieve economies of scale. Currently, a VAT charge between members of shared services may arise creating a barrier to the sharing of services. The exemption could, in certain circumstances, obviate this VAT charge, although the amendments to s.33 in 2015 to extend relief to NDPBs and certain charities resolves the issue where the amendments apply (see **Chapter 5 Contracted-Out Services**).

The Principal VAT Directive sets out the following conditions for Cost Sharing Exemption:

- the cost sharing group must be independent;
- members of a cost sharing group must make exempt and/or Non-Taxable supplies;
- supplies by the cost sharing group to its members must be at cost;
- the services supplied by the group to its members must be 'directly necessary' for the members' exempt and/or Non-Taxable supplies; and
- cost sharing, using the exemption, must not cause a distortion of competition.

ADMINSTRATION

3 ACCOUNTING FOR VAT

3.1 VAT Compliance

The primary objective of VAT accounting for the NHS is compliance on the "right tax at the right time" principle. There is never an apportionment of output tax, it is always payable in full but there may be an apportionment of the VAT incurred by an NHS organisation between its business activities and non-business activities, firstly as input tax and then as COS. Input tax is fully recoverable where attributable to taxable business supplies but it cannot be recovered where attributable to exempt business supplies. Where the VAT incurred cannot be attributed directly to business activities or taxable or exempt supplies, it must be apportioned. Essentially, output tax is straightforward according to the VAT liability of the supplies made, but calculating how much of the VAT incurred can be reclaimed either as COS or input tax is a more complex process.

3.1.1 The VAT Account

Regulation 32 (*VAT Regulations 1995 SI 1995/2518*) provides that every taxable person must keep a VAT Account:

- the VAT Account is to be divided into separate parts for each prescribed accounting period (i.e. VAT Return period);
- the VAT Account is to be divided into two parts, the VAT payable portion and the VAT allowable portion;
- the VAT payable portion includes a total of all output tax due, including tax on acquisitions from other Member States, and all corrections or adjustments allowed or required in the VAT Regulations; and
- the VAT allowable portion includes a total of all input tax allowable under VAT Act 1994 s.26, including tax allowable on acquisitions from other Member States, and all corrections or adjustments allowed or required in the VAT Regulations.

Keeping a VAT Account is a statutory requirement but it is also the key to a fully compliant VAT accounting system. A comprehensive and compliant VAT Account is an effective mechanism to ensure that an accurate declaration of VAT is made. This not only reduces the risk of an error giving rise to potential penalties but should also downgrade an organisation's risk status according to HMRC criteria (potentially reducing the frequency of HMRC visits, for example).

The inclusion of s.41 refunds in the VAT Account is not mandatory because COS is outside the scope of VAT but it is good practice to include all income and all expenditure. In addition to output tax and input tax calculated under Regulation 32 this also allows for the completion of the VAT 21, current business/non-business apportionment, the inclusion of any other relevant adjustments (such as an approved error correction notification) and the final calculation of VAT due for the period plus any COS refund to be claimed.

3.2 Compliance Checklist

The basic compliance checks for the preparation of a VAT Return are set out below:

3.2.1 Preliminaries

Income – ensure that all income (including cash income) is recorded in the VAT Account whatever the source or liability – include all central funding and grants as well as income from business activities or charges to the public.

Expenditure – ensure that all expenditure is recorded in the VAT Account whatever the activity or purpose – include all expenditure and purchases.

Liability – having checked that all income and all expenditure has been included in the VAT Account the VAT liability of each income stream or line of expenditure should be reviewed to ensure that it is correctly characterised i.e. is the income consideration for a taxable or exempt supply, and if taxable, at which rate? – is it non-business or otherwise outside the scope of VAT? – is the expenditure attributable to a business activity, and if so, taxable or exempt? – is it attributable to non-business activities? – or is the income or expenditure non-attributable or partially attributable?

3.2.2 Outputs

Output Tax – ensure that all output tax charged or chargeable on standard-rated taxable business activities is identified and included.

Tax Invoices – ensure that all sales invoices are retained (for six years) – electronic storage is an option.

Reduced-Rate – ensure that all reduced-rate income from taxable business activities is identified and that output tax is charged at the correct rate.

Zero-Rated – ensure that all zero-rated income from taxable business activities is identified and that output tax is not charged.

Exempt Supplies – ensure that all income from exempt business activities is identified and included and that output tax is not charged.

Bad Debt Relief – ensure that any claims for bad debt relief are included.

Credit Notes – ensure that a credit note is created for any credit adjustment arising where a debtor has been overcharged (if applicable).

3.2.3   Inputs

Input Tax – ensure that all allowable input tax attributable to business activities is identified and claimed where attributable to taxable supplies.

Tax Invoices – ensure that all purchase invoices have been retained (for six years) – electronic storage is an option.

Zero-Rated Purchases – ensure that zero-rating has been correctly applied by the supplier for any other purchases where appropriate.

Charitable Funds (Zero-Rating) – ensure that zero-rating has been correctly applied by the supplier to any purchases of qualifying equipment or services where these have been purchased with donated or charitable funds (see **12.5 Charitable Funds**).

Zero-Rating Certificates – ensure that these are issued and retained where appropriate (see **12.5 Charitable Funds**).

Reduced-Rate Purchases – ensure that the reduced-rate has been correctly applied by the supplier for any other purchases where appropriate.

Debit Notes – ensure that a debit note is created for any debit adjustment arising from a creditor overcharge (if applicable).

3.2.4   Tax Invoices

A Tax Invoice is the legal document which taxable persons must retain (for six years) as evidence of input tax entitlement (HMRC also require tax invoices to be retained for COS claims – although electronic storage is an option). A taxable person must supply another taxable person with a tax invoice where there has been a taxable supply. The requirement does not arise in relation to exempt supplies or non-business activities. If an NHS organisation makes a taxable supply to another taxable person, then a tax invoice must be issued. There is no corresponding requirement where supplies are made to unregistered persons or private individuals e.g. cash income (but a taxable person is entitled to receive a tax invoice for a cash purchase from an NHS organisation if appropriate and this should be provided upon request).

A valid tax invoice requires:
- a sequential unique reference number
- time of supply i.e. tax point
- date of issue
- name, address and VAT registration number of supplier
- name and address of recipient
- description of goods or services supplied

- quantity of goods or extent of services, rate of VAT and amount payable excluding VAT
- unit price (if applicable)
- gross amount excluding VAT
- rate of any discount offered
- total amount of VAT chargeable

In certain circumstances self-billed invoices may be issued (where the recipient prepares the tax invoice on behalf of the supplier). Prior approval from HMRC is not required but certain conditions must be complied with (see *VAT Notice 700/62*). Also where the consideration does not exceed £250 and the supply is within the UK a "less detailed" or simplified tax invoice can be issued (e.g. petrol receipts etc). All that is required for a simplified tax invoice is the name, address and VAT registration number of supplier, the time of supply, description of the goods or services, the total amount payable including VAT, the gross amount payable including VAT and the VAT rate applicable (see *VAT Notice 700*).

3.2.5   EU Supplies

EU Removals (Goods) – any removals of goods to other Member States should be checked for the correct treatment (zero-rated when supplied to VAT registered businesses in another Member State) (see **Chapter 11. International VAT**).

EU Acquisitions (Goods) – any acquisition of goods from within the EU should be checked for the correct treatment (Box 2 of the VAT Return) – if the acquisition relates to a taxable supply or is recoverable as COS (potentially as goods incidental to an eligible service) then VAT should be reclaimed either as input tax or COS in Box 4 of the VAT Return (net value in Boxes 7 and 9) (see **Chapter 11. International VAT**).

EU Reverse Charge (Services) – supplies of international services made (within the EU) – special care should be exercised over the supply of services made within the EU – there are complex rules on place of supply which determine in which Member State the VAT liability arises – where the place of supply is deemed to be another Member State the supply is outside the scope of UK VAT (Box 6 of the VAT Return) and the recipient would be required to account for the tax as a reverse charge (see **Chapter 11. International VAT**).

EU Reverse Charge (Services) – supplies of international services received (from within the EU) – special care should be exercised over the supply of services received from within the EU – there are general and special rules on the place of supply which determine in which Member State the VAT liability arises – where the place of supply is deemed to be the UK the VAT liability (output tax and input tax if appropriate) would have to be declared in the VAT Return (Boxes 1, 4, 6 & 7) (see **Chapter 11. International VAT**).

3.2.6   Non-EU Supplies

Exports (Goods) – any transactions outside the EU should be checked – exports of goods outside the EU are zero-rated provided that appropriate evidence of export is obtained and there would be a corresponding input tax entitlement under VATA 1994 s.26 (see **Chapter 11. International VAT**).

Imports (Goods) – any transactions from outside the EU should be checked – there are various provisions related to the relief of VAT on the importation of goods but normally VAT would be payable on importation – any input tax entitlement would be based on the relevant import documentation (see **Chapter 11. International VAT**).

Non-EU Reverse Charge (Services) – supplies of international services made (outside the EU) – special care should be exercised over the supply of services outside the EU – these will normally be outside the scope of VAT (rather than zero-rated) but there will nevertheless be a corresponding entitlement to input tax under VAT Act 1994 s.26 provided the supply is attributable to a taxable business activity (see **Chapter 11. International VAT**).

Non-EU Reverse Charge (Services) – supplies of international services received (from outside the EU) – special care should be exercised over the supply of services from outside the EU – with few exceptions the place of supply will be the UK and the VAT liability (output tax and input tax if appropriate) would have to be declared in the VAT Return (Boxes 1, 4, 6 & 7) (see **Chapter 11. International VAT**).

3.2.7   Contracted-Out Services

Contracted-Out Services – ensure that all COS entitlement for the period is identified and claimed.

EU & Non-EU Reverse Charge (COS) – include any COS entitlement arising from the output tax declared on eligible services received from either another Member State within the EU or outside (see **Chapter 11. International VAT**).

COS Underclaims – ensure that any COS underclaims for earlier periods are included (provided in time i.e. by 31 July following the end of the financial year).

COS Overclaims – ensure that any COS overclaims for earlier periods are included (HMRC do not apply the Treasury time limits to COS overclaims and will accept these out of time).

Capital Interims – ensure COS is claimed at the appropriate percentage on interim building certificates where an overall recoverable percentage has been identified (e.g. by advisers or in ProCure21 or ProCure21+) and, if appropriate, approved by HMRC.

Business/Non-Business COS Restriction – this should be completed and included in the period following the end of the financial year (the April VAT Return due by 31 May) in conjunction with the partial exemption annual adjustment (see **Chapter 7. Partial Exemption**).

3.2.8   Business Activities & Partial Exemption

Business/Non-Business Apportionment – complete the business/non-business apportionment for the period – this is a provisional monthly calculation and is subject to a longer period annual adjustment and it is also a necessary precursor to the partial exemption calculation – see **Chapter 6. Business Activities & Chapter 7. Partial Exemption**).

Partial Exemption – complete the partial exemption calculation for the period – this is a provisional monthly calculation and is subject to a longer period annual adjustment after the end of the financial year (unless a Combined Method has been agreed with HMRC – effective from 1 January 2011 – see **4.2 Business/Non-Business Apportionment**).

Business/Non-Business Annual Adjustment – this should be completed and included in the period following the end of the financial year (the April VAT Return due by 31 May) as a precursor to the partial exemption annual adjustment (unless a Combined Method has been agreed with HMRC – effective from 1 January 2011 – see **4.2 Business/Non-Business Apportionment**).

Partial Exemption Annual Adjustment – this should be completed and included in the period following the end of the financial year (the April VAT Return due by 31 May) – all of the monthly Partial Exemption calculations are provisional (unless a Combined Method has been agreed with HMRC – effective from 1 January 2011 – see **4.2 Business/Non-Business Apportionment**).

Partial Exemption *de minimis* – check the *de minimis* limit does not apply – if it does apply then all input tax attributable to exempt business activities may be recovered up to a maximum of £7,500 p.a. (unless a Combined

Method has been agreed with HMRC – effective from 1 January 2011 – see **4.2 Business/Non-Business Apportionment**).

Capital Items Adjustment – identify and include any capital Items – if appropriate complete the capital items adjustment (see **10.4 Capital Goods Scheme**) – the interval adjustment should be carried out in the May VAT Return due by 30 June.

3.2.9   Finalisation

Journals – ensure that all journals have been taken into account.

Adjustments – a final check on adjustments – depending on which financial year it relates to a miscellaneous adjustment may have an effect on the annual adjustment for the current financial year or it may fall outside – if so, it may necessitate a further adjustment to an earlier financial year if the value is material.

VAT Account – a final check that all income, expenditure, supplies and activities, journals and adjustments have been taken into account.

Error Correction Notifications – check that any approved ECNs are not included – these are dealt with separately outside the VAT Returns because they are corrections to an earlier period.

Business/Non-business Apportionment – check the business/non-business apportionment calculations.

Partial Exemption – check the partial exemption calculations.

VAT 21 – complete and submit the VAT 21 online.

VAT Return – complete and submit the VAT Return online.

3.2.10   The VAT Return

The VAT Return is the legal declaration of tax payable and tax allowable in any period. The content of a VAT Return is defined in Regulation 39 (*VAT Regulations 1995 SI 1995/2518*) and the definition does not include refunds under VAT Act 1994 s.41 (because these are not tax).

The VAT payable and VAT allowable portions of the VAT Account (Regulation 32 above) are carried through to the VAT Return:

In the box opposite the legend "VAT due in this period on sales and other outputs" shall be entered the aggregate of all the entries in the VAT payable portion of that part of the VAT account which relates to the prescribed accounting period for which the return is made, except that the total of the output tax due in that period on acquisitions from other

Member States shall be entered instead in the box opposite the legend "VAT due in this period on acquisitions from other EC Member States".

In the box opposite the legend "VAT reclaimed in this period on purchases and other inputs" (including acquisitions from other Member States) shall be entered the aggregate of all the entries in the VAT allowable portion of that part of the VAT account which relates to the prescribed accounting period for which the return is made.

The VAT Return is the legal declaration of output tax and input tax due under the statutory VAT Regulations and the VAT Act 1994. Because s.41 refunds are outside the scope of VAT and do not form part of a Value Added Tax Return the inclusion of COS claims in the VAT Return is an administrative practice only (for the processing of repayments by HMRC).

The VAT 21 (headed "Certificate of VAT Reclaimed Under Section 41(3) of the VAT Act 1994") is a form devised by HMRC to itemise COS refunds claimed in any prescribed period (technically, it is not part of a VAT Return but is submitted at the same time). From 1 April 2010 VAT 21s and VAT Returns are submitted online and HMRC have produced a guide to assist (*A step by step guide to VAT online filing for Government Departments and NHS Trusts* (HMRC 2010)). The total sum for each COS Heading is calculated and submitted online in an analytical table. The VAT 21 also includes the total amount of "Input tax on business activities" and the total amount claimed as COS is added to the input tax claim and automatically entered in Box 4 as part of the online submission process. Box 4 is calculated automatically from the VAT 21 entries. Boxes 3 and 5 are also automatically calculated when the remainder of the online VAT 100 has been completed.

The submission is finalised by electronic declarations that the information is "true and complete" with the obligatory warning that a "false declaration can result in prosecution". A VAT Return is a legal declaration and a significant responsibility for the authorised person who electronically "signs" or authorises it and it should be regarded as such.

3.2.11 VAT Management Plan

Creating a VAT Management Plan is good practice and enables the efficient management of VAT in relation to core activities and prudent VAT planning (it normally also results in improved levels of VAT recovery). It enables an NHS organisation to manage its relationship with HMRC (and professional advisers) and reduce risk. The plan should set out clear objectives in relation to the scheduling of core work and reviews, compliance checking procedures and planning opportunities.

A VAT Management Plan should include the following (on a financial year basis):

Update Meetings – there should be regular meetings with budget holders or finance managers to discuss developments and to update the VAT Management Plan for the coming financial year.

Compliance Systems – source data capture should be reviewed and checked to ensure that all data feeds through and that all formulas or calculations are correct and consistent.

VAT Account Review – the VAT Account should be checked to ensure that all formulas or calculations are correct and consistent.

VAT 21s Review – the VAT 21s should be checked to ensure that all formulas or calculations are correct and consistent.

VAT Returns Review – the VAT Returns should be checked to ensure that all formulas or calculations are correct and consistent.

COS Reviews – monthly, quarterly or annual schedule for reviewing COS claims – these should be planned in advance for the coming financial year.

July Deadline – backup reviews should be planned to ensure that all COS underclaims and overclaims have been finalised for 31 July each year.

Sales/Debtors Review – a review of outputs liabilities should be completed with particular emphasis on any new income streams – end of financial year.

Procurement Review – all capital expenditure on equipment, managed services contracts etc should be reviewed including any planned or future expenditure – with particular emphasis on any new procurements arising within the financial year.

Capital Planning Review – review the organisation's capital plans as far ahead as these are available e.g. three to five years if possible – this will enable informed consideration of the VAT implications on potentially significant expenditure to be undertaken at the earliest possible stage – in turn timeous VAT advice informs the decision making process.

Cold Takeaway Food – ensure the annual sample for the catering adaptation is completed – end of financial year.

Partial Exemption – review of PEX percentages – end of financial year.

Business Activities – review BA percentages e.g. the catering staff & visitors/patients ratio – end of financial year.

Capital Goods Scheme – review of CGS percentages and calculations – end of financial year.

Reduced Rate Fuel – this should be checked with Estates to ensure that all reliefs are up to date – end of financial year.

Updates & Information – the plan should include regular scheduled updates – advising of any significant changes with NHS implications – quarterly or end of financial year.

4 NON-BUSINESS ACTIVITIES

4.1 Non-Business Activities

Any income, transaction or activity which falls outside the scope of VAT Act 1994 s.4 is non-business (and thus outside the scope of VAT). Approx. 98% of NHS activities overall are non-business activities and outside the scope of VAT. Taxable business activities such as catering and parking represent approx. 1% of NHS activities and exempt private healthcare also represents approx. 1%. NHS legislation was summarised and consolidated in The National Health Service Act 2006. The NHS has three principal statutory duties: the provision of NHS healthcare; the provision of NHS accommodation e.g. hospitals or clinics etc; and, medical and dental clinical education. When provided for no consideration to the person receiving the supply or supplied within the NHS (irrespective of Divisional Registration) these activities are always non-business.

The main non-business activities of the NHS include:
- the supply of medical, dental and optical care or treatment to NHS patients (including drugs or any other goods or services supplied in the course of care or treatment etc). Care or treatment of NHS patients includes catering, hairdressing, laundry services, dressings, patients' clothing, the supply of prostheses and other appliances etc, occupational and other therapy and laboratory services etc.;
- the provision of hospital and other NHS accommodation (but not to external contractors such as GPs or dental practices);
- clinical education for the training of doctors, dentists, nurses and other medical staff (including in partnership or collaboration with Universities or other teaching institutions);
- the supply of drugs or other items supplied on prescription when dispensed in an NHS hospital to NHS patients (inpatients or outpatients);
- the supply of medical care or treatment under the Road Traffic Act; and
- the supply of medical care or treatment to non-EU patients (under a reciprocal health agreement).

Other minor non-business activities include:
- the first supply of NHS medical notes to solicitors, insurance companies and other interested bodies; and
- the supply of residential accommodation to staff under a Whitley Council agreement (at a subsidised and uneconomic rent).

HMRC have created three concessionary Divisional Registrations in England, Scotland and Wales. The effect of this is to treat NHS England, Scotland and Wales each as if it were a single taxable person (irrespective of the multiple separate legal entities which are members of the Divisional Registration). Supplies of any kind, including goods or services, within each concessionary Divisional Registration are treated as outside the scope of VAT because they are considered to be internal to the taxable person and are therefore disregarded (see **2.2 Divisional Registrations**).

Income from sources such as NHS funding, donations, charitable funds, grants etc. is outside the scope of VAT because it is not consideration for a supply (in the course or furtherance of any business). In *Vereniging Noordelijke Land en Tuinbouw Organisatie (CJEU C-515/07)* the Court of Justice of the European Union has created an intermediate concept of non-economic organisational "business" even though the activities of the organisation may be non-business or outside the scope of VAT. *Vereniging Noordelijke Land en Tuinbouw Organisatie* ended the use of the *Lennartz Mechanism (Lennartz (CJEU C-97/90))* in relation to NHS non-business activities. The Lennartz Mechanism allowed taxable persons to claim 100% of input tax at the time of purchase or acquisition of an asset and any non-business use was accounted for as a taxable self-supply over the life of the asset i.e. the taxable person charged itself proportionate output tax as an alternative to claiming a proportion of the input tax. From 22 January 2010 the Lennartz Mechanism is only available for a combination of business activities and private purposes (i.e. as an individual or for staff) wholly outside the taxable person's enterprise or undertaking (*HMRC Brief 2/10*).

The Treasury has published a list of activities which even if non-business were deemed by Direction to be business activities under s.41(2) when carried out by the NHS whether or not they fall under VAT Act 1994 s.4. Section 41(2) was repealed in Finance Act 2012 but it still applies to supplies between GDs. HMRC take the view that this will not result in any material change to the treatment of business activities in the NHS. The listed activities are only relevant where there is a consideration payable by the person receiving the supply and the supply is outside the NHS e.g. to the general public (catering or car parking) or to private patients (medical services) or GPs (rental of practice accommodation). Bodies governed by public law are treated as taxable persons where they engage in economic activities which may be in competition with private sector providers and the Direction was a mechanism to address any areas of uncertainty by deeming them to be business. After Finance Act 2012 this is now addressed by the insertion of s.41A to align s.41 with EU law (see **Appendix 1**). Any activity which is an economic activity under the Principal VAT Directive or falls under s.4 of the Act would have been a business activity irrespective of the Direction in any case but the change is intended to clarify the position in UK law.

4.2 Business/Non-Business Apportionment

Non-business activities are important in the NHS because although there is no tax entitlement for deductible VAT i.e. allowable input tax, there is a corresponding entitlement to claim s.41 refunds under the Treasury Direction in relation to the specified contracted-out services (it is a condition of eligibility that the VAT incurred is not for a "business purpose" i.e. it must be attributable to the non-business activities of the organisation). If VAT incurred is not wholly and exclusively attributable to non-business activities and is partly attributable to business activities (taxable or exempt) then an apportionment must be carried out both to determine the amount of allowable input tax and to restrict any COS claimed in relation to business activities (normally in relation to exempt business activities).

There was a change in the law in relation to business/non-business apportionment effective from 1 January 2011. The current default position is that the business/non-business apportionment is separate from the partial exemption calculation and should be carried out first on a basis determined by the taxpayer but which must result in a fair and reasonable attribution of input tax to taxable supplies (*VAT Notice 706/1*).

Technically, the method the taxpayer uses to calculate the business/non-business apportionment does not require the approval of HMRC (there is no provision in law which requires that HMRC approve a business/non-business apportionment method of itself) but, in practice, HMRC approve the method indirectly by approving the resulting input tax claimed as a fair and reasonable attribution to taxable supplies (it is the policy of HMRC not to agree methods of business/non-business apportionment where there is also an exempt element). The partial exemption calculation is then completed. If a Special Method of Partial Exemption (PESM) is used that requires the written approval of HMRC. Alternatively, the Standard Method can be used without the prior approval of HMRC but since this is generally disadvantageous in the NHS the use of an appropriate Special Method is recommended.

From 1 January 2011 a Combined Method provision was introduced (*VAT Notice 706/1 Partial Exemption*) which means that the business/non-business apportionment and partial exemption calculations may be combined into a single calculation subject to the approval of HMRC. HMRC will still agree special methods in relation to business/non-business apportionment but only where there are no exempt supplies (limited application in the NHS). Where there are exempt supplies HMRC will only agree a Combined Method (or a separate PESM). The Combined Method is a simplification which has administrative benefits both for HMRC (only a single approval required) and certain taxpayers e.g. charities and educational bodies (but not necessarily the NHS). There is no requirement to carry out a separate attribution for exempt supplies and non-business activities and similarly there is no *de minimis* calculation in the Combined Method (therefore exempt input tax up to £7,500.00 p.a. may be lost if a Combined Method is used and the organisation is *de minimis*).

Although a simplified approach may be advantageous for some NHS organisations in certain circumstances there is a general rule in VAT that the simpler the calculation, the less advantageous the result to the taxpayer (the Capital Banding Scheme is another example of this), therefore care should be exercised in deciding which method(s) of apportionment should be used. HMRC published a Framework for these calculations in October 2013 (see **Chapter 6. Business Activities** and **Chapter 7. Partial Exemption**), but the default position, which is established practice, may well achieve the best result for the NHS taxpayer. Historically, the NHS Compliance Team or its predecessors have not generally agreed business/non-business apportionment methods or required special methods of partial exemption to be formally approved. In practice, the methods are agreed and approved indirectly when HMRC approves the annual business activities and partial exemption claims. And because the NHS Compliance Team does not accept business activities claims without a corresponding partial exemption calculation these calculations must be completed at the same time in any case, but still technically separate (see **Chapter 6.** and **Chapter 7.** for a typical NHS business/non-business apportionment & partial exemption method).

5 CONTRACTED-OUT SERVICES

Contracted-out services (COS) is a Treasury refund mechanism of the amount of the VAT incurred on eligible services under VAT Act 1994 s.41(3). It is a form of funding and theoretically the Treasury budgets for amounts recoverable as COS in funding the NHS and Government Departments. HMRC administers COS recovery on behalf of the Treasury. It is important to reiterate that COS refunds are outside the scope of VAT and are not tax, specifically not input tax (i.e. there is no entitlement in tax law to receive the refund) and there is no overlap between the s.41 special legal regime and the VAT regime. The VAT regime is governed by UK law giving indirect effect to EU law whereas the COS regime is a compensation scheme arising from public policy in UK law (and while the UK remains a Member State of the EU, subordinate to EU law).

There are currently seven similar compensation schemes in the 28 Member States of the EU (*VAT in the Public Sector and exemptions in the Public Interest* TAXUD/2009/DE/316) including Austria, Denmark, Finland, France, Portugal, Spain and Sweden (eight in total including the UK). There are also other versions of VAT public sector compensation schemes outside the EU, notably in Canada, Australia and New Zealand. This is unlikely to be affected by the UK leaving the EU. Indeed, the opposite is the case because it is a wholly domestic provision. Previously, the European Commission has expressed concerns about such compensation schemes and expressed the view that they breach the EU's competition rules. This had placed a question mark over the long term future of s.41 refunds but when the UK leaves the EU the Commission would have no locus in relation to s.41.

5.1 Background

COS was introduced in 1983 as a result of government policy to open up the public sector to private sector competition in various areas of activity. Private sector organisations charging VAT for their services would have been at a competitive disadvantage against internal public sector providers which did not. The NHS and GDs were encouraged to contract-out services to the private sector which would have traditionally been performed in-house. It was recognised that many of these services would be subject to VAT and where they were acquired for 'non-business' purposes, the non-reclaimable VAT could act as a disincentive to contracting-out. The solution was to refund the VAT incurred on the charges by the private sector providers but only in limited areas and only for services (although s.41(3) actually refers to "goods or services").

It was decided to compensate the NHS (and GDs) by a direct refund mechanism, which is provided for in section 41(3) of the VAT Act 1994. Under this provision, the Treasury issues Directions, commonly known as the 'Contracting-Out Directions' which lists both the NHS organisations and GDs eligible to claim refunds of VAT, and the services on which VAT can be refunded. The most recent Treasury Directions date from 2 December 2002 (see **Appendix 2** & **Appendix 3**) although current revisions are pending. It contains a List of Eligible Services (see **Appendix 4**), a List of business activities (see **Appendix 5**) and a List of Eligible Departments (see **Appendix 6**). Treasury Directions are regularly published in the London, Edinburgh and Belfast Gazettes and the pending revisions will not take effect until published in the Gazettes (or on the HMRC website).

5.2   VAT Act 1994 section 41

Section 41(3) provides:

(3)   Where VAT is chargeable on the supply of goods or services to a Government department, on the acquisition of any goods by a Government department from another Member State or on the importation of any goods by a Government department from a place outside the Member States and the supply, acquisition or importation is not for the purpose—
   a.   of any business carried on by the department, or
   b.   of a supply by the department which, by virtue of section 41A, is treated as a supply in the course or furtherance of a business, then, if and to the extent that the Treasury so direct and subject to subsection (4) below, the Commissioners shall, on a claim made by the department at such time and in such form and manner as the Commissioners may determine, refund to it the amount of the VAT so chargeable.

(Reproduced in full at **Appendix 1**)

There are four conditions for eligibility for COS recovery:
(1)   the services are listed in the Treasury Refund Directions;
(2)   the services are not for a business purpose;
(3)   the historical capability to perform the service in-house existed anywhere within Government or the NHS (anywhere within Government rather within an individual NHS organisation or GD); and
(4)   the claim must be made within four months of the end of the relevant financial year i.e. by 31 July (previously 30 June) following the 31 March each year.

All of the conditions must be satisfied before an amount of VAT charged can be reclaimed as COS (for the purposes of s.41 and NHS organisation is a Government department).

Section 41(3) of the VAT Act 1994 refunds VAT 'if and to the extent that the Treasury so direct'. There may be occasions where the Directions are limited to a set of circumstances prevailing at a particular time. Where this has happened, the position is explained under the relevant Heading. Some Headings are seldom used, or not used in the NHS, and detailed explanations are not provided for these (but see *VAT & Government Departments* (Spiramus 2015) for further information if required).

5.3 Recent Developments

5.3.1 Call centre and contact centre services

For public bodies in general (i.e. not necessarily applicable to the NHS), the Treasury has agreed that COS refunds may be claimed for the following activities which will be included in the next revision of the Directions:

- Services provided through International Trade Advisers for UK Trade and Investment; and
- Services provided under Framework for Procuring External Support for Commissioners (FESC) other than:
  - supplies of computer services and professional services that are excluded from the scope of Headings 14 and 52 above, unless the Treasury directs otherwise, and
  - elsewhere, the supply of staff.

At date of publication certain Headings are not included in the online HMRC Manual VATGPB9700 because they are currently being drafted for the online manual; HMRC issued draft guidance for these Headings in October 2015 with further clarification on certain points issued in March 2016.

5.3.2 COS Tax Point

From 2016 COS recovery must now be based on the date of a tax invoice and not the date of payment, authorisation or registration of an invoice. HMRC require that all recoverable COS VAT on invoices dated on or before 31 March 2016 must have been recovered in the June 2016 VAT Return at the latest. The change in HMRC's policy means that any VAT incurred on invoices dated up to 31 March 2016 and not reclaimed by the June VAT return will be out of time and there will be no scope for recovery (and this will be the rule going forward until further notice).

In circumstances where a supply has been received and on which no VAT has been charged by the supplier and they subsequently issue a tax only invoice, the COS VAT can be recovered in the period in which the tax only invoice is received.

5.3.3   Budget 2015

Relief was extended to a variety of organisations in the 2015 Budget. Although not directly relevant to NHS organisations the relief now applies to certain associated or partner organisations including certain charities. The term 'charity' takes its meaning from the Finance Act 2010 Schedule 6.

5.3.4   Search and Rescue Charities

From 1 April 2015 search and rescue charities benefit from VAT relief under VAT Act 1994 s.33C and s.33D which means they will be eligible to recover VAT incurred on goods and services in relation to non-business activities (partial exemption still applies). Search and rescue charities are defined as charities whose main purpose is carrying out co-ordinated search and rescue, whose main purpose is to support, develop and promote the activities of charities established to search for and rescue people; or whose main purpose is to provide an air ambulance service.

5.3.5   Palliative Care Charities

From 1 April 2015 palliative care charities benefit from VAT relief under VAT Act 1994 s.33C and s.33D which means they will be eligible to recover VAT incurred on goods and services in relation to non-business activities (partial exemption still applies). The legislation defines palliative care charities.

5.3.6   Medical Courier Charities

From 1 April 2015 medical courier charities benefit from VAT relief under VAT Act 1994 s.33C and s.33D which means they will be eligible to recover VAT incurred on goods and services in relation to non-business activities (partial exemption still applies). The legislation defines medical courier charities.

5.3.7   Non-Departmental Public Bodies

Eligibility for COS refunds was also extended to NDPBs operating in a shared service context from 1 April 2015. This measure effectively extends the COS relief available to the NHS and GDs in relation to non-business activities to NDPBs (and possibly other organisations) operating in a shared service context (partial exemption still applies). Previously, NDPBs have had no special VAT relief and the VAT incurred has been an irrecoverable cost. This may have limited application in the NHS but may affect associated public bodies.

The overall policy is for public sector bodies to enter into shared services arrangements where possible for reasons of efficiency and cost-effectiveness. Where this happens the body or bodies providing services to the others engages in a business activity for VAT purposes, just as any supplier of this type of service does, and VAT is charged to the purchasers of the services. To date these services have mainly been in the fields of HR, recruitment and training, and IT services. There has been no provision to refund VAT to NDPBs sharing services with their parent GD or between themselves. With the expected wider take-up of shared services (including within the NHS and associated organisations), the intention is to ensure that these bodies are not at a VAT disadvantage when they enter into such arrangements. Because of competition issues, this will also include situations where they procure an eligible service directly from a private sector provider.

A new section 33E of VAT Act 1994 allows the refund of VAT incurred by named bodies on goods and services purchased, and goods imported or acquired, for their non-business purposes. Before a body can be named, it (or its parent GD) must have entered into an agreement with the Treasury to adjust the overall level of its public funding to take into account the VAT that will be recoverable. This is because such funding includes tax liabilities. Because it will not be possible to name bodies in primary legislation as and when such agreements are made with the Treasury the measure contains a power to make Treasury Orders to name the bodies. While it is expected that most bodies will be NDPBs the extension is not limited to them as there are other types of arms-length public body that may qualify. The Treasury consider it appropriate for these bodies to have the same level of VAT recovery as is available to the NHS and GDs under COS. Consequently, the Treasury (Contracting-Out) Directions which lists the eligible services upon which VAT can be recovered is also the Direction made for the same purpose under this measure.

5.4 Contracted-Out

COS Headings relate by definition to the provision of a specific service by an external contractor or supplier (i.e. contracted-out) rather than to costs incurred by an NHS organisation or GD in procuring the service for itself (although if services these may be recoverable under another COS Heading). This is fundamental: the service must be contracted-out to be eligible for recovery.

5.4.1 Exempt Business Activities

COS recovery is not allowed in relation to exempt business activities. For the NHS if an eligible service is partly attributable to an exempt business activity then it will be subject to restriction as part of the partial exemption calculation. If directly attributable to an exempt business activity (such as private patients) then COS recovery is not allowed.

5.4.2   Leasing or Hire of Equipment

Recovery on leasing or hire of equipment is only allowed under *Headings 25 and 26* in relation to photocopiers or reprographic equipment or vehicles on the condition that the hire or leasing includes repair and maintenance. Any other leasing or hire of equipment is not recoverable. There is a partial exception to this under *Heading 14* which allows recovery on the hire or rental of certain data land lines and private data circuits but not on equipment as such. Recovery on repair and maintenance included in a leasing contract is not allowed even where there is a separate contract unless there is no bar to the repair and maintenance being supplied by another provider (in which case it is recoverable).

5.4.3   Agency Staff

Recovery on agency staff hire is not allowed except in relation to nurses or auxiliaries under *Heading 41 – Nursing Services* (which may be exempt by concession in any case). Typical areas where recovery is not allowed are agency IT, finance and professional staff. However, there is a distinction between a supply of staff and a supply of services and it is advisable to analyse the nature of the supply because the charging mechanism for a staff agency or service company may be similar e.g. based on hours/days on site. A potentially eligible contract for services will mean that the service company controls the staff and has responsibility (and liability) for the performance of the service; otherwise the supply is likely to be one of staff and ineligible for recovery.

5.4.4   Minor COS Headings

Several of the COS Headings are of negligible importance (e.g. ceremonial services) or relate to primarily to exempt supplies (i.e. where VAT will not or should not be charged by the supplier). These include nursing services, childcare services and welfare services.

5.5   Managed Services

A managed service contract is one where an external contractor or supplier provides an eligible service on a managed basis usually including equipment or goods which would not be recoverable in its own right but the cost of which is included in the provision of the eligible service. Generally, the gross cost of a managed service is higher than the constituent elements (to reflect the management cost) but with COS recovery the net cost is often lower may be more cost effective overall. HMRC usually accept these in relation to administrative functions and technology e.g. IT and telephone systems, admin/records etc provided the service which is managed actually falls under a COS Heading (it is not enough that it is a service, it must be an eligible service). Where equipment is operated by the supplier's staff as part of the managed service contract the likelihood of approval for recovery is increased.

5.6 Repair and Maintenance

COS recovery is allowed on repair and maintenance on a range of activities e.g. the maintenance and non-structural repair of buildings (including gardens and grounds), the maintenance and repair of civil engineering works, the maintenance and repair of vehicles, plant, and equipment. Repair and maintenance means the reinstatement of the repaired item to its original state, and it therefore excludes any new work or new build construction. It includes the use of different or better materials where the original materials are obsolete and also incidental supplies of goods such as parts for vehicles, plant or equipment. Recovery is allowed on parts included under a repair and maintenance contract or where these are supplied as part of an ad hoc service. Recovery is not allowed on the installation of plant or equipment, nor on the replacement of a whole item of plant or equipment but is allowed on the repair by replacement of parts or components.

The repair and maintenance of buildings (including refurbishment and cleaning) is allowed under COS *Heading 35* but not new work (e.g. additions or alterations) or new build construction, extensions, installations or improvements (including preventive maintenance which improves the building). Substantial sums of COS may be recovered in this context and HMRC have issued detailed guidance (see **9.2 COS Capital**) and also devised a simplified Capital Banding Scheme in relation to larger projects up to £15m (see **9.2 COS Capital**). Routine and backlog maintenance are recoverable and there is a concession whereby any capital expenditure of a value of £5,000 or less (net) is eligible for COS recovery. Replacement of an eligible item would also be considered to be repairs and maintenance as long as that item is reinstated in the same location. Equally, any materials used would be considered to be an integral part of the service.

5.7 Incidental Supplies

VAT charged on goods supplied incidental to a service is also recoverable as COS e.g. parts supplied as part of a repair or maintenance service such as vehicle repairs or maintenance. To qualify for recovery on incidental goods the principal supply must be one of eligible services and all VAT charged is therefore recoverable as COS. Correspondingly, there is no COS recovery in relation to the corollary, a supply of services incidental to a principal supply of goods e.g. a maintenance service provided as part of a contract for the supply of equipment.

5.8 COS Time Limits

According to Treasury policy COS must be claimed within four months (previously three months) of the end of the financial year i.e. 31 July following 31 March (occasionally varied to take account of weekends etc, but otherwise a rigidly observed deadline) in order to preserve fiscal certainty in the public finances, that is, to ensure that there are no retrospective adjustments which would affect annual budgets. Until 1997 retrospective claims for up to six years could be made but in line with a general tightening of the VAT regime in response to Kenneth Clarke's "black hole" in Treasury VAT revenues (e.g. the introduction of the capping provisions in 1996/97) this was changed to the current financial year. Fiscal certainty applies equally to overclaims and underclaims of COS and in accordance with Treasury policy any adjustment (whether of overclaims or underclaims) must be made no later than the 31 July (plus 7 days for online filing) following the end of the financial year on 31 March (i.e. in the June VAT Return due by 31 July).

As part of the recent revision HMRC have allowed extended time limits (the four-year cap) where a revised interpretation applies and in certain circumstances:

- Where HMRC has instructed an NHS organisation or GD that it cannot claim COS VAT on a particular supply and this turns out to be incorrect – in these circumstances, the four-year cap applies.
- Where an NHS organisation or GD has asked whether a supply it has received is covered by a particular COS Heading, and by the time HMRC confirms that COS VAT is recoverable the time limits for claiming have passed – in these circumstances the four-year cap applies.
- Where there is uncertainty within the NHS (as a whole) or for GDs (as a whole) whether, in relation to a particular service, COS VAT can be recovered and this is not resolved by HMRC until after the time limits for claiming have expired – in these circumstances the four-year cap applies.

5.9 VAT Returns

HMRC have authority under VAT Act 1994 s.41 to determine the time, form and manner of claims and the Commissioners have determined that COS claims or adjustments must be made in an online VAT Return (although this is an administrative practice only because s.41 refunds are not technically part of a VAT Return). This means that it is not possible to make last minute submissions by email or error correction notification to HMRC Offices. This also means that, in practice, the June VAT return (due by the following 31 July) is the last Return in which an adjustment for the previous financial year (April – March) can be included. In exceptional circumstances it is possible to seek permission from HMRC to render an estimated July Return early i.e. by 31 July (rather than by 31 August when due) to avoid a potential loss of COS entitlement (*VAT Regulations 28 & 29(3) SI 1995/2518*).

5.9.1   Correction of COS Errors

The correction of a COS error is now treated as an error on a VAT Return and, at the discretion of the Commissioners on an administrative basis, is subject to the normal rules on ECNs (albeit that technically ECNs only apply to errors within the scope of the tax i.e. VAT errors (*VAT Notice 700/45/10)*). If under the ECN limits COS adjustments should be included in the current VAT 21 for inclusion in the current VAT Return but otherwise must be notified to the NHS Compliance Team.

5.9.2   Retention of Records

All records and supporting documentation relating to a refund of VAT on contracted-out services, including tax invoices, must be retained for a period of six years from the date the claim is made. Invoices may be scanned or transferred onto microfilm or microfiche, provided that copies can be easily produced and that there are adequate facilities for allowing HMRC to view them when required. Microfilm or microfiche records must also be kept for a period of six years from the date the claim is made. The six-year retention period for COS records parallels the requirement to retain VAT records for six years (*VAT Act 1994 Schedule 11 para 6(3)*). The agreement of HMRC must be obtained if records are to be destroyed within the six-year period (except where these are converted into electronic format).

5.10 COS Headings
VATGPB9750

COS Heading 1 - Accounting, invoicing and related services

This Heading concerns the outsourcing of all, or part, of an accounts department although it also covers the procurement of the type of services which would have been undertaken by an accounts department. The exclusions are functions which either had to be procured from external accountants or have since evolved as services supplied by external accountants. It would not include VAT incurred on external audit fees as, by their very nature, they would never have been performed in-house so could not be contracted out.

Includes any accounting or accountancy service performed by an external contractor or supplier, or any service in relation to invoicing or the preparation, processing or sending of invoices.

Accounting – includes the preparation of any type of financial accounts, statements or reports, bookkeeping or general financial record keeping.

Invoicing – includes the preparation, processing or sending of invoices (by an external contractor or supplier).

Tax Returns – includes the preparation of tax returns (but see below in relation to tax planning etc).

Excludes the services of external auditors in preparing audited annual accounts on the basis that a statutory audit by definition cannot be performed in-house. Only the statutory element of services provided by external auditors is ineligible. Other services such as value for money audits are eligible for recovery but the hire of accountants or tax advisers to carry out tax health checks or tax planning advice is specifically excluded. Other accounting services which by definition must be provided externally e.g. for regulatory purposes are not recoverable.

Notes – internal audit reports dealing with efficiency etc and advisory services such as management or financial consultancy are also currently eligible for recovery under *Heading 52*. The storage of financial records or invoices is recoverable under COS *Heading 63*.

References – HMRC VAT Manual VATGPB9750 (22 July 2016)

www.hmrc.gov.uk/manuals/vatgpbmanual/VATGPB9750.htm

VATGPB9770

COS Heading 2 - Administration of the following: Career development loans, Certificates of Experience, Government support payments to the Railway Industry Pension Funds, Grants and awards, Services supplied under the Companies Acts and the Patent and Trademarks Acts, Teachers' Superannuation Scheme, Vehicle Excise Duty refunds, Winter fuel payment scheme, Inherited State Earnings Related Pension Scheme, Student Loan Scheme, Fast Track Teaching Programme

Includes the administration by an external contractor or supplier of the following:
- Career Development Loans
- Certificates of Experience
- Government support payments to the Railway Industry Pensions Funds
- Grants and Awards

- Services supplied under the Companies Acts and the Patents and Trademark Acts
- Teacher's Superannuation Scheme
- Vehicle Excise Duty Refunds
- Winter Fuel Payment Scheme
- Inherited State Earnings Related Pension Scheme
- Student Loan Scheme
- Fast Track Teaching Programme

Excludes services other than those relating to the named programmes. New programmes can only be added to the list with the agreement of the Treasury.

References – HMRC VAT Manual VATGPB9770 (22 July 2016)

www.hmrc.gov.uk/manuals/vatgpbmanual/VATGPB9770.htm

VATGPB9790

COS Heading 3 - Administration and collection of toll charges

Includes the administration and collection of toll charges by an external contractor or supplier.

References – HMRC VAT Manual VATGPB9790 (22 July 2016)

www.hmrc.gov.uk/manuals/vatgpbmanual/VATGPB9790.htm

VATGPB9810

COS Heading 4 - Aerial photographic surveys and aerial surveillance

Includes the carrying out of aerial photographic surveys or surveillance by an external contractor or supplier (including satellite imagery and photographs).

References – HMRC VAT Manual VATGPB9810 (22 July 2016)

www.hmrc.gov.uk/manuals/vatgpbmanual/VATGPB9810.htm

VATGPB9830

COS Heading 5 - Agricultural services of the kind normally carried out by the Farming and Rural Conservation Agency

Includes the provision of agricultural services of the kind normally carried out by DEFRA by an external contractor or supplier or agricultural services of the kind normally carried out by the Farming and Rural Conservation Agency.

The wording of this Heading was amended in 2008 when the Farming and Rural Conservation Agency was abolished.

The Heading can be used by the relevant departments of the devolved administrations which have assumed responsibility for such activities from DEFRA.

References – HMRC VAT Manual VATGPB9830 (22 July 2016)

www.hmrc.gov.uk/manuals/vatgpbmanual/VATGPB9830.htm

VATGPB9850

COS Heading 6 - Alteration, repair and maintenance of road schemes, except (a) any works carried out pursuant to an agreement made under section 278 of the Highways Act 1980, or (b) works involving construction on land not already used for road schemes

Includes any service performed by an external contractor or supplier which may be reasonably construed as the alteration, repair or maintenance of an existing road.

Alterations – alterations to roads including the cost of materials and equipment (including hire) where this is part of a single (or composite) supply of services (and incidental to the supply of the services). Includes changing the layout of existing roads e.g. for the purposes of access or improvement.

Repair – repair of roads including the cost of materials and equipment (including hire) where this is part of a single (or composite) supply of services (and incidental to the supply of the services).

Maintenance – maintenance of roads including the cost of materials and equipment (including hire) where this is part of a single (or composite) supply of services (and incidental to the supply of the service).

Excludes new road construction (even for the purposes of access, the work cannot be new construction). Also excludes work pursuant to an agreement under Highways Act 1980 section 278 (which allows Highways Authorities to enter into agreements with private developers or third parties to pay for or carry out work in relation to public highways). Also excludes the gritting of roads in severe weather (revised from the previous guidance).

Notes – excludes materials, goods and the hire or purchase of equipment except where these are part of a single (or composite) supply of services and incidental to the supply of the services i.e. materials, goods or the hire or purchase of equipment purchased separately is ineligible for recovery.

5.10.1   Section 278 Agreements

Section 278 of the Highways Act 1980 allows a Highways Authority (HA) to seek contributions from developers towards the cost of works considered to be for the "common good". For example, these works could include the construction of a new slip road or roundabout.

Any work carried out by an HA under a section 278 agreement is a non-business activity for VAT purposes. This is because the HA has a statutory responsibility under the Highways Act 1980, to maintain the road on which the work is carried out. As such, the construction works form part of the HA's statutory responsibilities for maintaining the road.

Heading 6 of the Treasury's Contracting-Out Directions prevents the NHS and GDs from recovering VAT they incur when undertaking works under section 278 agreements.

As the HA is not able to claim a refund of the VAT under VAT Act 1994 section 41(3), it is a condition of the Section 278 agreement that the contributions they receive include irrecoverable VAT.

The HA cannot issue a VAT invoice to the bodies making contributions because it is seeking a reimbursement of costs and not making a supply. The contributor will be unable to recover any VAT element included in the contribution they pay to the HA. This is because the VAT amount does not relate to a supply, which has been made to the contributor. The contractor carrying out the works will always be making a supply to the HA.

5.10.2   Hybrid Road Schemes
"Hybrid Road Schemes" are works comprised of new construction together with improvements to the existing road schemes.

As the hybrid schemes involve two types of work, new construction and alteration, the costs must be separately identified for VAT purposes. This is because some of the VAT incurred on new construction undertaken in the hybrid scheme cannot be recovered.

It can sometimes prove difficult to separate the actual expenditure on new construction from that on alteration etc. HMRC allows an apportionment of costs to be made based on the terms of the additional contract.

In cases where it is not possible to directly attribute VAT elements, apportionment may be allowed. Hybrid road schemes are an example of a situation where permission to apportion the VAT has been granted.

References – HMRC VAT Manual VATGPB9850 (22 July 2016)

www.hmrc.gov.uk/manuals/vatgpbmanual/VATGPB9850.htm

VATGPB9870

COS Heading 7 - Broadcast monitoring services

Includes the provision of broadcast monitoring services by an external contractor or supplier such as:

- recording news and TV programmes which are relevant to the work of an NHS organisation;
- recording radio programmes;
- providing a digest of a departments coverage in the broadcast media; and
- social media monitoring e.g. Facebook, Twitter etc.

References – HMRC VAT Manual VATGPB9870 (22 July 2016)

www.hmrc.gov.uk/manuals/vatgpbmanual/VATGPB9870.htm

VATGPB9890

COS Heading 8 - Cartographic services

Includes the provision of mapping or cartographic services by an external contractor or supplier such as:

- mapping services;
- topographical surveys; and
- preparation of customised maps

References – HMRC VAT Manual VATGPB9890 (22 July 2016)

www.hmrc.gov.uk/manuals/vatgpbmanual/VATGPB9890.htm

VATGPB9910

COS Heading 9 - Cash in transit services

Includes any service performed by an external contractor or supplier providing cash in transit services for the safe or secure transport of cash or monies, including wage packeting case deliveries and associated equipment. Also includes the provision of security guards or secure vehicles for the safe or secure transport of cash or monies as part of a single (or composite) supply of services and incidental to the supply of the services.

Excludes supply or provision of security equipment or vehicles per se (including lease or hire).

Notes – the repair or maintenance of security equipment is recoverable under *Heading 37* and the provision of security guards for purposes other than the safe or secure transport of monies is recoverable under *Heading 60*.

References – HMRC VAT Manual VATGPB9910 (22 July 2016)

www.hmrc.gov.uk/manuals/vatgpbmanual/VATGPB9910.htm

VATGPB9930

COS Heading 10 - Catering

Includes the supply or provision of catering services by an external contractor or supplier (either in running an NHS organisation catering function or in relation to individual events) such as food prepared and facilities supplied by a contract catering service and:

- catering services for occasional functions;
- services associated with catering for occasional functions which form part of the supply of catering e.g. staff to serve food and drink, serving alcoholic beverages, hire of additional equipment (mobile kitchens, etc) to supplement the on-site facilities;
- vending machines when supplied as part of a catering contract;
- catering services for official functions e.g. receptions, dinners and banquets; and
- outsourced supplies of catering to NHS patients.

Excludes the purchases of food or drink and sandwich or food delivery services and the supply of catering staff. Also excludes supplies of catering to non-NHS patients (exempt).

Catering – a supply of catering is a supply of food which incorporates a significant element of service. The purchase of pre-packed food or retail food for patients or meetings e.g. sandwiches or snacks, would not be viewed as catering because there is no significant element of service in the supply, rather it would be viewed as a supply of goods. However, if the sandwiches or snacks are specifically prepared to order then that would qualify as catering.

Notes – the supply or provision of catering services to staff or visitors for a consideration or charge is taxable.

References – HMRC VAT Manual VATGPB9930 (22 July 2016)

www.hmrc.gov.uk/manuals/vatgpbmanual/VATGPB9930.htm

VATGPB9950

COS Heading 11 - Ceremonial services

Includes the provision of ceremonial or event management services by an external contractor or supplier such as:

- erecting seating and stands for dignitaries and the general public;
- putting up flags and bunting;
- hire of portable toilet facilities;
- putting up and dismantling crowd control barriers;
- hire of p.a. systems; and
- laying the "red carpet".

Excludes recovery on purchases of goods, for example:

- flags;
- flowers;

- red carpet;
- food or drink for hospitality purposes; and
- fireworks that are to be used in a display.

Notes – ceremonial services takes its everyday meaning e.g. opening new public buildings etc or hospital wing.

References – HMRC VAT Manual VATGPB9950 (22 July 2016)

www.hmrc.gov.uk/manuals/vatgpbmanual/VATGPB9950.htm

VATGPB9970

COS Heading 12 - Childcare services

Includes the provision of childcare or crèche/nursery services (including holiday play schemes) by an external contractor or supplier where the supply is for the benefit of the NHS organisation's own employees.

Excludes the administration fee on childcare vouchers.

Notes – the provision of childcare or crèche/nursery services in the course or furtherance of business and where the supplier is registered with OFSTED (under the Children Act 1989 as amended by the Care Standards Act 2000) is exempt under VATA 94 Schedule 9 Group 7 Item 9.

Supplies of childcare or crèche/nursery services by an eligible educational body are also exempt under VATA 94 Schedule 9 Group 6 Item 1.

Supplies of childcare or crèche/nursery services by a charity where charges are designed only to cover costs is outside the scope of VAT.

In principle, the service is otherwise standard-rated but exemptions from OFSTED registration are rare and it is unlikely that VAT would be charged on this service (or that an NHS organisation would engage a supplier not registered by OFSTED). COS recovery on the agency admin fee on childcare vouchers (taxable) is not allowed by HMRC.

References – HMRC VAT Manual VATGPB9970 (22 July 2016)

www.hmrc.gov.uk/manuals/vatgpbmanual/VATGPB9970.htm

VATGPB9990

COS Heading 13 - Collection, delivery and distribution services

Includes the provision by an external contractor or supplier of any form of collection, delivery, distribution (or storage) service, regardless of the nature of the items involved e.g. goods, packages or documents via internal distribution, courier services or carriage charges (separate from a supply of goods). Essentially, if an NHS organisation orders a specific collection or delivery (separate from a supply of goods) then that would be recoverable.

Also includes Royal Mail services where subject to VAT (historically exempt).

Excludes delivery charges as part of a supply of goods even where separately itemised on an Invoice. This would be part of a single (or composite) supply of delivered goods rather than an eligible service. Essentially, if a manufacturer or supplier includes a delivery charge as part of the purchase price this would not be recoverable.

References – HMRC VAT Manual VATGPB9990 (22 July 2016)

www.hmrc.gov.uk/manuals/vatgpbmanual/VATGPB9990.htm

VATGPB10010

COS Heading 14 - Computer services supplied to the specification of the recipient

This Heading applies to services supplied to an NHS organisation or GD in its procurement of an IT system to its own specifications or wider GD or NHS specifications.

The origins of this Heading lie in the outsourcing of entire IT systems by central government to the private sector. For this reason, the Heading does not cover in isolation the procurement of software or web design.

Because of the fast pace of technology, this Heading is not intended to be restricted to past practices; but instead to include modern methods of supplying an entire IT system. What is important is that the NHS organisation or GD is procuring an IT system designed to its specifications (or to wider GD or NHS specifications). Whether ownership of the hardware is or is not in the public sector, whether there is one supplier or several suppliers, whether the servers are or are not remote, does not affect this basic position.

Provided that the supply received is an IT system designed to the user's specifications, this heading applies even though some components of the package would – if supplied in isolation – be excluded from the Heading. The only exception is telephony, which is always excluded.

Includes:
- the provision by one or more suppliers of a fully managed and serviced computer infrastructure either using the recipient's own hardware or hardware provided by the supplier as part of the infrastructure;
- software support which forms part of a fully managed and serviced computer infrastructure;
- the development, implementation and support of bespoke software; and

- Hosting Computing Services, Archiving Communication Services, Data Communications Services, Desktop Communications Services, for example Picture Archiving Services (PACS), Ethernet Cable/Data lines and Cloud Computing.

Excludes:
- the supply and support of off-the-shelf software;
- licence fees except where integral to the provision of bespoke software or a fully managed and serviced computer infrastructure;
- the hire, installation or purchase of hardware alone;
- line rental as a separate supply unless as part of a fully managed and serviced computer infrastructure;
- telephony, which includes Voice Over Internet Protocol (VOIP);
- hire of computer consultants to add expertise to in-house IT teams; and
- web design where purchased as a stand-alone supply (this may be eligible for recovery under *COS Heading 49*).

5.10.3   'Fully managed and serviced computer infrastructure'
'Fully' is not to be read restrictively or taken to mean singular. A single IT initiative may be formed with reference to many 'mini' IT initiatives that make up the whole. Instead, the focus should be on the term "managed and serviced infrastructure".

'Stand-alone' contracts should be judged on their own merits. Variations to existing IT initiatives may be considered to be part of an overall IT initiative.

The 'fully managed and serviced' test will be satisfied where the recipient receives a package of services which are supplied and controlled by the supplier and where the risk of running the system and operating the service largely rests with the supplier.

5.10.4   'Bespoke software'
Bespoke software includes the creation of a new software package. This includes research and development, design and consultancy services. It may also include aftercare services such as updates and helpdesk facilities. It also includes the substantial modification of a pre-existing package of software to meet the needs of the recipient.

Non-qualifying 'off the shelf' software is taken to mean stock software such as "Microsoft Office" packages, Sage accounting software, etc. These generally require minor modification during implementation.

With any pre-existing software package, the key to qualification for VAT refund will be to consider whether the software package has been substantially modified.

5.10.5 Composite Supplies and Multiple Suppliers

VAT refunds under this Heading are permitted where the recipient contracts with more than one supplier, provided the services across the relevant supplier contracts dovetail together to provide a fully managed and serviced IT infrastructure. An example of this would be smaller contracts which when bundled together build up to one overall tower of fully managed and serviced IT infrastructure, this would also include any costs in relation to the build and support of the bespoke software which dovetails into the contract.

VAT on qualifying services received as part of wider supply that includes non-qualifying services or goods for a single all-inclusive charge, is not eligible for refund unless the qualifying services are supplied under a separately ordered, negotiated and contracted agreement. The exception to this is where a government department or NHS body receives a fully managed IT infrastructure service which includes telephony; in these situations, The Treasury requires the VAT incurred on the contract to be apportioned between telephony and IT services. The VAT which relates to the IT services can be recovered under COS *Heading 14* whilst any VAT incurred on telephony services cannot be recovered.

A VAT refund is permitted where goods are supplied as an integral part of qualifying services, are included in the contract for the qualifying services, and are ancillary to the qualifying services supplied.

References – Draft Guidance HMRC VAT Manual VATGPB10010 (12 October 2015)

VATGPB10030

COS Heading 15 - Conference and exhibition services

Includes the supply of a compound package of conference or exhibition services or facilities by an external contractor or supplier e.g. from a hotel or conference centre, including accommodation, meals, room hire etc. for a conference in relation to the non-business activities of an NHS organisation.

Conference – a planned large scale organised event usually attended by external delegates.

Exhibition – exhibition services include the provision of event management services by an external contractor or supplier e.g. audio visual services, event display and presentation services or the provision of reception and event staff as part of a single (or composite) supply of event management services.

Excludes the provision of accommodation *per se* by a hotel without the compound conference facilities (even if described as a "conference" or "delegate" rate) or the provision of meeting room hire of itself. There must be a supply of more than just accommodation and catering, the NHS organisation must receive a compound package e.g. the services of staff, room, equipment and catering etc.

Notes – if an NHS organisation holds a conference or meeting for which a charge is made to delegates and the conference or meeting does not relate to the non-business activities of the GD this could be an exempt supply because any conferencing or training (i.e. CPD) event held by an NHS organisation (as an "eligible body") would be exempt under Group 6 of VAT Act 1994 Schedule 9 and therefore any VAT incurred on costs would not be eligible for COS recovery. If the conference or meeting falls outside the definition of training or professional development, then it would be a taxable supply and there would be input tax entitlement (but output tax would be chargeable).

References – HMRC VAT Manual VATGPB10030 (22 July 2016)

www.hmrc.gov.uk/manuals/vatgpbmanual/VATGPB10030.htm

VATGPB10050

COS Heading 16 - Debt collection

Includes the provision of debt collection services by an external contractor or supplier e.g. by a professional debt collection agency, legal firm or bailiff services (revised from the previous guidance).

References – HMRC VAT Manual VATGPB10050 (22 July 2016)

www.hmrc.gov.uk/manuals/vatgpbmanual/VATGPB10050.htm

VATGPB10070

COS Heading 17 - Departmental staff records and payroll systems including administration and payment of pensions

Includes the provision of services by an external contractor or supplier to deal with departmental staff records and payroll systems or the administration or payment of pensions. Also actuarial services in respect of pensions, supplies by civil service pensions or similar bodies, or services supplied by government actuarial departments.

Excludes the administration of child care vouchers.

References – HMRC VAT Manual VATGPB10070 (22 July 2016)

www.hmrc.gov.uk/manuals/vatgpbmanual/VATGPB10070.htm

VATGPB10090

COS Heading 18 - Employment advisory services as directed by the Race Relations Act 1976

Includes the provision of employment advisory services as directed by the Equality Act 2010 by an external contractor or supplier including supplies by civil service policy (the Race Relations Act 1976 has been repealed).

References – HMRC VAT Manual VATGPB10090 (22 July 2016)

www.hmrc.gov.uk/manuals/vatgpbmanual/VATGPB10090.htm

VATGPB10110

COS Heading 19 - Engineering and related process services

Includes the provision of engineering and related process services by an external contractor or supplier, specifically in relation to manufacturing and the related commissioning processes.

Excludes the installation of plant and computer engineering.

References – HMRC VAT Manual VATGPB10110 (22 July 2016)

www.hmrc.gov.uk/manuals/vatgpbmanual/VATGPB10110.htm

VATGPB10130

COS Heading 20 - Environmental protection services of the kind normally carried out for the Department of the Environment, Food and Rural Affairs

Includes the provision of services by an external contractor or supplier in relation to environmental protection services of the kind normally carried out for the Department for Environment, Food and Rural Affairs (DEFRA).

References – HMRC VAT Manual VATGPB10130 (22 July 2015)

www.hmrc.gov.uk/manuals/vatgpbmanual/VATGPB10130.htm

VATGPB10150

COS Heading 21 - Estate management services

Includes the provision by an external contractor or supplier of estate management services such as a facilities management service or the management of a building complex, including arranging for the payment of rents or other charges, dealing with repairs and maintenance, arranging cleaning, security, post etc. The service would be a management service rather than the direct provision of specific services which are otherwise recoverable under COS *Heading 35 (repairs, maintenance, cleaning)* or COS

Heading 60 (security). It may also include utilities and equipment costs where these are part of a single (composite) supply or unitary charge.

Excludes separate recharges of utilities (supplies of goods).

Applies where an NHS organisation holds either the leasehold or the freehold on the property (or the equivalent under the law of Scotland).

References – HMRC VAT Manual VATGPB10150 (22 July 2016)

www.hmrc.gov.uk/manuals/vatgpbmanual/VATGPB10150.htm

VATGPB10170

COS Heading 22 - Export intelligence services

Includes the provision of export intelligence services by an external contractor or supplier.

References – HMRC VAT Manual VATGPB10170 (22 July 2016)

www.hmrc.gov.uk/manuals/vatgpbmanual/VATGPB10170.htm

VATGPB10190

COS Heading 23 - Filming, audio-visual and production services

Includes the provision of filming, audio-visual and production services by an external contractor or supplier for in-house training films, promotional videos for public awareness campaigns or filming or recording briefings, meetings or conferences etc.

References – HMRC VAT Manual VATGPB10190 (22 July 2016)

www.hmrc.gov.uk/manuals/vatgpbmanual/VATGPB10190.htm

VATGPB10210

COS Heading 24 - Health promotion activities

Includes the provision by an external contractor or supplier of health promotional activities, such as a health promotion campaign or health promotion advertisements.

Excludes VAT on costs incurred directly by an NHS organisation in carrying on health promotion activities itself unless these are otherwise eligible for recovery under another heading (e.g. the direct placement of health promotion advertisements is not eligible for recovery).

References – HMRC VAT Manual VATGPB10210 (22 July 2016)

www.hmrc.gov.uk/manuals/vatgpbmanual/VATGPB10210.htm

VATGPB10230

COS Heading 25 - Hire of reprographic equipment including repair and maintenance.

Under this Heading, 'reprographic' takes its everyday meaning and is the process of reproducing, reprinting, or copying graphic material especially by mechanical, photographic, or electronic means.

This Heading allows recovery on the hire, rental or lease of reprographic equipment (including multifunctional devices from May 2013) but only where the agreement or contract provides for repairs and maintenance and where the provider retains ownership and responsibility for the equipment.

Includes:
- hire, rental or lease of reprographic equipment where the charge is calculated on a 'copy 'or 'click' charge' basis and the provider retains ownership of the equipment, this also includes consumables provided as part of the 'click' or 'copy' charge;
- Multifunctional Devices (MFDs) which serve as printers, photocopiers and faxes.

Excludes:
- hire, rental or lease of reprographic equipment where the agreement or contract does not include repair and maintenance;
- hire of fax machines, as these are not primarily reprographic equipment;
- consumables supplied separately, for example, toner, fixing agents and copier.

References – Draft Guidance HMRC VAT Manual VATGPB10230 (12 October 2015)

VATGPB10250

COS Heading 26 - Hire of vehicles, including repair and maintenance

This Heading allows recovery where an NHS organisation or GD enters into a contract for the supply of a vehicle/vehicles and the repair and maintenance of these vehicles (by the supplier) is specified in the contract.

Includes contracts for the hire of pool cars, company cars or other vehicles where the contract includes repair and maintenance by the supplier. The requirement that the hire must be for a consecutive period of 30 days or more has been dropped.

Excludes hire of vehicles alone where the contract does not include repair and maintenance (however the VAT on the separate supply of repair and maintenance will be recoverable under *Heading 37*).

References – Draft Guidance HMRC VAT Manual VATGPB10250 (12 October 2015)

VATGPB10270

COS Heading 27 - Insolvency services

Includes the provision by an external contractor or supplier of insolvency services but only where it can be demonstrated that the insolvency practitioners are working under contract to an NHS organisation and that their services are being provided to the NHS. In many cases insolvency practitioners provide their services to the business under their supervision and therefore the supply is to that business.

References – HMRC VAT Manual VATGPB10270 (22 July 2016)

www.hmrc.gov.uk/manuals/vatgpbmanual/VATGPB10270.htm

VATGPB10290

COS Heading 28 - Interpretation and translation services

Includes the services of an interpreter or translator or the provision by an external contractor or supplier of interpretation or translation services such as simultaneous translation or interpretation services provided in person at events or meetings or via telephone or the translation of documents. Also includes sign language services.

References – HMRC VAT Manual VATGPB10290 (22 July 2016)

www.hmrc.gov.uk/manuals/vatgpbmanual/VATGPB10290.htm

VATGPB10310

COS Heading 29 - Issue of documents to, and control of, bingo halls and off-course bookmakers

Includes the services of issuing documents to, and control of, bingo halls and off-course bookmakers by an external contractor or supplier.

References – HMRC VAT Manual VATGPB10310 (22 July 2016)

www.hmrc.gov.uk/manuals/vatgpbmanual/VATGPB10310.htm

VATGPB10330

COS Heading 30 - Issue of documents under Wireless and Telegraphy Act

Includes the services of issuing documents under the Wireless Telegraphy Act by an external contractor or supplier.

References – HMRC VAT Manual VATGPB10330 (22 July 2016)

www.hmrc.gov.uk/manuals/vatgpbmanual/VATGPB10330.htm

VATGPB10350

COS Heading 31 - Laboratory services

This Heading allows recovery where an NHS organisation or GD has contracted-out its laboratory services. Laboratory services are defined as services of conducting scientific experiments, tests and investigations whether in a laboratory building or via a technological process.

Includes:
- drug testing;
- forensic testing;
- managed laboratory services.

Excludes:
- stand-alone supplies of laboratory consumables for example, reagents, chemicals and test tubes (supplies of goods);
- separate lease/hire of laboratory equipment.

The supply of laboratory pathology services that directly relate to the provision of healthcare for individual patients is exempt from VAT and thus there is no VAT to recover. This applies to all businesses that are state-regulated and supply laboratory pathology testing services, whether they supply the services to the NHS or to independent hospitals. The liability was clarified in GSTS Pathology LLP CO/3544/2013 (the supply was held to exempt despite the supply being via an intermediary and not directly to the individual patient).

References – Draft Guidance HMRC VAT Manual VATGPB10350 (12 October 2015)

VATGPB10370

COS Heading 32 - Laundry services

Includes the cleaning or laundering of clothing, linen and fabrics by an external contractor or supplier. Also, dry cleaning services, towel hire, towel cleaning services and the provision and exchange of linen on a regular basis for laundering (which remains the property of the company providing the service). Also, the cleaning and laundering of uniforms and fabrics.

Excludes the purchase of linen, clothing or fabrics or hire of same not including laundry services.

References – HMRC VAT Manual VATGPB10370 (22 July 2016)

www.hmrc.gov.uk/manuals/vatgpbmanual/VATGPB10370.htm

VATGPB10390

COS Heading 33 - Library services

Includes the provision of library services (such as the supply of information) by an external contractor or supplier e.g. a university or academic institution, including electronic or online library services or internet hosted library services and access to professional journals (including "subscriptions").

Excludes website subscriptions (but see above) and subscriptions to single publications or online journals or publications (i.e. where there is a subscription to a specific publication but not a library service).

Notes – subscription may be a misnomer in this context. A subscription normally is an ineligible service but if the "subscription" is actually a charge for online library services or online access to journals then it is eligible for recovery under this Heading. Subscriptions to websites or to an individual publication are not eligible.

References – HMRC VAT Manual VATGPB10390 (22 July 2016)

www.hmrc.gov.uk/manuals/vatgpbmanual/VATGPB10390.htm

VATGPB10410

COS Heading 34 – Maintenance and care of livestock and fauna in connection with the Royal Parks

Includes the services related to the maintenance and care of livestock and fauna in connection with the Royal Parks such as:

- veterinary costs
- tree surgeons' services
- vaccination programmes

References – HMRC VAT Manual VATGPB10410 (22 July 2016)

www.hmrc.gov.uk/manuals/vatgpbmanual/VATGPB10410.htm

VATGPB10430

COS Heading 35 – Maintenance, non-structural repair and cleaning of buildings

Includes the maintenance, repair or cleaning of buildings by an external contractor or supplier. Maintenance or repair relates to existing buildings, structures or premises as opposed to new construction or new work. Also includes cleaning of any kind e.g. domestic services as well as steam cleaning or window cleaning and also redecoration. Also the maintenance of gardens and grounds including tree surgery, grass cutting, surface maintenance, road cleaning and gardening (but not landscaping). Also any materials used in the repair or maintenance work.

Excludes new construction or new work as well as alterations, conversions, extensions, additions, or improvements. Also excludes initial decorating services and the separate purchase of cleaning materials. Also the supply or installation of goods, plant or equipment (plant means an immovable item which is genuinely fixed in the sense of being permanently incorporated into the structure of the building e.g. lifts, boilers and generators or other industrial equipment).

HMRC have produced the table below (**Annex A**) as a guide to recovery under *COS Heading 35* and also *COS Heading 37* where it relates to installed plant or equipment (see **9.2 COS Capital** and **9.4** for the **Capital Banding Scheme** in relation to larger projects).

ANNEX A

Subject	Description	Recovery	COS heading
Alarms	Repairing existing fire/burglar alarms	Yes	35
	Installation of fire/burglar alarms	No	
	Extension to current systems	No	
	Repair by partial replacement of parts within existing fire/burglar alarm	Yes	35
	The complete replacement of an existing system	No	
Asbestos	Removing asbestos	Yes	35
	Sealing in asbestos	Yes	35
Ceilings	Repairing existing ceiling/suspended ceiling	Yes	35
	Replacing existing damaged tiles in same location (within existing grids structure)	Yes	35
	Forming fire breaks in ceiling voids	No	
	Construction/installation of new ceilings/suspended ceilings.	No	
	Complete replacement of suspended ceiling structure	No	
Cleaning	Contract cleaning	Yes	35
Construction	Building new cool room	No	
	Construction of a new room	No	
	Building new extension	No	
	Major building improvements	No	
	Installation of a new damp proof course	No	
	Installation of a silicone based injection.	No	
	Single supply of scaffolding	No	
	Structural repairs not traditionally		

	performed in-house, as the work requires highly specialised skills.	No	
	Complete replacement of central heating and air conditioning systems	No	
Conversions	Converting an office space from small offices to open plan or vice versa	No	
Decorating	Repainting and decorating existing walls, windows etc to restore decorative order	Yes	35
	Re-painting existing external structure	Yes	35
	First time decoration	No	
	Resealing against damp and draughts	Yes	35
Doors	Fitting fire doors in corridors to form a fire break	No	
	Widening doors to allow wheelchair access	No	
	Blocking up old/existing doorways	No	
	Installing new doors/door frames where none existed previously	No	
	Installation of automatic/electric doors	No	
	First time fitting of fire doors in new buildings/extensions	No	
	Fitting fire doors in new partitions	No	
	Repairing by replacing existing doors/fire doors/door frames *	Yes	35
	Replacing existing doors with fire doors *	Yes	35
Electrical	*Electrical works would include items such as installation of luminaries, general lighting, small power, nurse call systems, electrical connections to other systems. VAT recovery will be dependent upon the context of the specific job being undertaken, e.g. if purely refurbishment, more scope expected for VAT recovery. If major alteration/reconfiguration, limited scope for recovery.*		
	Extension of wiring into new areas	No	
	Installation of new emergency lighting/fire signs	No	
	Installation/replacement of Building	No	

	Management System		
	Installing new/additional wiring and/or sockets	No	
	Installing new/additional wiring and/or light fittings	No	
	Installing new/addition cables/wiring for telephone/data lines	No	
	Complete removal and replacement of wiring back to distribution boards	No	
	Repair by replacing existing wiring/cabling, individual sockets and light fittings, if in exactly the same location *	Yes	35
	Portable Appliance Testing (PAT)	Yes	37
Equipment/ parts	Sterilisation of instruments and equipment	Yes	37
	Spare parts which are provided as part of the eligible repair and maintenance services	Yes	37
	Maintenance of security equipment	Yes	37
Fire Escapes	Replacing fire escapes	No	
	Repairing fire escapes	Yes	35
	Building new fire escapes	No	
Flooring	Breaking up existing concrete floors and subsequent relaying at a slight different floor level.	Yes	35
	Repairing existing stuck down flooring by rescreeding and resurfacing bonded fitted flooring, including stuck down carpet, carpet tiles, floor tiles and vinyl.	Yes	35
	Replacing worn flooring with the same type of covering i.e. replacing carpet with carpet, linoleum with linoleum. etc	Yes	35
	Supplying first time flooring	No	
	Installing plywood base to level floor	No	
Grounds	Upgrading worn floor covering, for example replacing linoleum with carpet, or replacing carpet with wooden flooring	No	

	Maintenance of grounds and gardens adjacent buildings	Yes	35
	Gardening	Yes	35
	Grass cutting	Yes	35
	Tree surgery	Yes	35
Incinerators	Landscaping/redesigning grounds	No	
	Repair of incinerator	Yes	37
	Installing new incinerator	No	
	Construction/extending height of chimney	No	
Insulation	Replacement of incinerator	No	
	Increasing thickness of existing lagging on incinerators	No	
	First time installing of insulation	No	
	Installing sound proofing panels	No	
	Repair by replacing lagging	Yes	35
Kitchen	Repair by resurfacing existing worktops and units	Yes	35
	Installing/building new kitchen units, cupboards etc.	No	
	Installing/building new work tops	No	
	Repair by replacing existing kitchen units, cupboards etc within kitchens/tea points *	Yes	35
Lifts	Repairs to existing lifts	Yes	37
	Replacement of lift	No	
	Installing a new lift	No	
Mechanical	*Mechanical works would include items such as pipe work, ductwork, heating units, chiller units, chilled water plant, air handling units, hot and cold water plant, compressed air systems, medical gases and soil and waste pipe work.*		
	Repairs to faulty systems (including parts)	Yes	37
	Replacement of system	No	
	Installation of new system	No	
	Alterations/additions and extensions to existing system	No	
	Fixing values and/or meters to existing/new radiators, pipes and taps	Yes	37

	to regulate temperate of hot water for patient safety/energy conservation purposes		
	Repair existing pipes/radiators	Yes	37
	Installation of new/addition pipes/radiators	No	
	Replacing water tanks	No	
	Building/installing new water tanks	No	
	First time installation of boiler	No	
	Replacement of boiler	No	
	Repair to boiler (including parts)	Yes	37
	Complete replacement of central heating system	No	
	Installation of new central heating system	No	
	Testing and Commissioning	No	
	Repairing by replacing existing pipes/radiators in same location *	Yes	35
Miscellaneous	Minor works of a repair and maintenance nature	Yes	35
	Disturbance works, where those works only need to be undertaken as a result of alterations to a building or as a result of new building works.	No	
	Fitting of fire hoses/extinguishers	No	
	Fitting of grilles, bars, locks, window film and security cameras	No	
	Installation of shelves	No	
	Replacement of shelves	No	
	Manufacturers warranties which are included in the purchase price of the goods, this is a single supply of goods	No	
	Maintenance contracts entered into after the manufacturer's warranty expires	Yes	37
Ramps	Repair existing ramps/handrails for access for the disabled	Yes	35
	Replacing/altering of ramps/handrails	No	
	Initial provision of ramps/handrails including replacement of stairs/steps by ramps	No	

Roads	Breaking up and removal of covers to existing manholes and their re-provision in the same place at a higher level	Yes	35
	Resurfacing existing non-fee paying car parks	Yes	35
	Resurfacing existing footpaths	Yes	35
	Relaying down to foundation of existing footpaths	No	
	Road cleaning	Yes	35
	Building new car park/footpath where one did not previously exist.	No	
Roofs	Maintenance of roofs including necessary access works	Yes	35
	Resurfacing/replacing/re-slating existing roof	Yes	35
	Re-felting of flat roofs	Yes	35
	Altering existing pitch i.e. replacing flat roof by pitch	No	
	Roofing over previous open space	No	
	Installation of canopy	No	
Sanitary ware	Repair of existing damaged washbasins and sanitary ware.	Yes	35
	Fitting new washbasins and sanitary ware.	No	
	Replacing existing systems in new locations or replacing bath by shower, toilet by wash basin etc	No	
	Replacement of sanitary back and side panels, vanity units, shower cubicles.	No	
	Replacement of existing damaged washbasins and sanitary ware in exactly the same place, i.e. toilet cistern by toilet cistern, sink by sink, bath by bath. This would not include replacement of sluices and hoppers *	Yes	35
Signs	Repairs to existing signs	Yes	37
	Repair by replacement signs	No	
	New signs necessary only as a result of a Trust merger	Yes	37

Walls	Repairing existing partitions	Yes	35
	Restoration of damaged plaster work/brick work	Yes	35
	Constructing new partitions/walls, altering partition layout	No	
	First time fitting of partitions in new buildings/extensions	No	
	Painting new walls/partitions	No	
	Repairing damaged tiles	Yes	35
	Tiling new areas	No	
	Repairs to wall-cladding	Yes	35
	Provision of wall-cladding/wall panels/wall protection rails	No	
	Replacement wall-cladding/wall panels/wall protection rails	No	
Windows	Window cleaning	Yes	35
	Repairing existing window frames and glass with similar items	Yes	35
	Bricking up windows or forming new window/window frames.	No	
	Installation of fitted blinds, curtains and curtain tracks	No	
	Replacement of fitted blinds, curtains and curtain tracks	No	
	Installation of combination window/blind units	No	
	Repair to fitted blinds, curtains and curtain tracks	Yes	37
	Replacement of windows within same aperture*	Yes	35
Woodwork	Repairs to dado /picture rail and skirting boards	Yes	35
	Replacement of dado /picture rail and skirting boards	No	
X-rays	Replacement of an X-ray tube or CT Tube*	Yes	37

*Exceptions to normal COS rules, where HMRC accept the concept of repair by replacement for the listed items only.

References – Draft Guidance HMRC VAT Manual VATGPB10430 (12 October 2015)

VATGPB10450

COS Heading 36 - Maintenance and repair of civil engineering works

Includes the maintenance and repair of civil engineering works by an external contractor or supplier. Civil engineering works include bridges, drains etc (but not roads).

Excludes the repair and maintenance of roads (which is covered by *Heading 6*), new civil engineering projects or work carried out under a s.278 agreement (see *Heading 6*) and winter road gritting and cleaning services.

References – HMRC VAT Manual VATGPB10450 (22 July 2016)

www.hmrc.gov.uk/manuals/vatgpbmanual/VATGPB10450.htm

VATGPB10470

COS Heading 37 - Maintenance, repair and cleaning of equipment, plant, vehicles and vessels

This Heading allows NHS organisations and GDs to recover VAT on:
- repair, maintenance and cleaning of equipment, plant, vehicles and vessels that they own, and/or;
- repair, maintenance and cleaning of equipment, plant, vehicles and vessels that are leased (provided that the repair and maintenance work is supplied under a separate contract or agreement from the lease) It does not have to be made by a different supplier. Where the lease and maintenance are provided by the same supplier, the contracts/agreements must not be interdependent on each other and must be separately enforceable.

For the purposes of COS recovery, the term 'vessels' includes ships and aircrafts and the term equipment includes computer equipment.

VAT incurred on the leasing or hire of equipment, plant, vehicles and vessels is not eligible for recovery. The only exceptions to this are COS *Headings 25 'Hire of reprographic equipment including repair and maintenance'* and *COS Heading 26 'Hire of vehicles, including repair and maintenance'*. In both these cases, the VAT is only recoverable on contracts that provide for the supply of the equipment/vehicles together with full repair and maintenance services.

Examples of what is included or excluded under *COS Heading 37* can be found at VATGPB10435 (**Annex A** above at *COS Heading 35*).

References – Draft Guidance HMRC VAT Manual VATGPB10470 (12 October 2015)

VATGPB10490

COS Heading 38 - Maintenance and repair of statues, monuments and works of art

Includes the maintenance and repair of statues, monuments and works of art by an external contractor or supplier such as cleaning, restoration, removal or relocation.

Excludes costs relating to the design and installation of new monuments.

References – HMRC VAT Manual VATGPB10490 (22 July 2016)

www.hmrc.gov.uk/manuals/vatgpbmanual/VATGPB10490.htm

VATGPB10510

COS Heading 39 - Medical and social surveys

Includes the supply of a medical or social survey by an external contractor or supplier. Also includes the provision of information from general surveys previously carried out.

Excludes costs incurred directly by an NHS organisation in procuring the service for itself unless these are otherwise eligible for recovery under another Heading and MORI polls as these have always been undertaken by independent external bodies to conduct opinion polls.

This Heading is specifically designed to allow recovery on surveys which were previously carried out in-house by GDs and which are now outsourced to private sector providers (and where the results are to be used in relation the non-business activities of the GD). This type of survey is most typically conducted amongst other public bodies such as local authorities, police authorities, health authorities and charities etc and the information obtained is used to inform future planning and policies. Other types of survey may also be eligible for recovery but the key criterion is to demonstrate that they are medical or social in nature and would have previously been undertaken in-house by an NHS organisation.

References – HMRC VAT Manual VATGPB10510 (22 July 2016)

www.hmrc.gov.uk/manuals/vatgpbmanual/VATGPB10510.htm

VATGPB10530

COS Heading 40 - Messenger, portering and reception services

Includes the supply of messenger, portering or reception services by an external contractor or supplier such as the internal movement of documents, mail or equipment. Also includes reception or receptionist services or appointment or reminder services.

Excludes the hire of telephone lines or telephone or switchboard equipment. Also excludes the supply of agency staff.

References – HMRC VAT Manual VATGPB10530 (22 July 2016)

www.hmrc.gov.uk/manuals/vatgpbmanual/VATGPB10530.htm

VATGPB10550

COS Heading 41 - Nursing services

This Heading is intended to allow recovery on nursing services in its widest sense and there is no requirement that the nursing staff must be providing medical care. The Royal College of Nursing defines nursing as "the use of clinical judgement in the provision of care to enable people to improve, maintain, or recover health, to cope with health problems, and to achieve the best possible quality of life, whatever their disease or disability, until death".

Includes the provision of nursing services or agency nursing staff:
- all grades of registered bank nurses, working on wards across the NHS
- healthcare assistants
- midwives and midwifery assistants
- phlebotomists
- theatre scrub nurses
- nurses employed by the 111 service

Operating Departmental Practitioners (ODPs) where due to the changes in the nature of their role they provide a nursing services (previously ODPs were excluded from COS Heading 41 as they were not providing a nursing service)

Excludes other types of medical professionals such as doctors, locums and other healthcare professionals or ambulance paramedics.

It should not be assumed that there is a VAT element included in the charge made for nursing services, as the supply may be exempt from VAT.

References – Draft Guidance HMRC VAT Manual VATGPB10550 (12 October 2015)

VATGPB10570

COS Heading 42 - Office removals

Includes the provision of an office removal service or office relocation services by an external contractor or supplier. Also hire of crates as part of a removal service.

Excludes the hire of crates without a corresponding removal service.

References – HMRC VAT Manual VATGPB10570 (22 July 2016)

www.hmrc.gov.uk/manuals/vatgpbmanual/VATGPB10570.htm

VATGPB10590

COS Heading 43 - Operation and maintenance of static test facilities, engineering and support services and test range industrial support and security/safety services including those acquired for the purposes of research and development

Includes the operation and maintenance of static test facilities, engineering and support services and test range industrial support and security/safety services including those acquired for the purposes of research and development by an external contractor or supplier.

References – HMRC VAT Manual VATGPB10590 (24 March 2015)

www.hmrc.gov.uk/manuals/vatgpbmanual/VATGPB10590.htm

VATGPB10610

COS Heading 44 - Operation and maintenance of stores depots

This Heading allows recovery where an external contractor is employed to operate and maintain a stores depot.

Includes monitoring stock levels, dealing with requisition requests and the day-to-day operation of stores.

Excludes the supply of the goods being stored.

Where there is a single contract for the operation and maintenance of stores depot and for the supply of the goods, VAT can only be recovered on the service element of the contract where this is shown as a separate charge on the invoice.

References – Draft Guidance HMRC VAT Manual VATGPB10610 (12 October 2015)

VATGPB10630

COS Heading 45 - Operation of hospitals, health care establishments and health care facilities and the provision of related services

This Heading concerns the operation of healthcare premises that have face-to-face dealings with patients. The contractor does not have to provide, and is unlikely to be providing, healthcare. Thus, the focus of the Heading is on the situation where the contractor provides a fully functioning building or facility within which medical and nursing professionals can treat and care for their patients. For example, the contractor may provide full facilities management support, IT support, catering, cleaning and security using its own employees (or the services of companies it sub-contracts work to). An agreement that consists of an ordinary premises lease with standard communal services only will not be covered by this Heading.

The origins of this heading lay in the type of PFI arrangement that was prevalent in the 1980s and 1990s. Over time, this type of arrangement has changed, either in terms of the level of services provided or the facility in which they are provided, but the principle remains unchanged – the contractor provides a sufficient level of services and support within the building or facility for the NHS (or other healthcare provider) to treat its patients. It covers PFI, PF2, Scottish Hub Procurement Arrangements, LIFT and non-PFI situations.

A hospital, healthcare establishment or healthcare facility is the building or facility which enables the medical and nursing professionals to treat and care for their patients such as:
- an entire hospital complex of buildings;
- part of a hospital complex of buildings;
- a discrete part of a hospital, such as a ward, a theatre suite, a radiology department, a renal dialysis suite, a diagnostic suite or an MRI unit;
- an off-site facility that provides services which would normally be carried out in a hospital or health care establishment; for example, an off-site facility for renal dialysis or diagnostic purposes;
- non-residential mental health facilities which are part of the healthcare offered by the NHS organisation.

Includes:
- the ancillary provision of equipment together with the service of operating and maintaining that equipment, for example heating, cooling and ventilation equipment; fire protection equipment; specialised lighting; nurse call systems; and medical gas supply piping;
- utilities when provided as a part of the whole package under the same contract and paid for within the single unitary charge - the utilities may be invoiced separately to the rest of the charges;
- hyperbaric chambers/mobile theatres, as long as these are supplied on a fully managed and serviced basis.

Excludes the hire of equipment alone or the separate supply of utilities.

References – Draft Guidance HMRC VAT Manual VATGPB10630 (12 October 2015)

VATGPB10650

COS Heading 46 - Operation of prisons, detention centres and remand centres, including medical services

Includes the operation of prisons, detention centres and remand centres, including medical services by an external contractor or supplier such as:

- the operation of a private prison
- the operation of a prison shop
- prisoner transport services
- the operation of prison hospitals

Excludes hostel accommodation.

References – HMRC VAT Manual VATGPB10650 (22 July 2016)

www.hmrc.gov.uk/manuals/vatgpbmanual/VATGPB10650.htm

VATGPB10670

COS Heading 47 - Passenger transport services

Includes the provision of passenger transport services by an external contractor or supplier e.g. any vehicle supplied with a driver etc taxis (where there is a standing contract), buses, minibuses etc. Also includes chauffeur driven vehicles and night car services.

Excludes costs incurred directly by an NHS organisation in procuring the service for itself unless otherwise eligible for recovery under another Heading. Also excludes the hire of vehicles without drivers or non-contracted taxi fares. Also excludes insurance, road tax and public transport or *ad hoc* taxi hires by staff.

References – HMRC VAT Manual VATGPB10670 (22 July 2016)

www.hmrc.gov.uk/manuals/vatgpbmanual/VATGPB10670.htm

VATGPB10690

COS Heading 48 - Pest control services

Includes the provision of a pest control service by an external contractor or supplier, such as disinfestation services, setting of traps, spraying insecticide and the removal of dead rodents.

Excludes the purchase of pest control substances, poisons, traps or materials.

References – HMRC VAT Manual VATGPB10690 (22 July 2016)

www.hmrc.gov.uk/manuals/vatgpbmanual/VATGPB10690.htm

VATGPB10710

COS Heading 49 - Photographic, reprographic, graphic and design services

This Heading allows recovery on contracted out photographic, reprographic, graphic and design services.

Includes:
- hire of a photographer
- design & printing of annual reports
- bulk copying services
- design and redesign of a website

Excludes:
- the purchase of photocopiers etc.
- printing of business cards and headed stationary (these may be recoverable under *COS Heading 61*)
- printing of office signage

References – Draft Guidance HMRC VAT Manual VATGPB10710 (12 October 2015)

VATGPB10730

COS Heading 50 - Preparation and despatch of forms

Includes the preparation and despatch of forms by an external contractor or supplier such as the design, printing and mailing of forms providing these services are provided within a single contract.

References – HMRC VAT Manual VATGPB10730 (22 July 2016)

www.hmrc.gov.uk/manuals/vatgpbmanual/VATGPB10730.htm

VATGPB10750

COS Heading 51 - Press cutting services

Includes the provision of a physical or electronic press cutting service by an external contractor or supplier.

References – HMRC VAT Manual VATGPB10750 (22 July 2016)

www.hmrc.gov.uk/manuals/vatgpbmanual/VATGPB10750.htm

VATGPB10770

COS Heading 52 - Professional advice or opinion on departmental efficiency or policy issues, legal advice or opinion and internal audit

This Heading is currently under review by the Treasury. HMRC advise that NHS organisations should continue to use the draft guidance issued in October 2015 and detailed below until further notice. The revisions are likely to include internal audit reports, legal opinion and management consultancy.

VAT is recoverable on the professional services of managers, advisers, experts, specialists and consultants in providing advice or information on how to put something into effect. The eligible services are therefore of an advisory nature, rather than of implementation, taking action following a recommendation, etc. In relation to building works and construction, the professional fees of architects and structural engineers are included, as is consultancy advice on planning site layouts and the services of solicitors, valuers and surveyors. VAT is eligible for a refund irrespective of whether the fees relate to repairs and maintenance or new construction or improvements or refurbishment etc.

But this category is not restricted to professional fees in connection with construction work and it also covers professional fees such as those in connection with computer consultancy work, including contract software development.

References – Draft Guidance HMRC VAT Manual VATGPB10770 (12 October 2015)

VATGPB10790

COS Heading 53 - Provision under a PFI agreement of accommodation, for office or other governmental use, together with management or other services in connection with that accommodation

This Heading covers PFI arrangements under which NHS organisations and GDs are supplied with fully serviced and managed accommodation by a single PFI provider. The most distinct element will be that risk is transferred from the NHS organisation or GD to the PFI provider. Consequently, the heading does not include leases granted by commercial landlords, even where they are landlord repairing and insuring leases.

Recovery under this heading is only allowed on utilities when provided as part of the supply of PFI accommodation and where the cost is subsumed within the single unitary charge (seen as a necessary incidental cost of providing the accommodation). Therefore, utilities provided outside the PFI unitary charge will not qualify for recovery under this Heading.

References – Draft Guidance HMRC VAT Manual VATGPB10790 (12 October 2015)

VATGPB10810 COS

Heading 54 - Publicity services

This Heading allows recovery on publicity services.

Includes:
- advertising campaigns other than recruitment adverts (which are covered by *COS Heading 57*);
- the use of a private publicity agency for dealing with the media;
- press releases;

- digital publicity services, for example illuminated portable posters and video walls.

Excludes:

- commissioning promotional items such as mugs, T-shirts, stickers etc (these are supplies of goods);
- the direct placing of an advertisement, for example in a newspaper.

References – Draft Guidance HMRC VAT Manual VATGPB10810 (12 October 2015)

VATGPB10830

COS Heading 55 - Purchasing and procurement services

This Heading allows recovery on purchasing and procurement services i.e. the procurement service charge.

Includes:

- negotiating procurement contracts;
- management and coordination of bulk orders;
- cloud based procurement services;
- government procurement services;
- where a buying agent or private firm is used for purchasing, then any VAT incurred on the buying agent's services would be eligible for recovery under this Heading.

Excludes the actual cost of the goods procured.

References – Draft Guidance HMRC VAT Manual VATGPB10830 (12 October 2015)

VATGPB10850

COS Heading 56 - Radio services

This Heading allows recovery on radio services.

Includes:

- radio broadcasting;
- radio bandwidth;
- contracting out of services connected to the running of a hospital radio;
- webcasting;
- provision of radio communications network for NHS Ambulance Trusts and handsets when supplied as part of the communications network.

Excludes:

- purchase of radios or radio equipment alone;
- the supply of car radios or radio masts.

References – Draft Guidance HMRC VAT Manual VATGPB10850 (12 October 2015)

VATGPB10870

COS Heading 57 - Recruitment and relocation of staff and other related services

This Heading allows recovery on recruitment and relocation of staff and other related services.

Includes:

- security vetting checks undertaken on employees including Disclosure and Barring Service (DBS) checks;
- staff relocation expenses where the department commissions the removal company;
- staff recruitment advertising commissioned via a recruitment agency;
- Civil Service Resourcing;
- if an agency is used to arrange for the recruitment of staff, the VAT would be refundable under this Heading (this would include services provided as part of a recruitment drive);
- where an NHS organisation opens a new hospital or moves to a new building and uses a private company to deal with the relocation of the staff.

Excludes:

- VAT incurred on removal firms hired by staff;
- placing recruitment adverts in a newspaper or on internet recruitment websites.

VAT incurred in respect of the recruitment of canteen staff would only be eligible for recovery under this Heading to the extent that it relates to the supply of catering for NHS patients as part of the provision of NHS healthcare.

References – Draft Guidance HMRC VAT Manual VATGPB10870 (12 October 2015)

VATGPB10890

COS Heading 58 - Research, testing, inspection, certification and approval work for the Health and Safety Executive

Includes research, testing, inspection, certification and approval work for the HSE by an external contractor or supplier.

Devolved administrations discharging functions on behalf of the HSE are eligible to recover COS under this Heading.

References – HMRC VAT Manual VATGPB10890 (22 July 2016)

www.hmrc.gov.uk/manuals/vatgpbmanual/VATGPB10890.htm

VATGPB10910

COS Heading 59 - Scientific work of the kind normally carried out for the Department of the Environment, Food and Rural Affairs and the Food Standards Agency

Includes scientific work of the kind normally carried out for the Department of the Environment, Food and Rural Affairs and the Food Standards Agency by an external contractor or supplier such as:

- testing contaminated food
- detection and verification of disease in animals
- detection and verification of plant disease
- inspection of diseased animal carcases

This Heading may be used by departments in the devolved administrations if they have taken over responsibility for work undertaken by DEFRA or the FSA.

References – HMRC VAT Manual VATGPB10910 (22 July 2016)

www.hmrc.gov.uk/manuals/vatgpbmanual/VATGPB10910.htm

VATGPB10930

COS Heading 60 - Security services

This Heading allows recovery for the security services.

Includes the provision of security guards and staff security surveillance equipment (CCTV, surveillance cameras), security patrols and the secure transport of equipment and lone worker monitoring of staff.

Excludes the purchase of security equipment only, security vetting (but this may be recoverable under *COS Heading 57*), the hire of security staff to supplement in-house security teams (for example to provide holiday cover) and the repair and maintenance of security equipment (but this may be recoverable under *COS Heading 37*).

References – Draft Guidance HMRC VAT Manual VATGPB10930 (12 October 2015)

VATGPB10950

COS Heading 61 - Services of printing, copying, reproducing or mailing of any documents or publications, including typesetting services

Includes:

- post opening services;
- franking;

- labelling services including printing of bespoke forms, labels, cards, reports, letterheads etc. (bespoke means from scratch designed specifically for the GD or NHS organisation);
- parcel X-raying services;
- photocopying services supplied by outside firms;
- services of mailing agencies;
- printing services or reproduction of documents or publications for example, annual reports;
- typesetting services;
- micro filming and microfiche services.

Excludes:
- post box hire;
- shredding machines;
- franking machines.

In the case of printing services, although the supply of the paper is a supply of goods, it is considered an intrinsic part of the service being provided (for example, it is impossible to receive the service of printed letterheads without the paper on which the letterhead is printed). Therefore, the VAT would be eligible for recovery on the total contract price, which will normally include that of typesetting, paper and the use of the printing or embossing machinery.

The initial supply of signs and names badges (also the complete replacement of) is not eligible for recovery (supplies of goods). Signs replaced because of the merger of NHS organisations or GDs would be recoverable, as would repairs to existing signs.

References – Draft Guidance HMRC VAT Manual VATGPB10950 (12 October 2015)

VATGPB10970

COS Heading 62 - Share Registry Survey

Includes the provision of share registry survey services by an external contractor or supplier.

References – HMRC VAT Manual VATGPB10970 (22 July 2016)

www.hmrc.gov.uk/manuals/vatgpbmanual/VATGPB10970.htm

VATGPB10990

COS Heading 63 - Storage, distribution and goods disposal services

Includes the provision of physical or electronic storage, distribution or goods disposal services by an external contractor or supplier, such as the archiving of documents or record storage and retrieval services. Also includes the storage of goods, equipment or stock etc or the distribution of goods, equipment or stock etc. and the destruction of documents or the disposal of goods, equipment or stock or incineration services. Also includes the storage of detained or seized items and their secure disposal, the accommodation of seized or detained animals in zoos or boarding kennels etc, the storage of employees' possessions when they are relocated, secure bulk shredding services and call-off stock.

Notes – Changes were introduced by the Finance Act 2012 which required the standard rate of VAT to be applied to supplies of storage facilities with effect from 1 October 2012 (VATLP17550).

www.hmrc.gov.uk/manuals/vatlpmanual/VATLP17550.htm

www.hmrc.gov.uk/manuals/vatlpmanual/VATLP17600.htm

References – HMRC VAT Manual VATGPB10990 (22 July 2016)

www.hmrc.gov.uk/manuals/vatgpbmanual/VATGPB10990.htm

VATGPB11010

COS Heading 64 - Surveying, certification and registration in connection with ships and relevant record-keeping and verification, issue of certification, cards, discharge books and campaign medals to seamen

Includes the services of surveying, certification and registration in connection with ships and relevant record-keeping and verification, issue of certification cards, discharge books and campaign medals to seamen by an external contractor or supplier.

References – HMRC VAT Manual VATGPB11010 (22 July 2016)

www.hmrc.gov.uk/manuals/vatgpbmanual/VATGPB11010.htm

VATGPB11030

COS Heading 65 - Training, tuition or education

Includes the provision of training, tuition or education by an external contractor or supplier such as the services of trainers or lecturers. Also includes packages which include room hire for training or accommodation for students. Also includes online training.

Excludes room hire for training or accommodation for students when supplied separately and training materials such as DVDs and stationery when supplied separately.

Notes – training provided by an eligible body is an exempt supply and therefore no VAT will be charged (*VAT Notice 701/30*). Eligible bodies include NHS and GDs, Universities, Further Education Colleges and other educational institutions, professional bodies and charities. In practice, VAT will only be charged on training by private sector businesses. Self-employed trainers or lecturers may not be registered for VAT.

References – HMRC VAT Manual VATGPB11030 (22 July 2016)

www.hmrc.gov.uk/manuals/vatgpbmanual/VATGPB11030.htm

VATGPB11050

COS Heading 66 - Transport research of the kind normally carried out for the Department for Transport

Includes the provision of transport research services of the kind normally carried out for the Department of Transport by an external contractor or supplier.

Departments in the devolved administrations which carry out functions delegated to them by the Department of Transport may recover VAT incurred on transport research under this Heading.

References – HMRC VAT Manual VATGPB11050 (22 July 2016)

www.hmrc.gov.uk/manuals/vatgpbmanual/VATGPB11050.htm

VATGPB11070

COS Heading 67 - Travel services, excluding hotel accommodation and fares

Includes the provision of travel services by an external contractor or supplier such as the making of travel arrangements by a travel agent or external booking agency and charges for the use of VIP lounges at airports or stations.

Excludes hotel accommodation and fares (public transport services are generally zero-rated). Also excludes third party hired cars and taxi fares.

References – HMRC VAT Manual VATGPB11070 (22 July 2016)

www.hmrc.gov.uk/manuals/vatgpbmanual/VATGPB11070.htm

VATGPB11090

COS Heading 68 - Travel and transport surveys, including traffic census counts

Includes travel and transport surveys, including traffic census counts, carried out by an external contractor or supplier.

References – HMRC VAT Manual VATGPB11090 (22 July 2016)

www.hmrc.gov.uk/manuals/vatgpbmanual/VATGPB11090.htm

VATGPB11110

COS Heading 69 - Typing secretarial, telephonist and clerical services including agency staff

This Heading covers the outsourcing of typing, secretarial, telephonist and clerical service functions. It does not include the hire of typists, secretaries, administration staff and agency staff, for example to fill short-term vacancies or supplement existing staff levels during busy periods.

The words 'including agency staff' needs to be read in the context of the whole sentence, rather than in isolation. The agency staff referred to in the heading are those of the company supplying outsourced typing, secretarial, telephonist and clerical services.

Includes the provision of typing services by a word processing bureau.

Excludes secondees, employee expenses, the hire of telephones, telephone lines, switchboard equipment etc, and the hire of agency staff (for example, to fill long-term or short-term vacancies).

References – Draft Guidance HMRC VAT Manual VATGPB11110 (12 October 2015)

VATGPB11130

COS Heading 70 - Waste disposal services

Includes the collection and disposal of waste, including the removal or disposal of ash, refuse and sludge by an external contractor or supplier. Also includes clinical waste disposal, incineration services, the hire of incineration facilities and the removal, conveyance, treatment or disposal of the contents of cesspools, septic tanks or similar, and the hire of rubbish bins, wheelie bins, skips or other receptacles where they are exchanged for empty ones by an external contractor or supplier. Also includes refuse collection, trade waste, feminine hygiene services and recycling services.

Excludes the purchase of waste disposal equipment or the hire without exchange or uplift of rubbish bins, wheelie bins or other receptacles, and the removal of waste from a building side post-demolition.

Notes – the disposal of construction or building waste is covered by *COS Heading 35* (but excludes post-demolition waste which is not recoverable).

References – HMRC VAT Manual VATGPB11130 (22 July 2016)

www.hmrc.gov.uk/manuals/vatgpbmanual/VATGPB11130.htm

VATGPB11150

COS Heading 71 - Welfare services

Includes the provision of care, treatment or instruction designed to promote the physical or mental well-being of elderly, distressed or disabled persons, including children and young persons by an external contractor or supplier. Also includes staff support and counselling services.

Notes – welfare services are generally exempt supplies and therefore no VAT would be charged by the supplier.

References – HMRC VAT Manual VATGPB11150 (22 July 2016)

www.hmrc.gov.uk/manuals/vatgpbmanual/VATGPB11150.htm

VATGPB11170

COS Heading 72 - Career guidance, mentoring, counselling and other related services to help people in to work or to retain work as part of the DWP/Jobcentre Plus Employment Programme, provided under sections 2 and 9 of the Employment and Training Act 1973

Includes career guidance, mentoring, counselling and other related services to help people in to work or to retain work as part of the DWP/Jobcentre Plus Employment Programme, provided under the Employment and Training Act 1973 sections 2 and 9 by an external contractor or supplier.

Notes – although this Heading refers to the DWP etc it is to be read as including any equivalent programme in Scotland, Wales or Northern Ireland.

References – HMRC VAT Manual VATGPB11170 (22 July 2016)

www.hmrc.gov.uk/manuals/vatgpbmanual/VATGPB11170.htm

VATGPB11190

COS Heading 73 - Services relating to Action Teams for Jobs and Employment Zones

The previous Heading which allowed recovery on "mentoring and counselling to help people in to work as part of the New Deal and ONE Programme" has been withdrawn. This is because activities which used to fall under this heading have largely been absorbed into the reworded Heading 72.

References – HMRC VAT Manual VATGPB11190 (22 July 2016)

www.hmrc.gov.uk/manuals/vatgpbmanual/VATGPB11190.htm

VATGPB11210

COS Heading 74 - Original research undertaken in order to gain knowledge and understanding

Whilst there is no general restriction under this Heading, the term 'original research' is interpreted as meaning research that:

(a) involves surveys, field tests or new research design thinking, interviews or observation conducted specifically in relation to the subject of the research (as opposed to merely collating existing data); and

(b) extends to secondary data analysis, interpretation (which may include options and/or recommendations) or a systemic review of evidence (rather than mere data gathering and recording).

References – Draft Guidance HMRC VAT Manual VATGPB11210 (12 October 2015)

VATGPB11230

COS Heading 75 - Inspection of woodland sites for approval of felling licence applications and of timber imports/imports using timber packing to prevent entry of foreign tree pests and diseases

Includes the inspection of woodland sites for approval of felling licence applications and of timber imports/imports using timber packing to prevent entry of foreign tree pests and diseases by an external contractor or supplier.

References – HMRC VAT Manual VATGPB11230 (22 July 2016)

www.hmrc.gov.uk/manuals/vatgpbmanual/VATGPB11230.htm

VATGPB11250

COS Heading 76 - Probation Services delivered under the Criminal Justice and Court Services Act 2000

Recovery under this Heading is allowed as a matter of policy. It is not in the Treasury (Contracting-Out) Directions and has not been published in the London, Edinburgh or Belfast Gazettes.

Includes probation services now delivered under the Offender Management Act 2007 by an external contractor or supplier (rather than the Criminal Justice and Court Services Act 2000).

References – HMRC VAT Manual VATGPB11250 (22 July 2016)

www.hmrc.gov.uk/manuals/vatgpbmanual/VATGPB11250.htm

5.11 Additional Recovery

In addition, the following services have been agreed by the Treasury for inclusion in the next revision of the Directions for the NHS and GDs and therefore COS may now be recovered in relation to these (mostly applicable to GDs).

(i) call centre and contact centre services:
- VAT incurred by consumer direct call centres recoverable from 1 April 2007 (no entitlement to recover prior to this date)
- all other call centres recoverable from 1 April 2011 (no entitlement to recover prior to this date)

Includes:

- when an NHS organisation contracts out the management and day to day operation of contact Centres and Call Centres to third parties, and
- on the associated costs which are recharged by their suppliers
- and on the outsourced operation of the NHS 111 service

Excludes overheads relating to the provisions of in-house call centres and contact centres.

(ii) services provided through International Trade Advisers for UK Trade and Investment.

Recovery from 1 April 2011 (no entitlement to recover prior to this date).

(iii) services provided under Framework for Procuring External Support for Commissioners (FESC) other than:

- supplies of computer services and professional services that are excluded from the scope of *Headings 14 and 52* above (unless Treasury directs otherwise).
- elsewhere, the supply of staff.

Recovery from 1 April 2007 (no entitlement to recover prior to this date).

6   BUSINESS ACTIVITIES

Any income, transaction or activity which falls within the scope of VAT Act 1994 s.4 is business (including by virtue of s.95 any trade profession or vocation and the provision by a club, association or organisation, for a subscription or other consideration, of the facilities or advantages available to its members, and the admission, for a consideration, of persons to any premises). There have been several cases in which the meaning of business in a VAT context has been examined.

In the NHS, any income, transaction or activity listed in the Treasury Taxing Direction revised in October 2008 was deemed to be a business activity (see **Appendix 4**). VAT Act 1994 s.41 was amended in the Finance Act 2012 to clarify the position under EU law (see **Appendix 1**). HMRC have indicated that there should be no material change in the application of s.41; merely that in its revised form it is more consistent with the Principal VAT Directive in relation to distortion of competition. About 2% of NHS activities overall are business activities and within the scope of VAT (although it should be remembered that the NHS as whole is a £2bn plus enterprise).

The main business activities of the NHS include:
- the supply of catering and food (see **6.1 Catering & Food**)
- private healthcare (see **6.2 Private Patients**)
- car parking (see **6.3 Car Parks**)
- supplies of drugs and pharmaceuticals (see **6.6 Pharmacy Supplies**)
- research and development (see **6.7 Research & Development**)
- supplies of accommodation and property (see **6.4 Property & Accommodation**)

If the income, transaction or activity does fall within the scope of the tax then output tax will be chargeable unless it falls within VAT Act 1994 Schedule 8 (Zero-Rated) or Schedule 9 (Exempt). All supplies of goods or services within the scope of the tax are standard-rated (20%) unless specifically excluded (if a supply falls within Schedule 7A – Reduced-Rate output tax will be chargeable at 5% rather than 20%). Theoretically, output tax charged is payable by the final consumer and therefore has no net effect on the position of the supplier. VAT incurred by a taxable person which is attributable to business activities will be input tax, but not necessarily allowable input tax.

For input tax to qualify as allowable under s.26 of the Act it must be:
- attributable to a taxable supply;

- attributable to supplies outside the UK which would be taxable supplies if made within the UK; and
- attributable to an exempt supply (but within the *de minimis* limits).

The entitlement to deduct arises in relation to goods acquired or services received for the purpose of business. This means that the taxable supply to which the input tax is attributable need not have actually occurred or be about to occur at the time the goods are acquired or services received. The intention to make a taxable supply also gives rise to the right to deduct. In certain circumstances that right also subsists where there is no subsequent taxable supply, but there are clawback and payback provisions under the VAT Regulations 1995 SI 1995/2518 where an intended taxable supply crystallises as an actual exempt supply or there is a change of use from taxable to exempt or vice versa (see *VAT Notice 706/1*).

Input tax is either directly attributable or indirectly attributable. Direct attribution means wholly and exclusively attributable to a supply whether taxable or exempt (or a supply above) and where taxable it should be claimed in full in the VAT Return for period in which it is incurred e.g. trading input tax such as vending machine supplies etc. direct input tax is not dependent on any method or special method and may be claimed without any further calculation or the approval of HMRC e.g. it is not necessary to wait for an annual business activities claim. Indirect attribution means partly attributable (to any degree) to taxable supplies (or a supply above) and partly attributable to exempt supplies or non-business activities or both. Indirect input tax may either be apportioned according a specific activity (sectorisation or partial attribution) or as part of all general and overhead costs (residual attribution).

Sectorisation can be a very accurate apportionment depending on the information available but it remains indirect attribution. Residual attribution identifies the final residual input tax entitlement where no specific apportionment is feasible on general costs and overheads. The more intensive the analysis, the more detailed the method, the more accurate the attribution.

Normally, the business/non-business apportionment is separate from the partial exemption calculation (the Combined Method now available is not generally recommended for NHS organisations) and should be carried out before it on a basis determined by the taxpayer but which must result in a fair and reasonable attribution of input tax to taxable supplies. The method the taxpayer uses to calculate the allowable input tax does not require the approval of HMRC because there is no provision in law which requires that HMRC approve a business/non-business apportionment method of itself but in practice HMRC approve the method indirectly by approving the resulting input tax claimed as a fair and reasonable attribution.

The main business activities of the NHS are covered under separate headings below from the perspective of the NHS as supplier, followed by the Treasury List. For the most part the remaining activities on the Treasury List are minor and peripheral.

All supplies are assumed to be made for a consideration and within the UK unless otherwise stated.

6.1 Catering & Food

6.1.1 Catering

The supply of catering to staff or visitors is the most significant business activity carried on by NHS organisations. It normally results in a significant output tax liability on the income (although there are both standard-rated and zero-rated supplies) and also in a significant (but proportionate) input tax entitlement on VAT incurred on costs directly and indirectly attributable to the taxable supplies as well as underpinning the residual input tax entitlement of the organisation in relation to general overheads (including capital expenditure). Where catering is contracted-out to a private contractor (e.g. in a PFI) there is a corresponding negative impact on overall input tax entitlement.

In the NHS catering is supplied to NHS patients, private patients and staff and visitors. Catering supplied to NHS patients in the course of healthcare is a non-business activity, catering supplied to private patients in the course of healthcare is an exempt supply, and catering supplied to staff and visitors (and NHS or private patients outside of healthcare) is a taxable supply. Catering means the supply of prepared food and drink consumed on the premises where supplied involving a significant element of service (*VAT Notice 709/1*). It includes supplies made in restaurants, cafes and canteens (excluding cold takeaway food) and food prepared and supplied for events and functions. It does not include the retail supply of food such as pre-packed sandwiches or groceries which are zero-rated supplies of goods, nor does it include the retail supply of confectionery, crisps, ice cream or alcoholic drinks which are standard-rated supplies of goods.

There is a potential anomaly in relation to supplies of catering to medical students. The teaching of medical students is a non-business activity. Supplies closely related to exempt education (including catering provided to students) are also exempt by virtue of VAT Act 1994 Schedule 9 Group 6. HMRC have noted that the concept of 'closely related' only applies to exempt supplies of education so although it may be expected that catering for medical students would be non-business as closely related to non-business teaching the HMRC position is that it must be taxable because there is no corresponding non-business 'closely related' provision.

The main aspects of catering as a business activity in the NHS are:
- catering on premises in staff (including students) and visitor restaurants, cafés or canteens etc (standard-rated);
- vending machine sales in staff and visitor restaurants, cafés or canteens etc (standard-rated – or partly zero-rated subject to a Retail Scheme apportionment – see *VAT Notice 727*);
- cold takeaway food sold in staff and visitor restaurants, cafés or canteens etc (zero-rated subject to a Retail Scheme apportionment – see *VAT Notice 727*); and
- catering for private patients (exempt).

Retail supplies as a business activity include:
- vending machine sales outside catering premises in common areas or thoroughfares (standard-rated or zero-rated depending on the product);
- trolley sales to NHS or private patients (standard-rated or zero-rated depending on the product);
- sales of food and groceries etc (predominantly zero-rated);
- sales of confectionery, crisps and ice cream etc (standard-rated); and
- (retail supplies may be made from the catering outlets as well as shops etc – see **Appendix 7. Reduced-Rate Supplies** and **Appendix 8. Zero-Rated Supplies**).

The following tests determine whether or not an activity is "catering" and therefore the liability of the supplies made (these may be standard-rated or zero-rated):
- does it fall within the ordinary meaning of catering?
- is it supplied for consumption on the premises?
- is it hot food?

The ordinary meaning of "catering" is the definition above. Following *Compass Contract Services UK Ltd (CA 2006)* the definition of "premises" was revised and limited to areas controlled by the supplier or areas specifically provided for the consumption of food e.g. a seating area adjacent to a catering outlet (historically, the definition was much wider). The significance of the redefinition is that if cold food is taken away from these areas e.g. from a canteen back to an office in the same building then that will qualify for zero-rating. Hot takeaway, however, is standard-rated and "hot" means heated for consumption above the ambient temperature (including where a microwave is provided for customers to heat the food themselves – it does not, however, include items cooked and allowed to cool). The main area of uncertainty is over the supply of cold food which is prepared and delivered e.g. sandwich platters or cold buffets. Casual or *ad hoc* sales of sandwiches or cold savouries in offices etc are regarded as zero-rated retail supplies but contracted or commissioned sales (for meetings etc) are regarded as standard-rated catering supplies.

6.1.2 Output Tax

Output tax is due on the standard-rated sales and there are two methods of calculating the proportions of standard-rated and zero-rated sales. Whichever basis is chosen the VAT Fraction (see **Appendix 11 – Definitions**) is then applied to the standard-rated proportion of sales to calculate the output tax due. The balance is zero-rated and no output tax is due on this.

The first method is the Point of Sale Retail Scheme (*VAT Notice 727*). This is potentially the most accurate method of accounting for VAT on mixed liability sales. It involves the use of separate tills or a till system capable of distinguishing between goods sold at different rates of VAT. It is, however, subject to human error and depends on the staff operating the tills to always ask whether the supply is "sit-in" or "takeaway" and always to record the liability of the supply correctly.

The second method is to use the Catering Adaptation Retail Scheme (*VAT Notice 727*). With the permission of HMRC this can be used where sales do not exceed £1m annually (from any single site – different sites could potentially use different Retail Schemes depending on circumstances), the result is fair and reasonable and HMRC are satisfied that it is impracticable to operate the Point of Sale Scheme.

(1) the first step is to add up Daily Gross Takings (including cash received, vouchers etc);

(2) the second step is to calculate the percentage of total supplies of catering which is standard-rated – this is done by keeping a representative sample of standard-rated and zero-rated sales – this means catering staff keeping a manual record of the types of supply made for a period (and every site would require its own representative sample taken) – normally a week's sample is satisfactory for HMRC and this should be updated annually – it should also take account of seasonal variations and fluctuations etc (if applicable);

(3) the third step is to apply the percentage of standard-rated sales derived from the sample to the Daily Gross Takings; and

(4) the fourth and final step is to apply the VAT Fraction to the standard-rated sales to calculate the output tax due.

There is a potential anomaly in relation to vending machines which has to be taken into account. Where these are sited outside catering premises e.g. in common areas or thoroughfares, sales are treated as retail supplies of goods and the liability is that of the product supplied. Where sited in staff and visitor restaurants, cafés or canteens etc the supply is regarded as standard-rated catering but subject to apportionment under the Retail Scheme used. Where this is the Catering Adaptation the representative sample taken should include any vending machine sales but if Point of Sale a separate and additional calculation will have to be carried out for the vending machine sales or all of the income may be incorrectly treated as standard-rated when it is partly zero-rated.

6.1.3 Input tax

Input tax is allowable on the direct and indirect costs attributable to taxable supplies of catering and food.

There are three levels of input tax recovery related to catering and food:

(1) full recovery on directly attributable input tax – such as the cost of retail purchases where these are standard-rated (e.g. confectionery etc) or costs attributable to a catering outlet which is fully taxable such as a restaurant, café or bistro which caters only to staff or visitors (or to patients outside of healthcare) – the zero-rated cold takeaway food does not normally give rise to a direct input tax entitlement because it is unlikely that VAT will have been charged on the purchases but zero-rated supplies are taxable supplies and there would be full input tax entitlement on attributable costs if the catering outlet is fully taxable;

(2) proportionate recovery on sectorised costs such as the catering cost centres – normally the same kitchen facilities are used for both patients (NHS or private) and the staff and visitors restaurants – where costs can be wholly and exclusively attributed to a fully taxable outlet then they would fall into the category above but this is not normally the case except for peripheral and self-contained outlets such as coffee shops etc – generally an apportionment has to be made to determine the taxable catering percentage – normally this information will be provided by the catering manager or supervisor typically on the basis of the ratio of NHS/private patient meals prepared to meals sold in the catering outlets to staff and visitors – this varies according to outlet and circumstances – this percentage is then applied to the sectorised costs and that proportion of the VAT incurred is allowable input tax; and

(3) residual recovery on general overheads – in this context the residual input tax entitlement arises as a proportion of VAT incurred on general non-attributable overheads for the organisation as a whole (any VAT

incurred on costs which has been taken into account above should be excluded).

Proportionate recovery on capital expenditure will also be allowable – significant sums of VAT may be incurred in relation to capital expenditure and this area of entitlement is often overlooked – the entitlement arises in relation to taxable supplies made or intended to be made irrespective of whether the project is refurbishment, new build, alteration, extension etc (unlike eligibility for COS recovery) – the amount of input tax allowable will depend on the proportion of the VAT incurred which relates or will relate to taxable supplies – further calculations will be necessary to determine this proportion – but typically it would be based on a floorspace analysis and ratio (excluding the common areas of buildings which are non-attributable) – from 1 January 2011 any capital project with a net value in excess of £250,000 and including a business element (taxable or exempt) falls within the Capital Goods Scheme (**10.4 Capital Goods Scheme**).

6.2   Private Patients

Supplies to private patients are business supplies to individuals or organisations outside the NHS Divisional Registration. Private healthcare is an exempt supply and the supply of goods closely related to private healthcare as part of a package of care (including drugs) is also exempt. Private healthcare is the main exempt business activity in the NHS and as such gives rise to most of the partial exemption restriction applied to COS recovery. Government has abolished the private patient cap (Health & Social Care Act 2012) and proposed a significant increase in private patient income in the NHS which, if implemented, would have a corresponding impact on the overall VAT position of the NHS.

Following *d'Ambrumenil (CJEU C-307/01)* medical care was redefined from 1 May 2007 to services provided where the primary purpose is the protection, maintenance or restoration of the health of the person receiving the service. Previously, medical services supplied by persons on a statutory medical register were exempt under Group 7 of VAT Act 1994 Schedule 9 but the position in relation to non-medical related services was unclear. The revision meant that non-medical but related services which were hitherto exempt supplies became standard-rated supplies.

The liabilities of supplies related to private patients are as follows:

6.2.1   Medical Services

- medical services supplied to a private patient (including non-EU patients where there is no reciprocal health agreement) when performed by a person enrolled on a statutory medical register and where the primary purpose of the service is the protection, maintenance or restoration of the health of the person receiving the service (exempt);

- provision of a package of care including medical services, nursing services, accommodation and catering etc for private inpatients (exempt);
- healthcare or nursing services supplied to a private patient when performed by a person not enrolled on a statutory medical register where that person is under the direct supervision of a person enrolled on a statutory medical register (exempt);
- healthcare or nursing services supplied to a private patient where supplied in a hospital, hospice or nursing home (exempt);
- healthcare or nursing services supplied to a private patient when performed by a person not enrolled on a statutory medical register where that person is not under the direct supervision of a person enrolled on a statutory medical register and where not supplied in a hospital, hospice or nursing home (standard-rated);
- goods including drugs, dressings and appliances etc supplied to a private patient in connection with medical or surgical treatment as part of a package of care (exempt); and
- goods supplied to a private patient (but not on prescription) and not as part of a package of care (standard-rated).

6.2.2   Cosmetic Services

- cosmetic services supplied to a private patient when performed by a person enrolled on a statutory medical register or an unregistered person directly supervised by a person enrolled on a statutory medical register and where the primary purpose of the service is the protection, maintenance or restoration of the health of the person receiving the service (exempt);
- cosmetic services supplied to a private patient when performed by a person enrolled on a statutory medical register or an unregistered person directly supervised by a person enrolled on a statutory medical register and where the primary purpose of the service is not the protection, maintenance or restoration of the health of the person receiving the service (standard-rated); and
- cosmetic services supplied to a private patient when performed by a person not enrolled on a statutory medical register where that person is not under the direct supervision of a person enrolled on a statutory medical register (standard-rated).

6.2.3   Drugs & Prescriptions

- qualifying goods dispensed (including letting on hire) on the prescription of an approved practitioner by a registered pharmacist to a private patient for personal use (zero-rated);
- qualifying goods dispensed (including letting on hire) on the prescription of an approved practitioner by a registered medical practitioner to a private patient for personal use (standard-rated);
- "qualifying goods" means any goods (including drugs) designed or adapted for use in conjunction with any medical or surgical treatment except hearing aids, dentures, spectacles and contact lenses;
- "direct supervision" means supervision provided to meet the medical needs of the patient, where the supervisor is a person enrolled on a statutory medical register, where the supervisor has a direct relationship with the staff performing the service, where the supervisor is available for the whole time the care is provided, where the supervisor decides on the level of care to be provided, where the supervisor demonstrably monitors the work of the unregistered staff and where not more than 2,000 hours per week of staff time are supervised by a single health professional;
- "approved practitioner" means registered medical practitioner, dentist, community practitioner nurse prescriber, nurse independent prescriber, optometrist independent prescriber, pharmacist independent prescriber or supplementary prescriber; and
- "personal use" means for the personal or domestic use of an individual and explicitly excludes use by an individual while being provided with medical or surgical treatment, or any form of care, as an inpatient or resident of, or whilst attending, a hospital, nursing home or other approved institution.

6.2.4   Occupational Health

- occupational health services provided to private patients when performed by a person enrolled on a statutory medical register and where the primary purpose of the service is the protection, maintenance or restoration of the health of the person receiving the service e.g. post-employment medicals in relation to the health and medical fitness of the employee, post-employment training and advice to promote and maintain the health and medical fitness of employees (exempt); and
- occupational health services provided to private patients when performed by a person enrolled on a statutory medical register and where the primary purpose of the service is not the protection, maintenance or restoration of the health of the person receiving the

service e.g. pre-employment medicals in relation to the health and medical fitness of the prospective employee, post-employment medicals in relation to pension schemes, ergonomic and risk assessments, advice or helpline services, counselling or lifestyle assessments (standard-rated).

6.2.5   Patient Transport
- ambulances services provided to private patients (for sick and injured persons) in vehicles designed for that purpose (exempt); and
- patient transport or taxi services provided to private patients (standard-rated).

6.2.6   Administrative Services
- associated or administrative services supplied to private patients when performed by a person enrolled on a statutory medical register and where the primary purpose of the service is not the protection, maintenance or restoration of the health of the person receiving the service e.g. medical reports, passport applications, medico-legal services (standard-rated);
- access to the medical records of a private patient – where provided under a statutory duty e.g. Data Protection Act 1998, Access to Medical Reports Act 1988 or the Access to Health Records Act 1990 (non-business);
- access to the medical records of a private patient – where provided otherwise than under a statutory duty e.g. Data Protection Act 1998, Access to Medical Reports Act 1988 or the Access to Health Records Act 1990 (standard-rated);
- medical certificates provided for a private patient where the primary purpose of the service is the protection, maintenance or restoration of the health of the person receiving the service e.g. certificate of fitness to travel (exempt); and
- medical certificates provided for a private patient where the primary purpose of the service is not the protection, maintenance or restoration of the health of the person receiving the service e.g. certificates re pensions, personal injury litigation, medical negligence litigation or in relation to professional or sporting activities (standard-rated).

6.2.7   Output Tax
Output tax is due on standard-rated supplies made to private patients.

6.2.8   Input Tax
Input tax is allowable on the direct and indirect costs attributable to taxable supplies made to private patients.

There are three levels of input tax recovery related to private patients:

(1) full recovery on directly attributable input tax – such as VAT incurred on the purchase of drugs supplied on prescription to private outpatients (zero-rated or standard-rated);

(2) proportionate recovery on sectorised costs such as the pharmacy cost centres – the recovery percentage could be calculated on the basis of proportionate quantities of drugs supplied or income related to taxable supplies – this percentage is then applied to the sectorised costs and that proportion of the VAT incurred is allowable input tax; and

(3) residual recovery on general overheads – in this context the residual input tax entitlement arises as a proportion of VAT incurred on general non-attributable overheads for the organisation as a whole (any VAT incurred on costs which has been taken into account above should be excluded).

Proportionate recovery on capital expenditure will also be allowable – the entitlement arises in relation to taxable supplies made or intended to be made irrespective of whether the project is refurbishment, new build, alteration, extension etc (unlike eligibility for COS recovery) – the amount of input tax allowable will depend on the proportion of the VAT incurred which relates or will relate to taxable supplies or supplies which would be taxable supplies if performed in the UK – further calculations will be necessary to determine this proportion – but typically it would be based on a floorspace analysis and ratio (excluding the common areas of a building which are non-attributable) – from 1 January 2011 any capital project with a net value in excess of £250,000 and including a business element (taxable or exempt) falls within the Capital Goods Scheme (see **10.4 Capital Goods Scheme**).

6.2.9   Partial Exemption

The majority of costs related to private healthcare are attributable to exempt supplies and no input tax entitlement arises. The partial exemption restriction in relation to input tax is normally neutral because exempt input tax (as opposed to COS) will not usually have been previously claimed. The exempt supplies attributable to private patients are the main source of COS restriction in the NHS. The impact of this can be reduced by accurate attribution. For example, identifying private wards or costs which are directly attributable to private patients and excluding these. Equally, there should be no restriction on costs directly attributable to non-business activities.

6.3 Car Parks

The supply of parking facilities to staff, visitors or patients is standard-rated. The income from car parking can be significant. Output tax is due on the income (although penalties may be outside the scope of VAT) but there is also a significant (but proportionate) input tax entitlement on VAT incurred on costs directly and indirectly attributable to the taxable supplies as well as contributing to the residual input tax entitlement of the organisation in relation to general overheads (including capital expenditure). Where car parking is contracted-out to a private contractor (e.g. in a PFI) there is a corresponding negative impact on overall input tax entitlement.

6.3.1 Output Tax

Output tax is due on the standard-rated charges for parking. The VAT Fraction is applied to the standard-rated income to calculate the output tax due.

Excess charges can be treated in two ways. If an excess charge is a penalty for exceeding time of stay, then it can be treated as outside the scope of VAT and no output tax is due. Accordingly, the VAT Fraction should only be applied to the standard-rated proportion of the income. However, if the car parking facilities can continue to be used after the original time of stay has expired on payment of an additional amount then that is regarded as an additional standard-rated consideration. Accordingly, the VAT Fraction would be applied to the full amount of the income received because it is all standard-rated. The liability is dependent on the terms and conditions of parking and these should be clearly displayed.

Where car parking services are contracted-out this can either be on a profit share basis or a right over land is granted to the contractor. Where an NHS organisation receives a commission on the parking charges this will normally be a profit share arrangement and will be standard-rated. Leases of car parks are also standard-rated.

6.3.2 Input Tax

Input tax is allowable on the direct and indirect costs attributable to taxable supplies of car parking.

There are two levels of input tax recovery related to car parks:

(1) full recovery on directly attributable input tax. Apart from construction costs (see below) maintenance costs on open car parks are generally minimal. However, if there is a multi-storey car park then there may be associated utilities and maintenance costs and any VAT incurred on these would be recoverable in full as allowable input tax.

(2) residual recovery on general overheads. In this context, the residual input tax entitlement arises as a proportion of VAT incurred on general non-attributable overheads for the organisation as a whole (any VAT incurred on costs which has been taken into account above should be excluded).

However, a recent case (*Vehicle Control Services Ltd [2016] UKUT 316*) suggests that apportionment may be required where there is a significant level of income outside the scope of VAT.

Proportionate recovery on capital expenditure will also be allowable. The entitlement arises in relation to taxable supplies made or intended to be made (therefore normally full recovery) irrespective of whether the project is refurbishment or new build (unlike eligibility for COS recovery) e.g. the resurfacing of an existing car park or the construction of a new one. From 1 January 2011 any capital project with a net value in excess of £250,000 and including a business element (taxable or exempt) falls within the Capital Goods Scheme (see **10.4 Capital Goods Scheme**).

Before 1 January 2012 the supply of parking to staff under a salary sacrifice scheme was outside the scope of VAT and would have been regarded as a non-business Activity requiring apportionment of input tax (if applicable). However, following *Astra Zeneca UK Ltd (CJEU C-40/09)* supplies to employees previously regarded as outside the scope of VAT are now regarded as business supplies and if standard-rated, output tax will be due. Because the supply of parking is standard-rated, output tax is now due on any such salary sacrifice arrangement (it was always due on salary deduction arrangements and remains so).

6.4   Property & Accommodation

This section deals with business supplies of land and property by the NHS. Supplies of land and property are exempt (*VAT Act 1994 Schedule 9 Group 1*) unless an option to tax (*VAT Act 1994 Schedule 10*) is exercised. The supply of land and property is one of the most complex areas of the tax because of the underlying complexity of property law (see *VAT Notice 742*). The tax position reflects the underlying legal position. Because of this it is always prudent to take VAT advice in relation to any property transaction in the same way that legal advice would be taken (i.e. when a lease is drafted or a sale proposed or as part of the planning process).

The main supplies of land and property as a business activity by the NHS are:

- supplies of accommodation to businesses e.g. leased retail premises, serviced or unserviced (exempt or standard-rated);

- supplies of accommodation to partnership organisations e.g. Universities, Further Education Colleges, local authorities, police and fire authorities (exempt or standard-rated);
- supplies of practice accommodation to GP and dental practices (exempt or standard-rated);
- supplies of accommodation to charities (exempt or standard-rated);
- NHS LIFT (exempt or standard-rated);
- supplies of residential accommodation e.g. to resident staff (non-business or exempt);
- disposals of land or property e.g. sales of land or buildings (exempt or standard-rated).

(Supplies of land and property within the NHS are non-business)

6.4.1   Supplies of Accommodation

Where an NHS organisation rents out or leases property or grants a licence to occupy for a consideration there will be an exempt supply. If the option to tax is exercised, the supply is standard-rated. Option to tax is nearly always advisable from the perspective of the supplier (for example, it is intrinsic to LIFT Projects) because it gives rise to full input tax entitlement and all of the VAT incurred on costs attributable to the taxable supply of land or property is recoverable. Conversely, if the supply is not taxed and remains exempt none of the VAT incurred on costs attributable to the exempt supply of land or property is recoverable either as input tax or COS. In relation to land or property these sums can be significant. From an NHS perspective option to tax should be considered first as the likely best option (although see below for consideration of the commercial impact).

However, from the perspective of the recipient, the purpose for which they use the accommodation will determine whether a taxed transaction is cost effective, for example, an opted lease for retail premises would be standard-rated and because the recipient is a fully taxable business the effect is neutral because the recipient could recover input tax in full. If the recipient was, for example, a University (which makes predominantly exempt supplies), and the leased premises are used to make predominantly exempt supplies the allowable input tax would be minimal or even nil, thus the output tax charged by the supplier would become an additional irrecoverable cost. The status and activities of the recipient will influence their decision making i.e. whether or not they can recover input tax. This is a prime example of the duality of the tax and why every transaction should be considered from both an output and input perspective.

Thus the liability of the supply by the NHS would be either exempt or standard-rated and where opted and standard-rated input tax would typically be recoverable by the recipient as follows:

- supplies of accommodation to businesses making taxable supplies e.g. leased retail premises (serviced or unserviced) – full input tax recovery by the recipient;
- supplies of accommodation to Universities or FECs making exempt or predominantly exempt supplies (or using the accommodation for non-business activities) – minimal or nil input tax recovery by the recipient;
- supplies of accommodation to Universities or FECs making taxable or predominantly taxable supplies – full or partial input tax recovery by the recipient;
- supplies of accommodation to local authorities, police and fire authorities e.g. in a LIFT Project – full VAT recovery under VAT Act 1994 s.33 by the recipient (but nil or minimal input tax recovery *per se*);
- supplies of practice accommodation to GP and dental practices (making exempt or predominantly exempt supplies – minimal or nil input tax recovery by the recipient (but the irrecoverable VAT charged may be refunded under practice arrangements);
- supplies of accommodation to charities making exempt or predominantly exempt supplies e.g. welfare services – minimal or nil input tax recovery by the recipient;
- supplies of accommodation to charities making taxable or predominantly taxable supplies e.g. a tearoom or coffee shop – full or partial input tax recovery by the recipient.

The option to tax is disapplied in relation to the following and output tax should not be charged:

- supplies of accommodation to charities for non-business activities (the option is not disapplied where a charity uses the accommodation for office purposes – nor in relation to other non-business activities such as NHS Healthcare e.g. in LIFT projects);
- supplies of residential accommodation e.g. to resident staff.

6.4.2   The NHS as Landlord

Where an NHS organisation makes supplies of accommodation it is likely that there will be an associated supply of services. Again the complexity of the tax position reflects the underlying complexity of property law. The principal liabilities are set out here but it is prudent to take tax advice should when entering into any contract or rental agreement with tenants particularly when these involve inducements, reverse premiums, variations, surrenders, reverse surrenders, dilapidation payments or indemnity payments (with or without associated services – see *VAT Notice 742*).

The liability of services provided by landlords for non-domestic property are as follows:

General Service Charges – general services provided as part of a lease follow the liability of the main supply of accommodation – typically a service or maintenance charge connected with the external fabric or common areas or parts of the building (as opposed to demised areas of the property for individual occupants) – and paid for by all the occupants through a common service charge (exempt or standard-rated where an option to tax has been exercised).

Insurance – if the landlord is the policy holder then the insurance payment from the tenant to the landlord is part payment for the main supply of accommodation and follows the liability of the main supply (exempt or standard-rated).

Insurance – if the tenant is the policy holder then the insurance payment from the tenant to the landlord and then paid by the landlord on behalf of the tenant is a disbursement and therefore outside the scope of VAT (non-business).

Rates – if the landlord is the rateable person then the rates payment from the tenant to the landlord is part payment for the main supply of accommodation and follows the liability of the main supply (exempt or standard-rated).

Rates – if the tenant is the rateable person then the rates payment from the tenant to the landlord and then paid by the landlord on behalf of the tenant is a disbursement and therefore outside the scope of VAT (non-business).

Telephones – if the account is in the name of the landlord then any charge for telephones by the landlord is a payment for a supply of services (standard-rated).

Telephones – if the account is in the name of the tenant then any payment from the tenant to the landlord and then paid by the landlord on behalf of the tenant is a disbursement and therefore outside the scope of VAT (non-business).

Reception/Switchboard – an inclusive charge under the lease for reception or switchboard facilities is part payment for the main supply of accommodation and follows the liability of the main supply (exempt or standard-rated).

Office Services – an inclusive charge under the lease for office services or facilities is part payment for the main supply of accommodation and follows the liability of the main supply (exempt or standard-rated).

Office Services – a separate charge for office services or facilities is a payment for a supply of services (standard-rated).

Fixtures & Fittings – an inclusive charge under the lease for fixtures and fittings is part payment for the main supply of accommodation and follows the liability of the main supply (exempt or standard-rated).

Fixtures & Fittings. A separate charge for fixtures and fittings is a payment for a supply of goods (standard-rated).

Utilities – a separate charge for un-metered supplies of fuel and power is treated as an additional payment for the main supply of accommodation and follows the liability of the main supply (exempt or standard-rated).

Utilities – a separate charge where the landlord operates secondary credit meters is payment for a supply of fuel and power (standard-rated for non-domestic premises – reduced-rate for domestic premises).

Management Charges – a separate charge for the management of a development or administering the collection of services charges is treated as an additional payment for the main supply of accommodation and follows the liability of the main supply (exempt or standard-rated).

(see *VAT Notice 742*)

The liability of services provided by landlords for domestic residential property are as follows (except where provided to staff under a Whitley Council Agreement at a subsidised and uneconomic rent (non-business activity)):

General Service Charges – mandatory services related to the upkeep of common areas on an estate of dwellings or the common areas of multi-occupied dwelling e.g. nurses' or doctors' residences are treated as ancillary to the main supply of residential accommodation (exempt).

Utilities – a separate charge for un-metered supplies of fuel and power is treated as an additional payment for the main supply of residential accommodation (exempt).

Utilities – a separate charge where the landlord operates secondary credit meters is payment for a supply of fuel and power (reduced-rate).

(see *VAT Notice 742*)

6.5   NHS LIFT

Local Improvement Finance Trusts are now an established component of the NHS Primary Care investment strategy (NHS LIFT). LIFT is a joint venture between the public and private sector to build and operate new and fit for purpose primary care premises (usually with associated public or third sector partners e.g. local authority social services, fire and police authorities or charities). For each LIFT a joint venture company (LIFTCO) is formed with shareholders including the NHS, private sector partners, the Department of Health and Partnerships UK (therefore the NHS does not supply the accommodation directly but as part of the LIFTCO). The private sector partners are normally responsible for construction and management of the building. LIFTCO will exercise the option to tax to recover the input tax on construction and ongoing maintenance costs. This is fundamental and output tax will be charged on the rent and service charges (including utilities and equipment) irrespective of the status of the occupants (see above for recipients).

If an NHS organisation sublets part of a LIFT, then option to tax should be considered in the normal way. Option to tax applies to a taxable person and a specified property (whether land or a building). Another taxable person is not bound by that option to tax insofar as they make business supplies in relation to the land or building. Therefore, a sublet by a tenant in a taxed building is not obliged to opt to tax the sublet (nor is it automatically opted). Conversely, a sublet by a tenant in an untaxed building can be opted by the tenant. If the tenant is an NHS organisation and does not actually opt to tax the sublet the supply will be exempt and there will be a restriction on any COS entitlement under *COS Heading 45* (see *VAT Notice 742A*).

6.5.1 Sales of Land or Buildings

Except in relation to the sale of the freehold of a non-domestic building which is less than three years old (standard-rated) where an NHS organisation sells land or buildings there will be an exempt supply. If the option to tax is exercised the supply is standard-rated. If standard-rated output tax would be chargeable on the full value of the supply (and any Stamp Duty Land Tax payable on the transaction would be charged on the gross value). But option to tax is virtually always advisable for the supplier because it gives rise to full input tax entitlement and all of the VAT incurred on costs attributable to the taxable supply of land or property is recoverable. Conversely, if the supply is not taxed and remains exempt none of the VAT incurred on costs attributable to the exempt supply of land or property is recoverable either as input tax or COS. In relation to sales of land or property these sums can be significant. From an NHS perspective option to tax should always be considered first as the likely best option.

For example, the VAT on demolition and site clearance costs would be recoverable as input tax where an option to tax is exercised (and these costs are not eligible for COS recovery). VAT on legal fees and other professional fees is not recoverable as COS in relation to an exempt supply even where the ultimate purpose of the transaction is NHS healthcare or a non-business activity. The rule in relation to input tax or COS recovery is that for direct attribution there must be a direct and immediate link to the supply or activity. Therefore, VAT incurred where there is a direct and immediate link to an exempt supply as part of a project with an ultimate NHS healthcare purpose will not be allowable input tax or be eligible for COS recovery, but if the transaction is taxed all of the VAT incurred is allowable input tax.

6.5.2   Output Tax
Output tax is due on taxable supplies of land or property.

6.5.3   Input Tax
Input tax is allowable on the direct and indirect costs attributable to taxable supplies of land or property.

There are three levels of input tax recovery related to supplies of land or property:
(1) full recovery on directly attributable input tax – such as VAT incurred on construction, demolition, site clearance, professional fees, peripheral works, maintenance costs, utilities or any other cost directly attributable to the taxable supply etc.;
(2) proportionate recovery on sectorised costs – such as the administration of estates and facilities or leased practice accommodation. Further calculations will be necessary to determine this proportion, but typically it would be based on a floorspace analysis and ratio. This percentage is then applied to the sectorised costs and that proportion of the VAT incurred is allowable input tax; and
(3) residual recovery on general overheads. In this context the residual input tax entitlement arises as a proportion of VAT incurred on general non-attributable overheads for the organisation as a whole. Any one-off sales or purchases of land or property should be excluded as incidental. Therefore, the residual input tax entitlement will only arise in relation to ongoing supplies of land or property such as leased accommodation (any VAT incurred on costs which has been taken into account above should be excluded).

Input tax entitlement arises in relation to taxable supplies made or intended to be made irrespective of the type of supply. The amount of input tax allowable will depend on the proportion of the VAT incurred which relates or will relate to taxable supplies. Further calculations will be necessary to determine this proportion in each project, but typically it would be based on a floorspace analysis and ratio (excluding the common areas of buildings which are non-attributable). From 1 January 2011 any capital project with a net value in excess of £250,000 and including a business element (taxable or exempt) falls within the Capital Goods Scheme (See **10.4 Capital Goods Scheme**).

6.6 Pharmacy Supplies

Unless subject to qualification or exclusion business supplies of drugs and pharmaceuticals are standard-rated. This is an area with multiple liabilities depending on the circumstances. It is a significant source of error in relation to unclaimed input tax attributable to taxable supplies. Drugs or pharmaceuticals supplied or administered in connection with medical or surgical treatment as part of a package of NHS care (including supplied by an NHS hospital or nursing home to inpatients or persons attending the hospital or nursing home for care or treatment) is a non-business activity.

The liabilities of pharmacy supplies as a business activity by the NHS are:

- drugs or pharmaceuticals supplied to a private patient in connection with medical or surgical treatment as part of a package of care – and following *Dr Beynon & Partners (HL 2004)* this includes the administration of drugs or pharmaceuticals in the course of treatment (exempt)
- drugs or pharmaceuticals supplied by a hospital or nursing home in the course of private care or treatment to:
  - an inpatient
  - a person attending the hospital or nursing home for care or treatment
  - any other person or establishment where the item is for use by, or in connection with, care or treatment provided to inpatients of or persons attending a hospital or nursing home – see *VAT Notice 701/31 (exempt)*
- (by concession) drugs or pharmaceuticals supplied by a pharmacist within a hospital or nursing home provided:
  - the items are designed or adapted for use in connection with medical or surgical treatment
  - the items are dispensed by a pharmacist in the normal way on the prescription of an approved medical practitioner (see **6.2 Private Patients** for the definition of an approved medical practitioner)

- the items are intended for self-administration (i.e. personal use) by the person named on the prescription (see **6.2 Private Patients** for the definition of personal use)
- the items are supplied separately from, and do not form any part of any medical services, treatment or care provided in the hospital or nursing home
- in the case of NHS prescriptions, the pharmacist is acting under the NHS Pharmaceutical Regulations, and is reimbursed for the dispensed items via community pharmacy services – see *VAT Notice 701/31/11* para 2.8 (zero-rated)
- drugs or pharmaceuticals supplied to a private hospital (standard-rated)
- drugs administered at by a nurse at the home of a patient where the drugs have been dispensed by a pharmacist and the supply is one of the dispensed drugs alone and not medical care or treatment (following *Healthcare at Home Ltd (VTD 20379)*) (zero-rated)
- drugs or pharmaceuticals supplied to an external organisation e.g. a University, private sector business or another NHS organisation outside the Divisional Registration (standard-rated)
- drugs or pharmaceuticals supplied to a private patient (but not on prescription) and not as part of a package of care (standard-rated)
- drugs or pharmaceuticals dispensed on the prescription of an approved practitioner by a registered pharmacist to an NHS or private patient for personal use (zero-rated)
- drugs or pharmaceuticals dispensed on the prescription of an approved practitioner by a dispensing doctor to an NHS or private patient for personal use. Applies only to authorised dispensing doctors in relation to qualifying patients. Dispensing doctors cannot dispense to other patients and other doctors are not authorised to dispense (zero-rated)
- drugs or pharmaceuticals dispensed (including letting on hire) on the prescription of an approved practitioner by a registered medical practitioner to a private patient for personal use (standard-rated)
- drugs or pharmaceuticals supplied to a charity for use in relation to providing care, or medical or surgical treatment, or engaging in medical research (zero-rated)

(see *VAT Notice 701/31*)

6.6.1 Output Tax

Output tax is due on standard-rated supplies of drugs or pharmaceuticals.

6.6.2   Input Tax

Input tax is allowable on the direct and indirect costs attributable to taxable supplies of drugs or pharmaceuticals (standard-rated and zero-rated).

There are three levels of input tax recovery related to pharmacy supplies:

(1) full recovery on directly attributable input tax – VAT incurred on the supply of drugs where these are standard-rated or zero-rated;

(2) proportionate recovery on sectorised costs such as the pharmacy cost centres. The recovery percentage could be calculated on the basis of proportionate quantities of drugs supplied or income related to taxable supplies – this percentage is then applied to the sectorised costs and that proportion of the VAT incurred is allowable input tax; and

(3) residual recovery on general overheads. In this context the residual input tax entitlement arises as a proportion of VAT incurred on general non-attributable overheads for the organisation as a whole (any VAT incurred on costs which has been taken into account above should be excluded).

Proportionate recovery on capital expenditure will also be allowable e.g. in relation to a project which includes a pharmacy. The entitlement arises in relation to taxable supplies made or intended to be made irrespective of whether the project is refurbishment, new build, alteration, extension etc (unlike eligibility for COS recovery) – the amount of input tax allowable will depend on the proportion of the VAT incurred which relates or will relate to taxable supplies or supplies which would be taxable supplies if performed in the UK. Further calculations will be necessary to determine this proportion, but typically it would be based on a floorspace analysis and ratio (excluding the common areas of a building which are non-attributable). From 1 January 2011 any capital project with a net value in excess of £250,000 and including a business element (taxable or exempt) falls within the Capital Goods Scheme (**10.4 Capital Goods Scheme**).

6.7   Research & Development

Supplies of research are taxable but were exempt until 1 August 2013 where supplied by an eligible body to an eligible body (these include Universities and other educational institutions, GDs and charities as well as NHS organisations). It is often an international activity, both within and outside the EU, which gives rise to different liabilities.

Research means original investigation undertaken in order to gain knowledge and understanding. It does not include consultancy or business efficiency advice, the collection or recording of data or statistics without analysis and interpretation, market research or polling, the writing of software or routine testing or analysis of materials, components or processes. (*VAT Notice 701/30*).

The VAT liabilities related to research are as follows:

- supplies of research in the UK e.g. to a pharmaceuticals company (standard-rated)
- supplies of research to a recipient outside the UK but within the EU (outside the scope but with input tax entitlement under VAT Act 1994 s.26)
- supplies of research to a recipient outside the EU (outside the scope but with input tax entitlement under VAT Act 1994 s.26)
- clinical trials involving a significant element of patient care and when performed or supervised by a person enrolled on a statutory medical register and where the primary purpose of the service is the protection, maintenance or restoration of the health of the person receiving the service (exempt)
- clinical trials not involving a significant element of patient care (standard-rated)

If the research is carried within the NHS for the purpose of NHS healthcare it is a non-business activity. Grants provided by Government or donations by charities or private individuals to fund research are not regarded as consideration for a supply in the course or furtherance of business and are therefore outside the scope of VAT. Grant funding or donations remain outside the scope of VAT even where intellectual property rights are transferred, since the transfer of IPRs of itself does not constitute a consideration (*VAT Information Sheet 04/08*). As a consequence of the withdrawal of the exemption in 2013, supplies of research will either be standard-rated or non-business.

If research is funded partly from grants and partly by funding from commercial organisations, supplies will be generated where benefits are actually provided in return for funding contributions and therefore mixed funding of this kind may result in some funding contributions being outside the scope of VAT and others being consideration for supplies in the course or furtherance of business. It is not the status of the person providing the funds that determines the liability, but whether that person receives any benefit in return for the payment. Where there is collaborative funding by a research council to a research partnership this is normally paid to a single representative body which then distributes the funding to the other partners. An administrative arrangement of this kind does not create a supply for VAT purposes and remains outside the scope of VAT. However, any sub-contracting to third party non-partners does create a supply in relation to the services provided to the partnership and the liability will depend on the kind of services supplied (*VAT Information Sheet 04/08*).

6.7.1   Output Tax

Output tax is due on supplies of research in the UK where it is a business supply. The international place of supply rules in relation to services within the EU were amended from 1 January 2011 (assuming the supply is to a taxable person (i.e. a "relevant business person". It is unlikely that research services would be supplied to an unregistered private individual).

Research falls under the cultural, artistic, sporting, scientific, educational and entertainment services provisions. From 1 January 2011 research services are taxed where the customer is established.

This means that output tax if due would be declared by the recipient in the member state where the recipient is established under the reverse charge provisions (see **11.4.3 Reverse Charge**) and the supply by an NHS organisation to an EU recipient would be outside the scope of VAT but with input tax entitlement under VAT Act 1994 s.26.

6.7.2   Input Tax

Input tax is allowable on the direct and indirect costs attributable to taxable supplies of research and supplies outside the UK which would be taxable supplies if performed in the UK.

There are three levels of input tax recovery related to taxable supplies of research (and to supplies outside the UK which would be taxable supplies if made in the UK):

(1) full recovery on directly attributable input tax – such as the cost of equipment, materials and related services attributable to a taxable supply of research;

(2) proportionate recovery on sectorised costs such as the research cost centres e.g. laboratory costs or utilities and other overheads. The recovery percentage could be calculated on the basis of floorspace, staff time or income related to taxable supplies or supplies outside the UK which would be taxable supplies if performed in the UK. This percentage is then applied to the sectorised costs and that proportion of the VAT incurred is allowable input tax; and

(3) residual recovery on general overheads. In this context the residual input tax entitlement arises as a proportion of VAT incurred on general non-attributable overheads for the organisation as a whole (any VAT incurred on costs which has been taken into account above should be excluded).

Proportionate recovery on capital expenditure will also be allowable e.g. a project which includes a research laboratory or facility. The entitlement arises in relation to taxable supplies made or intended to be made irrespective of whether the project is refurbishment, new build, alteration, extension etc (unlike eligibility for COS recovery). The amount of input tax allowable will depend on the proportion of the VAT incurred which relates or will relate to taxable supplies or supplies which would be taxable supplies if performed in the UK. Further calculations will be necessary to determine this proportion, but typically it would be based on a floorspace analysis and ratio (excluding the common areas of a building which are non-attributable). From 1 January 2011 any capital project with a net value in excess of £250,000 and including a business element (taxable or exempt) falls within the Capital Goods Scheme (see **10.4 Capital Goods Scheme**).

6.8   The Treasury List

Until the repeal of VAT Act 1994 s.41(2) in Finance Act 2012 the activities listed below listed below were deemed to be business activities by a GD by Treasury Direction (revised October 2008). The Treasury List now only has effect between GDs and does not apply in relation to any other business supplies.

Any activities:
- which may not amount to the carrying on of a business but where there may be competition with the private sector (other taxable persons carrying on a business);
- whether goods or services; and
- where supplied for a consideration (i.e. where a charge is made)
- were deemed to be business activities (it may have been, for whatever reason, that the activity did not fall within the scope of tax but by virtue of the Treasury Direction was deemed to be a business activity).

The Treasury Direction did not apply where there was a statutory duty, or where there was no consideration (these remained non-business). Equally, the Treasury Direction had no effect where an activity was an economic activity under the Principal VAT Directive or fell under VAT Act 1994 s.4. In those circumstances, it would have been of itself a business activity; the Treasury Direction only removed the uncertainty where an activity may have been construed as a non-business activity.

HMRC take the view that the repeal of s.41(2) will not result in any material change in the treatment of business activities by the NHS or GDs and the liability notes set out below assume supplies made within the United Kingdom and for a consideration. Although the most recent

Treasury (Contracting-Out) Directions were issued in December 2002, deemed business activities were revised in October 2008.

All business supplies within the UK are taxable and standard-rated unless specifically excluded (see **Appendix 7. Reduced-Rate Supplies**, **Appendix 8. Zero-Rated Supplies** and **Appendix 9. Exempt Supplies**).

All supplies below are assumed to be made for a consideration and within the UK unless otherwise stated.

Accommodation, including property acquisition and disposal and any related services
Supplies of commercial accommodation are exempt unless an option to tax is exercised in which case standard-rated:
- the leasing or letting of land or property including government offices (exempt)
- acquisition or purchase of land or property including government buildings (exempt or standard-rated where an option to tax is exercised by the vendor)
- disposal or sales of land or property including government buildings (exempt or standard-rated where an option to tax is exercised (with Treasury permission)
- professional services related to land or property e.g. legal, architects, surveyors etc (standard-rated)
- Freehold sales of new (up to three years old) commercial buildings are standard-rated irrespective of an option to tax (see **Chapter 10. Land & Property**).

Administration Services
Supplies of administrative services are standard-rated, including administration services related to financial services or the management of funds (including funds in trust) unless the services provided qualify for exemption as a financial service:
- general administration services (standard-rated)
- management, office, accounting or payroll services (standard-rated)
- administration services for shared services organisations (standard-rated)
- administration services for trading subsidiaries (standard-rated)
- administration of funds in trust (standard-rated)
- financial services administration (standard-rated)

(see *VAT Notice 701/49 Financial Services*)

Admission to Premises and to Events, e.g. Entertainments, Air Displays etc

Supplies of admissions to premises and events are standard-rated including any kind of admission charge, concerts, open days, guided tours and firework displays.

However, the cultural exemption may apply to public or non-profit making bodies (eligible bodies) in certain circumstances and therefore the admission charges would be exempt (although not mandatory). Public bodies in this context include GDs, NDPBs listed in the Cabinet Office publication 'Public Bodies' and local authorities. However, exemption cannot apply where the exemption of admission charges would be likely to distort competition to the disadvantage of a commercial supplier of similar services, or the public body enters into a joint venture or profit/income-making arrangement with anyone other than another public or eligible body.

An example of a joint venture which would not qualify for exemption is one where the local authority acts as a ticket broker for a commercial promoter or has a profit/income sharing arrangement with that promoter for a qualifying performance. An example of a joint venture which would qualify for exemption is one where the local authority sells tickets for a qualifying performance on behalf of an eligible body.

HMRC takes the view that it is entitled (under the terms of current EC agreements) to take a national and overall view of competition where admissions to the various cultural activities are supplied by public bodies. It is necessary therefore to establish at the outset whether commercial suppliers of cultural activities may be placed at relative disadvantage if similar supplies made by a particular public body are treated as exempt. However, once this has been done it is not necessary to apply this test to each future separate performance.

To satisfy the non-distortion requirement in order to exempt admissions of a qualifying nature a public body must take steps to notify all identifiable commercial suppliers of related facilities or performances. For example, a local authority will need to identify from its business rating, planning, taxation and other records, any such supplier within its geographical area of responsibility and to notify in writing its intention of introducing exemption to all those suppliers. This could be by individual letter or by public notice in the local press for the authority's geographical area, which will need to specify a date (for example, 30 days) by which any objection to exemption has to be lodged. The public body can start to exempt the supplies advertised for exemption but must retain copies of the relevant correspondence and advertisements for future examination.

Where there is an objection and the public body still wishes to exempt admission charges and disagrees with the objection, the public body should forward details of the intended exemption together with copies of the relevant correspondence to HMRC but it should not exempt any supplies which are in dispute until the matter has been resolved. In identifying commercial suppliers who may be disadvantaged by exemption, a public body will only need to look at museums, galleries, art exhibitions and zoos or theatrical, musical and choreographic performances in isolation. For example, a public body wishing to exempt admission charges to a museum would have to demonstrate that it would not disadvantage commercial museums, galleries, art exhibitions and zoos within its geographical area, but would not have to take account of commercial theatrical, musical and choreographical performances.

Correspondingly, in judging whether exemption of theatrical performances of a cultural nature would disadvantage a commercial supplier, it will be sufficient for the public body to take account of all commercial suppliers of theatrical, musical or choreographic performances within its geographical area. It will not be necessary to take account of commercial museums, galleries, art exhibitions or zoos.

(see *VAT Notice 701/47*)

Advertising or Publicity Services
The liability of supplies of advertising or publicity services are as follows:
- advertising services (other than to charities) (standard-rated)
- sponsorship (but not donations) (standard-rated)
- donations (outside the scope of VAT)
- distribution of advertising material (standard-rated)
- rights over land for advertising space (a licence to occupy) e.g. hoardings, boards, display stands etc (exempt)
- rights over land for advertising space (a licence to occupy) e.g. hoardings, boards, display stands etc (standard-rated where an option to tax has been exercised)
- advertising services supplied to charities (zero-rated)

Archives
Supplies of archiving services are standard-rated including the archiving, maintaining and updating of records.

Attendance of Staff at Court (or any similar place)
Supplies of staff attendance at court are standard-rated including expert witness services and medico-legal services (standard-rated).

Bankruptcies and Insolvency Services
Supplies of professional services in relation to bankruptcy or insolvency are standard-rated.

Broadcasting Services
Supplies of broadcasting services are standard-rated.

Car Leasing
Supplies of car leasing services are standard-rated.

Catering, including supplies from vending machines
Supplies of catering are standard-rated or zero-rated depending on the type of activity.

Community Tradeable Emissions Allowances (in return for payment pursuant to section 16 of the Finance Act 2007 where such allowances could also be obtained from the Private Sector)
Supplies of community tradeable emissions allowances are zero-rated.

(*The Value Added Tax (Emissions Allowances) Order 2009*)

Computer Services or Goods
Supplies of computer services or goods are standard-rated.

Concessions for Catering or Other Services
Supplies of concessions for catering or other related services are standard-rated where there is a concession with profit share e.g. retail outlets or where there is a concession as a right over land (where an option to tax has been exercised) e.g. retail outlets (a licence to occupy).

Supplies of concessions for catering or other related services are exempt where there is a concession as a right over land (where no option to tax has been exercised) e.g. retail outlets (a licence to occupy).

(see **Chapter 10. Land & Property**)

Conferences, Exhibitions and Related Facilities or Services
Supplies of conference, exhibition or related facilities services are standard-rated including the provision of lecturers and speakers, the organisation of exhibitions or displays or the hiring of space or other accommodation for conferences or exhibitions (where an option to tax has been exercised).

Supplies of conference, exhibition or related facilities services are exempt in relation to the organisation of educational or professional conferences (e.g. for Continuing Professional Development) or seminars as an eligible body (see *VAT Notice 701/30 Education & Vocational Training*) or the hiring of space or other accommodation for conferences or exhibitions (where no option to tax has been exercised).

(see **Chapter 10. Land & Property**)

Construction, Alteration, Demolition, Repair or Maintenance Work, Civil Engineering
Work, Any Related Services or Goods

(see **Chapter 10. Land & Property**)

Contract or Procurement Services
Supplies of contract or procurement services are standard-rated.

Copying or supply of any Reproductions or Documents
Supplies of extracts from printed books, booklets, pamphlets, leaflets, second or additional copies of patients' notes or X-rays supplied to solicitors, insurers or other external organisations or the use of photocopiers or other reprographic equipment are standard-rated.

Supplies of printed books, booklets, pamphlets, leaflets, brochures, newspapers, magazines, journals, periodicals are zero-rated.

Copyright, Patents or Licences to Manufacture
Supplies of copyright, patents or licences to manufacture are standard-rated.

Delivery or Distribution Services
Supplies of delivery or distribution services are standard-rated.

Drainage Work
Supplies of drainage works or services are standard-rated (see **Chapter 10. Land & Property**).

Electronic Transfer of Data
Supplies of the electronic transfer of data are standard-rated.

Export of Goods and Related Services
(see **Chapter 11. International VAT**)

Filming, Replay or Recording Services
Supplies of film or recording services or similar are standard-rated.

Financial and any Related Services
Supplies of financial services are exempt (but related services such as administration and bookkeeping are standard-rated).

Fishing Licences or Permits
Supplies of fishing licences or permits are normally standard-rated. supplies of fishing licences or permits are sporting right i.e. the right to take game or fish from land. The supply of sporting rights is normally standard-rated. However, if the sporting rights form part of a supply of land, there are occasions when the liability of the sporting rights will follow the liability of that land (i.e. exempt or standard-rated). Finally, in certain circumstances if there is a separate charge for fish taken then that may be zero-rated.

Fire Service Assistance
Supplies of fire service assistance are standard-rated.

Freight Transport
Supplies of freight transport services are standard-rated.

Fuel and Power
Supplies of non-domestic fuel are standard-rated and supplies of domestic fuel are reduced-rate.

Government Car Service
Supplies of a government car service are standard-rated.

Grant or Assignment or Surrender of any Interest in or Right over Land, or of any Licence to do anything in relation to Land
(see **Chapter 10. Land & Property**)

Grant of a Right to Inspect Records
Supplies of a right to inspect records are standard-rated.

Goods, including goods manufactured within a government department and sold to its staff and to other customers, stores, surplus, or other equipment

Supplies of goods are standard-rated except where specifically reduced-rate or zero-rated (see **Appendix 7. Reduced-Rate Supplies** and **Appendix 8. Zero-Rated Supplies**). The liability of the supply may depend on the status of the recipient e.g. supplies of pharmaceuticals to charities (zero-rated).

Grave Maintenance
Supplies of grave maintenance services are standard-rated.

Grounds Maintenance
Supplies of grounds or garden maintenance services are standard-rated.

Hairdressing
Supplies of hairdressing for staff or the public are standard-rated.

Heating
Supplies of non-domestic fuel are standard-rated and supplies of domestic fuel are reduced-rate.

Hire of Vehicles, Machinery or Equipment, With or Without Operator Crew
The following supplies of the hire of vehicles, machinery or equipment, with or without operator crew are standard-rated:
- hire of an NHS or GD vehicle (designed or adapted to carry less than 10 passengers) with or without a driver e.g. cars
- hire of an NHS or GD vehicle (designed or adapted to carry less than 10 passengers) without a driver e.g. coaches or minibuses
- private use on hire of an NHS or GD vehicle (designed or adapted to carry less than 10 passengers) e.g. cars
- private use on hire of an NHS or GD vehicle (designed or adapted to carry less than 10 passengers) e.g. coaches or minibuses
- hire of NHS or GD machinery or equipment (with or without operator crew)

The following supplies of the hire of vehicles, machinery or equipment, with or without operator crew are zero-rated: hire of an NHS or GD vehicle (designed or adapted to carry not less than 10 passengers) with a driver e.g. coaches or minibuses.

Passenger transport charges (e.g. by bus, rail, air or sea) are normally zero-rated. Where an NHS organisation or GD supplies qualifying passenger transport services (e.g. a coach or minibus with a driver) that would be zero-rated but the hire of an NHS or GD vehicle without a driver would be standard-rated.

Hydrographic, Cartographic and Similar Services
Supplies of hydrographic, cartographic and similar services are standard-rated.

Information or Statistical Services
Supplies of information or statistical services are standard-rated.

Charges made for the provision of information requested under the Freedom of Information Act 2000 is not treated as being a taxable supply provided that the information can only be provided by that specific NHS organisation or GD and is not available from any other source (outside the scope of VAT).

Inspection Services
Supplies of health and safety inspection services are standard-rated.

Laboratory Services Including Analysis and Testing of Any Substance
The following supplies of laboratory services including analysis and testing of any substance are standard-rated:

- testing and analysis services when performed by a person not enrolled on a statutory medical register;
- testing and analysis services when performed or supervised by a person enrolled on a statutory medical register and where the primary purpose of the service is not the protection, maintenance or restoration of the health of the person receiving the service;
- writing of scientific reports when performed by a person not enrolled on a statutory medical register;
- writing of scientific reports when produced or supervised by a person enrolled on a statutory medical register and where the primary purpose of the service is not the protection, maintenance or restoration of the health of the person receiving the service;
- laboratory services (including X-ray services and analyses and the processing of urea) supplied by unqualified technicians working without supervision; and
- laboratory services (including X-ray services and analyses and the processing of urea) when performed or supervised by a person enrolled on a statutory medical register and where the primary purpose of the service is not the protection, maintenance or restoration of the health of the person receiving the service.

The following supplies of laboratory services including analysis and testing of any substance are exempt:

- testing and analysis services when performed or supervised by a person enrolled on a statutory medical register and where the primary purpose of the service is the protection, maintenance or restoration of the health of the person receiving the service;
- writing of scientific reports when produced or supervised by a person enrolled on a statutory medical register and where the primary purpose of the service is the protection, maintenance or restoration of the health of the person receiving the service; and
- laboratory services (including X-ray services and analyses and the processing of urea) when performed or supervised by a person enrolled on a statutory medical register and where the primary

purpose of the service is the protection, maintenance or restoration of the health of the person receiving the service.

Laundry Services
Supplies of laundry services are standard-rated e.g. to staff or an external organisation or business.

Licensing, Certification, Authorisation or the granting of any rights other than rights over Land
Supplies of grants of Crown Copyright or software licences are standard-rated supplies of services.

Manufacturing, Assembling and Other Services
Supplies of manufactured products e.g. during industrial or occupational therapy, are standard-rated.

Medical Services
Supplies of medical services are exempt when performed or supervised by a person enrolled on a statutory medical register and where the primary purpose of the service is the protection, maintenance or restoration of the health of the person receiving the service:
- medical practitioners (including with limited registration);
- ophthalmologic opticians or dispensing opticians;
- osteopaths or chiropractors;
- qualified nurses and midwifes;
- dispensers of hearing aids;
- dentists, dental auxiliaries and dental technicians; and
- pharmaceutical chemists.

Membership Subscriptions
The liability of membership subscriptions reflects the benefit(s) members receive in return.

There may be a principal benefit and therefore a single supply with a single VAT liability (i.e. that of the principal benefit) or there may be a multiple supply and an apportionment will be necessary to reflect the different liabilities of different components of the supply. Membership benefits can be standard-rated, zero-rated, exempt or, in certain circumstances, non-business.

Non-profit making bodies (e.g. charities) making a single supply which comprises a mixture of benefits with different VAT liabilities are allowed to apportion their subscriptions to reflect the value and VAT liability of each individual benefit.

(see *VAT Notice 701/5 Clubs & Associations*)

Meteorological and Related Services

Supplies of weather forecasts or the provision of data relating to weather or climate change, or the use of computer modelling to simulate weather conditions or climate change are standard-rated.

Mortuary Services

Supplies of mortuary services, storage of remains and post-mortem examinations are standard-rated.

A post-mortem carried out under Coroners Act 1998 s.19 (i.e. an appointment by the coroner) is outside the scope of VAT.

Nursery and Daycare Facilities

The provision of childcare or crèche/nursery services by a supplier not registered with OFSTED (under the Children Act 1989 as amended by the Care Standards Act 2000) is standard-rated.

The provision of childcare or crèche/nursery services by a supplier registered with OFSTED (under the Children Act 1989 as amended by the Care Standards Act 2000) is exempt.

Supplies of childcare or crèche/nursery services by an associated charity where charges are designed only to cover costs is outside the scope of VAT.

Occupational Health Services

The following supplies of occupational health services are standard-rated:
* manufactured goods or equipment e.g. from industrial or occupational therapy;
* pre-employment medicals in relation to the health and medical fitness of the prospective employee;
* post-employment medicals in relation to pension schemes;
* ergonomic and risk assessments;
* advice or helpline services; and
* counselling, lifestyle assessments, health and safety audits

The following supplies of occupational health services are zero-rated:
* food produce e.g. from industrial or occupational therapy.

The following supplies of occupational health services are exempt:
* post-employment medicals in relation to the health and medical fitness of the employee; and
* post-employment training and advice to promote and maintain the health and medical fitness of employees.

Passenger Transport

The following supply of passenger transport is standard-rated:

- transport in any vehicle with driver or crew designed or adapted to carry less than 10 passengers e.g. taxis or private hire cars

The following supply of passenger transport is zero-rated:
- transport in any vehicle with driver or crew designed or adapted to carry not less than 10 passengers e.g. coaches or minibuses

Payroll and Pension Administration Services
Supplies of payroll or pension administration services, payment of salaries and wages, deductions from employees pay for insurance premiums, mortgage repayments, Trade Union subscriptions or in compliance with an attachment of earnings order.

Pest or animal control
Supplies of pest control or animal control services are standard-rated.

Photocopying Services
The following supplies of photocopying services are standard-rated:
- extracts from books, booklets, pamphlets, leaflets;
- second or additional copies of patients' notes or X-rays supplied to solicitors, insurers or other external organisations; and
- the use of photocopiers or other reprographic equipment.

The following supplies of photocopying services are zero-rated:
- books, booklets;
- pamphlets, leaflets, brochures; and
- newspapers, magazines, journals, periodicals.

Photographic Services
Supplies of photographic services are standard-rated.

Port, airport or harbour services and related goods
Supplies of services provided for the handling of ships or aircraft in a port, customs and excise airport or outside the UK are zero-rated. Includes salvage, pilotage and towage services. Also includes port and harbour dues, dock and berth charges, aircraft landing, parking and housing fees.

Postal, packing or distribution services
Supplies of postal services provided by the Royal Mail subject to a universal service obligation are exempt (excludes courier and parcel services).

Other postal, packing or distribution services that are not subject to a universal service obligation are standard-rated (including courier and parcel services).

Professional services including those of any manager, adviser, expert, specialist or consultant

Supplies of professional services are standard-rated including:

- legal, accounting, IT or computing, management, administration or other advisory or consultancy services;
- medico-legal services including arbitration, mediation, conciliation and services provided to insurers or claimants, the preparation or consideration of medical reports in relation to claims or disputes; and
- scientific testing or analysis (e.g. drugs or materials).

The following supplies of professional services are exempt when performed by a person enrolled on a statutory medical register and where the primary purpose of the service is the protection, maintenance or restoration of the health of the person receiving the service:

- medical practitioners (including with limited registration);
- ophthalmologic opticians or dispensing opticians;
- osteopaths or chiropractors;
- qualified nurses and midwifes;
- dispensers of hearing aids;
- dentists, dental auxiliaries and dental technicians; and
- pharmaceutical chemists.

Publications

The following supplies of publications are standard-rated:

- electronic publications e.g. ebooks, CDs, DVDs, microfilm, microfiche etc. ;
- stationery e.g. letterheads, forms, cards, compliment slips, envelopes, invoices etc.; and
- calendars, posters

The following supplies of publications are zero-rated:

- printed books, booklets;
- pamphlets, leaflets, brochures; and
- newspapers, magazines, journals, periodicals.

Radio or Communication Services

Supplies of radio, communications or broadcasting services are standard-rated.

Recruitment Services

Supplies of recruitment services are standard-rated.

Research, Testing, Experimentation, Sampling or Other Related Laboratory Services

Supplies of research, testing, experimentation, sampling or other related laboratory services are standard-rated.

Supplies of research, testing, experimentation, sampling or other related laboratory services funded by grants or donations are non-business activities.

The exemption for research supplied between eligible bodies under VAT Act 1994 Schedule 9 Group 6 was abolished on 1 August 2013.

Repair or Maintenance of Machinery, Equipment or Other Goods

Supplies of repair or maintenance services for non-qualifying goods or equipment are standard-rated.

Supplies of repair or maintenance services for qualifying goods or equipment are zero-rated (see **Appendix 8. Zero-Rated supplies**).

Searches

Supplies of search services are standard-rated.

Secondment of Staff for Services obtainable from the Private Sector

Supplies of staff are standard-rated. A supply of staff is the provision to another person, for payment, of the services of an individual who is contractually employed by the supplier. This applies whether the terms of the individual's employment are set out in a formal contract or letter of appointment, or are on a less formal basis. The determining factor is that the staff are not contractually employed by the recipient but come under their direction.

Secretarial Services

Supplies of secretarial services are standard-rated including typing services and the taking of minutes.

Transcription Services

Supplies of transcription services are standard-rated.

Security Services and Related Goods

Supplies of security services and related goods are standard-rated, including the provision of security guards, the installation of security systems such as door key pads, CCTV, security lighting etc.

Shipping Services

Supplies of shipping services including the preparation of import/export documentation and allowing the use of freight containers are standard-rated.

However, these supplies are subject to the place of supply rules and depending on the status of the recipient (i.e. business or consumer) and the nature of the supply the place of supply may not be the UK and therefore the supply would be outside the scope of UK or, potentially, outside the scope of EU VAT altogether if performed for a recipient established outside the EU.

(see **Chapter 11. International VAT**)

Slaughter, Rendering and Disposal of Animals
Supplies of the slaughter, rendering and disposal of animals are standard-rated.

Supplies of animal products for human consumption are zero-rated.

(see *VAT Notice 701/40 Food Processing Services*)

Social Services
Supplies of social services are exempt including welfare services. Welfare services are defined as services directly connected with the provision of care, treatment or instruction designed to promote physical or mental welfare of elderly, distressed or disabled persons i.e. not medical care (see **Appendix 9. Exempt Supplies**).

(see *VAT Notice 701/2 Welfare*)

Statistical Services, including the Collection, Preparation and Processing of Data
Supplies of statistical services are standard-rated including the collection, preparation and processing of data, the preparation of statistical reports, medical or social surveys and statistical data processing.

Statistical services of themselves are standard-rated however if the services form part of a single (or composite) supply of research services the liability will follow that of the principal supply.

Storage Facilities and Related Services
Supplies of storage or warehousing services are standard-rated.

Telecommunications
The liability of supplies of telecommunications are as follows:
- private use by employees (standard-rated);
- income from payphones including rented payphones (standard-rated);
- commission on payphones where an option to tax has been exercised (standard-rated);
- right over land e.g. for the siting of a mast where an option to tax has been exercised (standard-rated);

- commission on payphones where no option to tax has been exercised (exempt); and
- right over land e.g. for the siting of a mast (exempt).

Training, Tuition or Education and Any Related Goods or Services

The liability of supplies of training, tuition or education and any related goods or services provided by an NHS organisation or GD as an eligible body is as follows:

- goods and services not closely related to education or not for the direct personal use of the student e.g. training CDs, DVDs (standard-rated)
- goods and services not closely related to education or not for the direct personal use of the student e.g. textbooks and training materials (zero-rated);
- education and vocational training including lectures, seminars, conferences and symposia (exempt);
- first aid courses, paramedic training and other medical training etc (exempt); and
- goods and services closely related to education and for the direct personal use of the student e.g. textbooks and training materials, accommodation, catering and transport (exempt).

Training and tuition when provided by an eligible body is an exempt supply and NHS organisations and GDs qualify as eligible bodies. Supplies of goods and services essential to providing the training or tuition are also exempt as supplies closely related to education. (*VAT Notice 701/30 Education & Vocational Training*).

Transfer of Milk Quota Leases

The transfer of a milk quota lease (without a corresponding right over land) is a standard-rated supply of services.

Translation Services

Supplies of translation services are standard-rated, including the supply of oral interpreters or written translations.

Tree Planting and Afforestation

Supplies of tree planting, afforestation and forest management are standard-rated.

Vehicle Conversions

Supplies of converting a vehicle for the personal use of a disabled individual are zero-rated.

Vehicle Servicing and Maintenance
Supplies of vehicle servicing and maintenance services (including any parts supplied) are standard-rated.

Supplies of vehicle servicing and maintenance services for qualifying vehicles (including any parts supplied) are zero-rated (see **Appendix 8. Zero-Rated Supplies**).

MOT Tests are outside the scope of VAT (but any repairs which require to be carried out to pass an MOT are taxable).

Verification of particulars of births, marriages or deaths
Supplies of duplicate copies of birth, death or marriage certificates or confirming information on application forms and other official forms are standard-rated.

Waste Disposal
The following supplies of waste disposal services are standard-rated:
- incineration of waste products;
- removal, conveyance, treatment or disposal of the contents of cesspools, septic tanks or similar receptacles, where supplied to industrial customers; and
- removal of industrial waste not discharged into sewers.

The following supplies of waste disposal services are zero-rated:
- removal, conveyance, treatment or disposal of the contents of cesspools, septic tanks or similar receptacles, where supplied to non-industrial customers

Water   (Supplies of Water and Ice)
The liability of supplies of water or ice is as follows:
- water or ice supplied to industrial users (standard-rated);
- water or ice supplied to non-industrial users is zero-rated;
- mineral water or bottled water (standard-rated);
- ordinary water supplied in bottles as a drought alleviation or other emergency measure (zero-rated); and
- distilled or deionised water and water of similar purity (standard-rated).

(see *VAT Notice 701/16 Water and Sewerage Services*)

Weighbridge Services
Supplies of weighbridge services are standard-rated.

7 PARTIAL EXEMPTION

Partial exemption is an apportionment of input tax between taxable supplies and exempt supplies subject to the VAT Regulations 1995 SI 1995/2518 Part XIV – Input Tax and Partial Exemption. It does not apply to COS and the use of the term "partial exemption" in relation to the exempt element of the business/non-business COS restriction is a misdescription (**4.2 Business/Non-Business Apportionment**).

A business which makes exempt supplies (and the NHS is a business in this context) cannot reclaim all of its input tax and must use an approved partial exemption method which will be either the Standard Method (which does not require the prior approval of HMRC) or a Special Method (which does require the prior approval of HMRC). The Standard Method is not generally recommended for the NHS. This is principally because the Standard Method is based on an apportionment of income. In the NHS some 98% of income is funding for expenditure i.e. at cost, whereas business income includes an element of profit which is distortive. Use of the Standard Method, in practice, understates the taxable % and overstates the exempt % to the disadvantage of an NHS organisation (see *VAT Notice 706/1*).

The following are excluded from the calculation:
- supplies of capital goods or assets used for the purposes of the business whether or not subject to the capital goods scheme (see **10.4 Capital Goods Scheme**) – this may include medical equipment exclusively used for business activities e.g. in relation to private patients;
- incidental financial transactions or income e.g. bank interest received;
- incidental land and property transactions e.g. a one-off sale of land (but generally not an ongoing supply of accommodation etc);
- any self-supply made e.g. a reverse charge supply (see 3.2.5 **EU supplies** and **3.2.6 Non-EU supplies**);
- EU acquisitions (see **3.2.5 EU supplies**); and
- any transaction on which output tax is not chargeable by Treasury Order (*VAT Act 1994 s.25*) or any transactions which are not supplies for VAT purposes (as deemed by Treasury) e.g. the transfer of a business or part of a business as a going concern (TOGC).

Technically, partial exemption calculations should be completed monthly on a provisional basis with an annual adjustment in either Month 12 (the March VAT Return due by 30 April) or Month 13 (the April VAT Return due by 31 May) for the "longer period" i.e. the financial year (the requirement does not apply to the Business/Non-Business Apportionment calculations). However, as a concession to the NHS, HMRC allow these calculations to be completed on the basis of annual submissions in arrears.

Historically, HMRC have not generally required Special Methods of Partial Exemption (PESMs) to be formally approved. In practice, the methods are agreed and approved indirectly when HMRC approves the annual business activities and partial exemption claims. Because HMRC does not accept business activities claims without a corresponding partial exemption calculation, these calculations must be completed at the same time and as part of the same calculation in any case, but still technically separate. The next section contains a typical method of calculating the business/non-business apportionment and partial exemption which gives a fair and reasonable result. Although the Combined Method *per se* is not recommended for NHS organisations this calculation is carried out in combination with the partial exemption calculation and the result is the same or similar. The Combined Method has the disadvantages of requiring HMRC approval for the business/non-business apportionment method as well as the partial exemption method and at the same time the *de minimis* rule is disapplied.

The objective of the calculation is to identify the proportion of allowable input tax an organisation is entitled to reclaim over the financial year (output tax is not affected or apportioned). VAT is allowable input tax if consumed in the making of taxable supplies or otherwise allowable under VAT Act 1994 s.26. This cannot be ascertained directly from the data available (and the calculation is ultimately limited by the quality of the data available). Therefore, a proxy is used to calculate it indirectly e.g. income or outputs, but also potentially floorspace or transaction ratios, staff time ratios or purchases and inputs. It should always be remembered that the objective of the calculation is to identify allowable input tax and, therefore, the more accurate the proxy and the greater the correlation with allowable input tax, the more accurate the calculation will be and by definition, the more fair and reasonable the result.

7.1 Business Activities

7.1.1 Outputs

Analyse income to identify the total income of the organisation, the taxable income (standard-rated, reduced-rate and zero-rated) and the exempt income (from the income codes in the nominal ledger or the annual accounts).

7.1.2 Incidental Income

Exclude any income which is incidental or excluded (or outside the scope of VAT and which does not relate to a specific non-business activity) e.g. donations, grants, finance interest received, proceeds from one-off sales of property etc, sales of capital assets or capital goods – where these do not relate to a specific or general activity, either business or non-business (from the income codes in the nominal ledger or the annual accounts).

7.1.3 Private Patient Income

Private patient income should also be excluded if the appropriate data is available. It is not incidental but the exempt % related to private patients is more accurately calculated on the basis of activity rather than income/outputs e.g. by using the Finished Consultant Episode (FCE) figures or Occupied Bed Days (OBD) where these are available because private patient income includes a significant element of profit (e.g. on professional fees). The VAT incurred and consumed on the cost of an NHS or private procedure is the same or similar but the income received in relation to that procedure will differ greatly. If income/outputs is used as proxy in this context the effect will be distortive.

7.1.4 Non-Attributable Income

Exclude non-attributable income. This is funding income which relates to the overall activities of the organisation but which cannot be directly attributed to any specific business activity or non-business activity e.g. funding for general administration costs, estates, premises and general overheads (the proportion of non-attributable income can be calculated from the annual accounts using either the proportion of costs applied to non-attributable residual areas or the proportion of staff applied to non-attributable residual areas).

The non-attributable income is excluded because any fair and reasonable method should be capable of reverse analysis. For example, if an NHS organisation is 1% taxable and 1% exempt it does not follow that it is 98% non-business. Reverse analysis will show that it is probably only about 73% non-business, the remaining 27% being 2% business (taxable or exempt) and 25% non-attributable or residual (i.e. it relates proportionately to business supplies as well as to non-business activities). This means that the taxable and exempt percentages would be calculated as 1/75 rather than 1/100. If a calculation fails the reverse analysis test then it is distortive and the result will be less accurate and less fair and reasonable. The non-attributable income is deducted from the total income. The taxable and exempt income values remain constant.

7.1.5   Non-Business, Taxable & Exempt Percentage
The remainder should only include income attributable to non-business activities and income attributable to taxable and exempt business activities. There is a fundamental difference between non-business income and business income. non-business income is funding for expenditure (at cost) and business income is the proceeds of sales including an element of profit. The non-business, taxable and exempt residual % can then be calculated.

7.1.6   Sectorisation
The sectorised taxable and exempt percentages should then be calculated e.g. the catering staff & visitors/patients taxable % (different outlets may have different ratios) or a pharmacy or telephones taxable %. The sectorised taxable or exempt % will depend on the circumstances of the organisation and its activities.

7.1.7   Input tax – Direct Attribution
VAT incurred which is directly attributable (wholly and exclusively or 100%) to taxable supplies should be identified through a cost centre analysis from the accounts payable and general ledger. This VAT is allowable input tax (but it is not eligible for COS recovery – although it may have already been claimed as COS where it relates to an eligible service).

VAT incurred which is directly attributable (wholly and exclusively or 100%) to exempt supplies should be identified through a cost centre analysis from the accounts payable and general ledger. This VAT is not allowable input tax (nor is it eligible for COS recovery).

VAT incurred which is directly attributable (wholly and exclusively or 100%) to non-business activities should be identified (cost centre analysis from the accounts payable and general ledger). This VAT is non-input tax and no allowable input tax entitlement will arise in relation to this VAT but it will be eligible for COS recovery and it will not be subject to the partial exemption COS restriction.

7.1.8   Input Tax – Partial Attribution
VAT incurred which is partially attributable (sectorised %) to taxable supplies should be identified (cost centre analysis from the accounts payable & general ledger). The sectorised taxable % is applied to the sectorised VAT to calculate the allowable taxable proportion. This VAT is allowable input tax (but it is not eligible for COS recovery – although it may have already been claimed as part of a COS claim where it relates to an eligible service).

VAT incurred which is partially attributable (sectorised %) to exempt supplies should be identified (cost centre analysis from the accounts payable & general ledger). The sectorised exempt % is applied to the sectorised VAT to calculate the exempt proportion. This VAT is not allowable input tax (nor is it eligible for COS recovery).

7.1.9   Input Tax - Residual

VAT incurred which is non-attributable or residual should be identified through a cost centre analysis from the accounts payable & general ledger. Any VAT already identified as directly or partially attributable is excluded in calculating the non-attributable or residual VAT (VAT on general overheads, premises and admin costs).

The taxable residual % is applied to the non-attributable or residual VAT to calculate the allowable residual input tax (not eligible for COS recovery, although it may have already been claimed as part of a COS claim where it relates to an eligible service).

The exempt residual % is applied to the non-attributable or residual VAT to calculate the residual exempt input tax. This VAT is not allowable input tax (nor is it eligible for COS recovery).

The non-business % is applied to the non-attributable or residual VAT to calculate the residual non-input tax (eligible for COS recovery).

7.2   Partial Exemption *De Minimis*

The *de minimis* limits apply in each VAT Period and therefore in every provisional monthly calculation but are adjusted in the longer period annual adjustment for the financial year. If a taxable person is *de minimis* then all input tax is allowable under VAT Act 1994 s.26 including input tax directly attributable to exempt supplies (the *de minimis* limits do not apply to COS – although by concession HMRC allow full COS recovery where the restriction plus exempt input tax falls within the *de minimis* limits). Any NHS organisation with private patients or significant exempt supplies of land and property to tenants will not be *de minimis*. Where exempt input tax (including all directly attributable, partially attributable and residual exempt input tax) is not more than £625 per month on average (£7,500 annually) and not more than 50% of all input tax then the *de minimis* rule applies, and all input tax is recoverable.

7.3   Calculation of Allowable Input Tax

The total allowable input tax can now be calculated by adding the directly attributable allowable input tax, the partially attributable allowable input tax and the non-attributable or residual allowable input tax.

If the calculation is a longer period annual adjustment, then any input tax already claimed in VAT Returns for the period (and relevant to the period) should be deducted (any input tax claimed in the financial year which relates to another financial year should be excluded e.g. a business activities approval related to another financial year or an Error Correction Notification claim related to another financial year).

Ensure that all directly attributable and partially attributable allowable input tax has been identified and included. This is allowable in relation to taxable supplies but it will be normally be unascertained as input tax at the point of purchase (see **2.2 Divisional Registrations**). The entitlement to recover will only become apparent at a later stage when the taxable supply is made e.g. drugs or pharmaceuticals purchased in bulk. input tax on these purchases cannot be identified at the time of purchase and the only mechanism is a reverse calculation from the taxable supplies made e.g. sales of goods or equipment, telephone charges, drugs or pharmaceuticals sold or resold, recharges of utilities to tenants etc (taking into account any mark-up or profit margin). This applies both to direct and indirect input tax arising from direct attribution, partial attribution and residual VAT). This is a significant area of error in NHS VAT where input tax entitlement is lost or unclaimed. If there is a taxable supply, there will be allowable input tax and the objective of any fair and reasonable method is to identify the value of that allowable input tax as accurately as possible.

7.4   Business/Non-Business COS Restriction

In the same way that the VAT on purchases of goods and services for the purposes of business often cannot be identified at the time of purchase, the correct treatment of services used both for the purposes of exempt business activities and non-business activities generally cannot be ascertained when received, and on eligible services the COS will have been claimed in full. Therefore, a COS adjustment has to be carried out later, either in a monthly provisional calculation with a longer period annual adjustment or in a single longer period annual adjustment. This is normally misdescribed as "partial exemption" but it is actually a calculation to identify COS which has been claimed in error in relation to business activities (albeit exempt). COS which has been claimed in error in relation to taxable business activities is equally irrecoverable as COS, but will be recoverable as allowable input tax. However, mischaracterisation can lead to compliance errors and other errors in the business activities & partial exemption calculations and therefore accuracy is important.

The COS claimed in the period or financial year should be totalled. Only COS recovered in relation to VAT partially attributable to exempt supplies or non-attributable or residual VAT should be included in the restriction. Any COS directly attributable to non-business activities is fully recoverable. VAT incurred which is partially attributable to exempt supplies will have been identified by cost centre analysis from the accounts payable & general ledger (at inputs above) and this includes VAT on goods as well as services. Any COS claimed on the eligible services in the period or financial year will be subject to the restriction i.e. reduced by the sectorised exempt %. Equally, COS claimed on eligible services in relation to non-attributable or residual VAT will have been identified in the same way above and should be reduced by the exempt residual %.

7.5 Submission & Approval

If the calculations have been carried out on a monthly provisional basis with a longer period annual adjustment there is no requirement to submit the calculation to HMRC for approval. Alternatively, as a concession to the NHS, HMRC allow these calculations to be completed annually in arrears and submitted for approval with an ECN. The monthly provisional calculation with a longer period annual adjustment is the recommended approach because it is technically correct and fully compliant.

VAT AND THE NHS

8 NHS FRAMEWORK

HMRC published a framework for NHS business activities and partial exemption in October 2013. The main content is reproduced below and the full guidance (including worked examples) is published on the HMRC website:

https://www.gov.uk/government/publications/partial-exemption-frameworks/partial-exemption-frameworks

The framework is essentially a version of the Combined Method (see **Chapter 4. Non-Business Activities**) and is therefore not recommended for NHS organisations unless there are only minor taxable activities with minimal input tax entitlement.

Framework for NHS Bodies VAT Recovery Calculation Methods

Version 1 - October 2013

Introduction

This Framework is not mandatory and does not replace the content of VAT Notice 706/1 (Partial Exemption), but adopting its principles will enable HM Revenue & Customs (HMRC) more readily to give approval for a VAT recovery method for which a Statutory Declaration has been made. The Framework has been prepared by working with the Health Finance Managers Association (HFMA), the representative body for the tax affairs of NHS Trusts, and is jointly owned and supported by HFMA and HMRC.

Where this Framework refers to an 'NHS Trust' that term should be taken to include any relevant NHS body, including Health Boards in Scotland and Wales.

There is an attached flowchart of this method which illustrates the flow of VAT through an NHS Trust and highlights some of the key considerations that a Trust's recovery method can be used to address.

This Framework has been published by HMRC on its website. Further useful information, for example the VAT streams, is available on the TISonline website.

VAT and NHS Trusts

The principal activity of NHS Trusts is the provision of healthcare for no consideration carried out under statutory regulation. This is a non-business activity. Normally the VAT on expenditure used exclusively for non-business activity is irrecoverable. However, s41 of the VAT Act 1994 provides a special refund scheme for NHS Trusts whereby the VAT incurred on certain Contracted Out Services (COS) used for non-business activity may be reclaimed.

NHS Trusts also make business supplies. These include exempt supplies such as the provision of healthcare for a consideration to private patients and taxable supplies such as the supply of catering to staff and visitors. VAT on expenditure used solely to make exempt supplies cannot be recovered. VAT on expenditure used exclusively to make taxable supplies is recoverable under s26 of the VAT Act 1994.

The VAT on expenditure used partly for business purposes and partly for non-business purposes should normally be apportioned using a business/non-business (BNB) method of apportionment. The VAT that relates to business purposes should then be further apportioned between taxable supplies and exempt supplies using a partial exemption (PE) method. However, HMRC can approve a single method that is a combined method covering both your business/non-business and your partial exemption calculations. This is to save the cost of seeking approval of two separate methods. It also helps to make sure a fair recovery of VAT overall as the calculations can be considered in their entirety.

Most NHS Trust costs are used for a mix of taxable, exempt and non- business purposes and the VAT incurred has to be apportioned. This means that all VAT expended should be identified. A recovery method normally has three further steps:

- first, a direct attribution of VAT on costs;
- second, a calculation to determine the amount of non-attributable input VAT incurred against COS headings that relates to non-business activities and which may be reclaimed under s41 of the VAT Act 1994.
- third, a combined business/non-business (BNB) and partial exemption method to calculate the proportion of non-attributable input VAT (both COS VAT and non-COS VAT) that relates to taxable business activities and is recoverable under s26 of the VAT Act 1994.

The third step involves using a recovery method that has to be approved in writing for the individual Trust by HMRC.

Please note that the VAT recovery methods Trusts use are combined business/non-business and partial exemption methods. The partial exemption *de minimis* limit does not apply if a taxpayer has a combined method of this type so Trusts have to make any input tax restriction suggested by the calculation.

The Principles of VAT Deduction under a combined BNB and PE method

Direct attribution is the identification of VAT on supplies that are:

- wholly used, or to be used, in making taxable business supplies; or
- wholly used, or to be used, in making exempt business supplies; or
- wholly used, or to be used, in non-business activities.

Trusts are encouraged to use their existing accounting systems and practice to directly allocate as many costs as they can when implementing methods based on the ideas set out in this Framework. Normally HMRC will accept that costs such as fuel and power, telephone bills and auditors' fees form part of the general overheads of a Trust; in other words, they are costs which are used to support all of the Trust's activities. The input VAT on general overheads is known as residual VAT.

Allocation refers to dividing residual VAT between sectors in a recovery method. For example, a Trust might incur VAT on crockery, kitchen equipment and catering staff supplied by an agency. If it had a VAT recovery method which treated catering as a separate sector it would allocate those costs to the catering sector.

Apportionment means dividing residual VAT between non-business, taxable and exempt supplies. This is done using a proxy calculation. Where an activity has been sectorised, only the income generated in that sector would be used in the proxy calculation for that sector and this income would be excluded from any calculations for other sectors.

Income values based methods are the default proxy calculation. They are generally reliable because they:
- values change as the level of activity changes;
- rely on readily available records; and
- figures are easily verified.

Trusts wishing to use a proxy other than one based on income values should be prepared to show HMRC:
- why an incomes based method gives a result that is not fair and reasonable; and
- how the proposed alternative proxy successfully addresses that issue.

For example, calculations based on meal numbers in catering outlets do not make good proxies because they are difficult to define and audit. Often they do not use like-for-like values; for example, a full meal and a snack may both be counted as one 'meal' without taking into account how the taxed costs of providing a full meal compare with those of providing a snack.

HMRC accepts the use of Occupied Bed Days (OBDs) as a valid method for calculating the split of costs used to care for NHS and private patients. NHS Trusts may wish to apply for methods that allow for the OBDs calculation to be made once at the end of the tax year with the result applied provisionally in each return made during the subsequent tax year. Any changes in the OBDs figure for the subsequent figure can then be adjusted for as part of the normal longer period adjustment that all recovery methods include.

To determine the extent of taxable business use that carries a right to deduct input tax a recovery method must be fair and reasonable. It must:
- reflect how goods or services are used to make taxable supplies
- be simple to operate and easy to check
- be easily understood but respond to foreseeable changes.

HMRC will only approve a recovery method if it is accompanied by a Declaration on which the Trust states that to the best of its knowledge and belief the method produces a fair and reasonable input tax recovery. Annex C sets out in detail the steps that an NHS Trust are advised to take to ensure that their proposal is fair and reasonable.

A Trust always has to get prior written approval from HMRC before changing its method.

Sectors

A Trust may wish to consider sectorising an activity in its recovery method if:

(a) the activity is subject to segmental accounting and uses tax in a different way to that suggested by the result of a global calculation; or

(b) the result of a global calculation is substantially different to the result of an attribution which represents the extent to which the goods and services are used to make taxable supplies while performing that activity.

HMRC normally regards a substantial difference to be £50,000, or half of the Trust's input tax (excluding its COS VAT) and at least £25,000. A Trust may feel that one or more of its activities should be sectorised when these guide figures are not reached. In such situations it should discuss the position with HMRC with a view to agreeing whether sectorisation is appropriate in those circumstances.

Distorting Supplies

Values-based methods work on the premise that each £ value of output supply uses the same amount of VAT-bearing residual cost. However, occasionally a supply will use a disproportionate amount of residual cost thereby distorting the entire method.

The main characteristic of a distorting supply is that very little taxed cost is used to generate the value of the income received. When considering whether a supply is distortive it helps to ask the following questions:

- how does this supply's value change the recovery rate?
- how much extra input tax does that imply should be recovered or restricted?
- does that reflect the tax actually incurred on the taxed costs of that supply?

Once a distorting supply has been identified, a Trust should consider how it should be treated in the recovery method. The income should either be excluded, or its impact limited through the creation of a sector.

Provisional Recovery

A Trust that has not sought or does not seek approval for a partial exemption special method, or a combined business/non-business and partial exemption method, may find itself defaulting to the standard partial exemption method. In such circumstances the Trust will have to make:

(a) a claim under section 41 of the VAT Act for VAT that is recoverable under the arrangements for Contracted out Services;

(b) a calculation under section 24(5) of the VAT Act to work out how much of its input VAT is used to support the making of business supplies; and

(c) a calculation under regulation 101 of the VAT Regulations 1995 to work out how much of its input tax is used to support the making of taxable supplies.

Trusts are reminded that use of the previous year's recovery percentage became part of the standard method with effect from 1 April 2009.

It is recommended that a Trust asks for provisional recovery to be a feature of its special recovery method. Provisional recovery means that the previous year's recovery percentage can be applied in all tax periods during the current tax year.

This can ease the administrative burden for a Trust because the full calculation only has to be made once each year. The revised figure is applied to the tax year as part of the longer period adjustment that forms part of all partial exemption, and combined business/non-business and partial exemption, methods.

A Trust that does not apply for provisional recovery has to determine its recovery percentage each individual tax period.

NHS Trusts and the Capital Goods Scheme (CGS)

In many cases the CGS will not affect assets acquired by NHS Trusts (or assets on which a Trust spends money) because the scheme does not apply to assets which are wholly used for non-business purposes.

However, if a Trust does have any CGS items it needs to be aware of the impact of a new recovery method. Specifically, CGS adjustments may be required where a new method results in a recovery rate that is higher or lower than that allowed under the previous method. If a Trust has any questions about whether it has a CGS item, or about how to apply the CGS, it is welcome to contact HMRC.

Other Matters

Ordinarily the value of VAT incurred on purchases, recognised at the tax point, should be used when making a recovery method calculation. Purchase figures derived from trial balances may, because of any accruals and prepayments, differ slightly. Also, such values may fail to recognise situations where purchases from unregistered suppliers, or zero-rated supplies, form part of the trial balance figure. Using the trial balance figures to approximate the value of purchases may therefore produce a difference which would affect a Trust's recovery of VAT.

However, after representations from HFMA, HMRC has agreed that for some Trusts the possible loss of accuracy arising from the use of trial balance figures, when compared to using purchase figures with precise tax points, is outweighed by the additional work required to produce exactly precise information.

If a Trust wants to use figures from the trial balance it will need to agree with HMRC that they may do so. In situations where there is a possibility that any purchases from unregistered suppliers, or zero-rated purchases, may prove significant, for example if the Trust has a significant catering spend, HMRC will work with a Trust to find a practical way in which to gather sufficient information to ensure a fair and reasonable result from the VAT recovery method calculation.

An NHS Trust may need to change its recovery method if new circumstances arise. Even if the change involves amendment to an existing method such changes will normally require formal approval by HMRC. A Declaration is required for any new method.

Where a Trust changes, or anticipates changing, its legal entity it should contact HMRC.

This Framework will be updated regularly adding details and further topics as needed. Readers wishing to suggest improvements and new topics should write to HMRC Deductions and Financial Services Policy Team, 100 Parliament Street, London SW1A 2BQ.

Seeking approval for a VAT recovery method

C1.   Have you taken reasonable steps?

The person making a Statutory Declaration that a proposed VAT recovery method would give a fair and reasonable attribution of input tax has to state that they have taken reasonable steps to ensure that they have all relevant information relating to the proposed method. If you have to make a Declaration you might want to check that you have covered the points in paragraphs C2 to C5.

C2.   Have you considered whether your method needs sectors?

You should consider a sector if:

(a) an activity is subject to segmental accounting and uses tax in a different way to that suggested by the result of a single calculation covering all of the Trust's activities or

(b) the result of a single calculation covering all of the Trust's activities is substantially different to the result of an attribution which represents the extent to which the goods and services are used, or to be used by you, in making taxable supplies while performing that activity. HMRC normally regards a substantial difference to be £50,000, or half of your input tax (excluding your COS VAT) and at least £25,000. Please see paragraph 16 of this Framework for more detail on this point.

C3.   Have you prepared a worked example of your proposed method?

HMRC prefers to receive a worked projection of how your proposed method will work in practice, using real figures, and also an explanation why you feel your proposed method gives a fair and reasonable result. HMRC might not be able to give approval for a proposed method if there is uncertainty about its methodology in the absence of any documented projection of the result that the proposed method would generate.

C4.   Have you designed your method using the Framework and HMRC guidance?

If your proposal is not based on the VAT recovery method in this Framework HMRC will still fully consider it without preconceptions over its acceptability. However, it is not unreasonable to expect that more detailed enquiries will be made and the proposal fully tested.

C5.   Have you made your declaration?

You will need to make a statutory Declaration in accordance with the law (set out in Regulation 102(9), SI 1995/2518). You should be able to do so if you have taken the reasonable steps described in paragraphs C2 to C4 to ensure that your proposed method gives a fair and reasonable result.

9   CAPITAL EXPENDITURE

9.1   VAT & Capital Expenditure

VAT incurred on capital expenditure is a significant proportion of the overall VAT incurred by NHS organisations and, depending on the type of project, there may be VAT recovery either as input tax or COS, potentially even up to 100%. The supply of land and property is one of the most complex areas of the tax because of the underlying complexity of property law. The tax position reflects the underlying legal position. Because of this it is always prudent to take VAT advice in relation to any capital expenditure in the same way that legal advice would be taken (i.e. as part of the planning process).

Input tax incurred in relation to capital expenditure is allowable where it is attributable to taxable supplies. Significant sums of VAT may be incurred in relation to capital expenditure and this area of entitlement is often overlooked. The input tax entitlement arises in relation to taxable supplies made or intended to be made irrespective of whether the project is refurbishment, new build, alteration, extension etc and supersedes any eligibility for COS recovery (i.e. the input tax entitlement should be calculated first and any COS recovery calculation carried out on the remainder). Taxable supplies may include a catering outlet within the project or commercial letting where an option to tax has been exercised (thus the entitlement does not arise only where an option to tax has been exercised – any taxable business activity will create an entitlement to allowable input tax).

The amount of input tax allowable will depend on the proportion of the VAT incurred which relates or will relate (i.e. is intended to relate) to taxable supplies. This proportion would typically be calculated on a floorspace analysis and ratio (excluding the common areas of a building which are non-attributable) e.g. 5% taxable, 75% NHS, 20% non-attributable – this would result in a taxable ratio of 5:80 rather than 5:100 which equals 6.25% rather than 5% (the non-attributable element is disregarded).

From 1 January 2011 any capital project with a net value in excess of £250,000 and including a business element (taxable or exempt) falls within the capital items adjustment (see **10.4 Capital Goods Scheme**) although the effect is neutral if there are no taxable supplies. The majority of NHS capital projects apart from minor works or refurbishments will now fall within the Capital Goods Scheme and the input tax entitlement calculated via the capital items adjustment.

9.2 COS Capital

COS recovery is allowed on the maintenance, repair or cleaning of buildings by an external contractor or supplier under Heading 35. Maintenance or repair relates to existing buildings, structures or premises and includes refurbishment but does not include new construction or new work such as alterations, extensions, additions, or improvements. Repair by replacement is also excluded except where specified in the revised HMRC guidance as is the supply or installation of goods, plant or equipment (plant means an immovable item which is genuinely fixed in the sense of being permanently incorporated into the structure of the building e.g. lifts, boilers and generators or other industrial equipment).

Until 1 April 2012 any project where the VAT exceeded £50,000 had to be submitted to HMRC for prior approval (with appropriate documentation e.g. Bills of Quantity or plans/drawings etc), but HMRC have now dropped this requirement.

Any minor project under £5,000 (net of VAT) is treated as repair and maintenance under a concession agreed with between HMRC and the Department of Health. DoH Circular EL (90) P64 defines such work as "individual works schemes for the initial provision, extension improvement or adaptation (including upgrading), renewal, replacement or demolition of buildings, building elements (e.g. roofs), external works, engineering services or plant." Each project, however, must be complete and self-contained. A large project cannot be split into individual elements to bring the cost down, per element, to below £5000. It will only apply where the project is undertaken in its own right and not as part of a larger project.

Capital projects of any value may be analysed in detail under the COS rules, but where the project falls within the terms of the Banding Scheme (see below) then this may be considered as an alternative approach. The recoverable elements of any project or scheme (including where appropriate Preliminaries, Mechanicals and Electricals) may be recovered under *COS Heading 35* and any other eligible services under the appropriate Heading e.g. *COS Heading 60* for site security services.

Professional services are recoverable in full where these are supplied separately from the project (but see *COS Heading 52* for proposed changes) but professional services supplied as part of a design & build scheme are not usually recoverable because design & build normally means new build and therefore there would be no eligibility for COS recovery. Where there are recoverable elements within a design & build scheme then there would be proportionate recovery. Professional services included in a design &

build scheme are part of a single (or composite supply) and eligibility for COS recovery follows that of the principal supply.

In lower value projects a single analysis of the project as a whole is sufficient. However, in larger projects interim invoices will be received from the contractor and the recoverable percentage is applied to the VAT incurred on each interim invoice. Larger projects should also be reviewed before the end of each COS year (31 July) to ensure that there have been no material changes to the costs of the project or the recovery percentage (and also at the conclusion of the project).

9.3   Bill of Quantities

Typically, a Bill of Quantities will contain the following elements:

- Preliminaries
- Mechanicals
- Electricals
- Works
- Contingencies

To calculate the recoverable COS:

Analyse the Works line by line for recoverable elements on the building works and calculate a Works % excluding Preliminaries, Mechanicals, Electricals, Contingencies and Retention (the Works % does not apply to Preliminaries, Mechanicals, Electricals, Contingencies or Retention).

Analyse the Preliminaries line by line for recoverable elements and calculate a Preliminaries % (if it is not possible to analyse the Preliminaries the Overall % below can be applied).

Analyse the Mechanicals line by line for recoverable elements and calculate a Mechanicals % (the value of Mechanicals can be significant but scope for recovery is limited except where there is repair by replacement).

Analyse the Electricals line by line for recoverable elements and calculate an Electricals % (the value of Electricals can be significant but scope for recovery is limited except where there is repair by replacement (see **Annex A** at *COS Heading 35*).

Calculate a proportionate Overall % from the Works %, the Preliminaries %, the Mechanicals % and the Electrical %.

The Overall % is then applied to all expenditure e.g. interim certificates (including Contingencies and Retention – and Preliminaries where there is no analysis).

HMRC offer an alternative approach in their Draft Revised Guidance (issued 12 October 2015):

Recovery of VAT on a Line by Line Basis

Go through Bill of Quantity/Tender documents etc. and decide what is fully-recoverable, non- recoverable and Pot (mixed - unable to separate).

With Preliminaries – if you have a detailed breakdown and can separately identify qualifying items (professional services, security etc.), these can be added to the fully-recoverable figure, with the rest in non-recoverable, or the whole figure can be added to Pot (mixed).

This is an either/or, what you cannot do is strip out fully recoverable and add rest to Pot.

If a piece of work can be easily differentiated between fully/non recoverable e.g. "Supply & fit 20 doors (16 replacement/4 new)", 80% of price can be added to fully-recoverable and 20% to non-recoverable. If the description just says "Supply & fit 20 doors", this would be added to the Pot.

When this is completed, the formula to find out the provisional percentage recovery on all interim payment invoices is:

$$\text{Fully-recoverable} = \% \text{ Fully-recoverable} + \text{non-recoverable}$$

Headings such as Provisionals, Overheads & Profit, Contractors margin etc. should be placed in the Pot; Contingencies should be ignored until the end of the project, when it will become clear if any have been spent. Capital projects should be reviewed annually or at the end of the project whichever is sooner. Where work is carried out to meet H&S or fire regulations, this does not mean you can just claim back everything. The work must still be listed on repairs and maintenance list to qualify for recovery.

9.4   The Banding Scheme

Capital projects up to £15m qualify for the Capital Banding Scheme. Projects of this value may be complex and different rates of banding can be applied to the separate elements of the project to calculate a rationalised overall percentage. For example, a high value project may include an element of new build, an extension, major and minor alterations to existing buildings and refurbishment of existing buildings. The Capital Banding Scheme can be applied proportionately to each element of the project to calculate an Overall %. The scheme only applies to the actual construction works. Other costs such as professional services may be recovered separately as appropriate to the type of project.

9.4.1 New Build
Complete new construction from scratch or making use of the foundations of an existing building, where the whole of the former building has been demolished to ground level. **0%**

9.4.2 Extensions
Where a building is enlarged or extended and that enlargement or extension creates new space. **5%**

9.4.3 Major Alterations
Works to an existing building where major work has taken place to the fabric of the original building including the replacing of much of the internal/external configuration. **20%**

9.4.4 Minor Alterations
Work to an existing building where the alterations are incidental to and have occurred as a result of repair or maintenance work. **40%**

9.4.5 Refurbishment/Repair and Maintenance
This is general upkeep to and refurbishment of existing building where the works do not result in any alteration or additions. **75%**

With effect from 1 April 2012 HMRC dropped the requirement that any project (including under the Capital Banding Scheme) where the VAT exceeds £50,000 must be submitted for prior approval.

The advantage of the Capital Banding Scheme is simplification; the disadvantage is potential loss of COS entitlement because a more detailed analysis may produce a more accurate result. COS recovery is only allowable in relation to non-business activities. If the project relates directly or indirectly to exempt supplies, then there will be a restriction on COS recovery e.g. the letting of commercial property on which an option to tax has not been exercised (normally calculated on the basis of a floorspace analysis and ratio).

9.5 Private Finance Initiative
VAT on unitary charges under the Private Finance Initiative for the operation of hospitals, healthcare establishments and healthcare facilities and any related services are recoverable under *COS Heading 45* (but COS recovery is only allowable in relation to non-business Activities. If the PFI project includes exempt supplies directly or indirectly then there will be a restriction on COS recovery e.g. where there are private patient wards within a PFI building). Under PFI the level of services provided is irrelevant, unitary charges are recoverable under *COS Heading 45* even on a "hard PFI" and recovery is also allowed on the provision of utilities and

ancillary equipment as part of the unitary charge or related eligible services in a separate or associated contract.

PFI projects take many forms, but essentially they all begin with a land transaction where the NHS grants a right over land (lease or licence) to the PFI contractor via a Special Purpose Vehicle (SPV) for an extended period (e.g. 25 years). The SPV will construct the hospital etc on the land (usually still owned by the NHS) and on completion operates the building, normally providing all or a range of the ancillary services required (although these can be sub-contracted or even provided by the NHS itself under a "hard PFI" arrangement e.g. catering, security, domestic services etc). The initial grant of the right over land is an exempt supply by the NHS to the SPV unless an option to tax is exercised (recommended – see below). The SPV then invoices the NHS organisation via a single unitary charge plus VAT (normally monthly) for the service of operating the building (a taxable supply). After the contractual period ends the PFI building normally becomes the property of the NHS organisation.

Again the tax position reflects the underlying legal position and because of this it is always prudent to take VAT advice in relation to any PFI project in the same way that legal advice would be taken. PFI projects are normally very high value projects lasting for decades and it is good practice to reduce the tax risk by being able to make informed decisions based on the appropriate tax advice at the right time.

9.6   NHS LIFT

VAT on charges to NHS organisations as part of a LIFT project is recoverable as COS under *COS Heading 45*. Local Improvement Finance Trusts were launched in 2001 when the Department of Health commenced a national joint venture with Partnerships UK to develop and encourage a new market for investment in primary care and community-based facilities and services. A national strategy was devised to improve the condition of the primary care estate, and thereby to improve the quality of service to patients. The NHS LIFT approach was intended to involve the local health community in developing a strategic service plan, incorporating its local primary care service needs and relationships with, for example, intermediate care, and local authority services.

For each LIFT a private sector partner is identified through a competitive procurement, and then a Joint Venture (JV or LIFTCO) established including the local NHS organisations, the private sector partner and the national JV established between the Department of Health and Partnerships UK. The private sector partner is responsible for property development and management, construction and services contracting and project management. The integration of the planning of estates requirements with a service strategy for the local health economy, and the involvement of the private sector partner in planning future estates requirements to meet that strategy as well as in managing and delivering services, were key changes introduced by the LIFT approach.

The services provided by the LIFT, alongside the on-going planning and liaison on existing and future requirements, include, for example: investment in new one-stop health centres; providing an integrated range of primary and intermediate care services; leasing premises to individual primary care service deliverers, such as GPs, on flexible terms that can respond and adapt to changing requirements over time; management of the facilities provided, such as maintenance over the whole life of the assets, providing all energy and utility requirements, and potentially cleaning and equipping premises. The LIFTCO is responsible for collecting its income from occupants and end users of services (although the NHS organisation is a shareholder/partner in LIFTCO) and output tax will be charged on this because the option to tax will normally have been exercised.

9.7   ProCure21+

The ProCure21+ National Framework is a framework agreement sponsored by the Department of Health with various Supply Chains (Principal Supply Chain Partners or PSCPs) selected via an OJEU Tender process for capital investment construction schemes. ProCure21+ has an arrangement with HMRC in relation to COS recovery on the ProCure21+ National Framework. input tax recovery is not covered by the arrangement nor are capital goods scheme calculations. From 1 January 2011 every P21+ Project will be a capital Item and fall within the Capital Goods Scheme (see **10.4 Capital Goods Scheme)**.

A mechanism for COS recovery has been agreed with HMRC which, although not allowing recovery on design & build *per se*, is an arrangement which would not normally be eligible for recovery in a non-P21+ Project. Therefore, there are tax advantages in taking the P21+ route. One feature of P21+ is that there are nominated internal NHS P21+ VAT Advisors, endorsed by HMRC and the DoH and their services are provided at no cost to the NHS organisation. However, the P21+ arrangement does not include input tax or the Capital Goods Scheme and it has been confirmed that the P21+ VAT Advisors do not undertake or monitor the 10-year capital item interval adjustments which may arise from a P21+ Project. There is, therefore, a potential compliance risk area in relation to the Capital Goods Scheme and a potential loss of input tax entitlement. In order for an NHS organisation to ensure compliance the P21+ COS calculations would have to be taken into account in completing any capital items adjustments or input tax claims.

COS recovery is allowed on the professional fees of the Principal Supply Chain Partner under *COS Heading 52* and on other fees charged on savings made. It is also allowed in relation to the recoverable elements of Site Administration and Site Facilities services (Preliminaries) and Risk Allowances (Contingencies). HMRC have not clarified the position of P21+ in the event that the proposed changes to *COS Heading 52* are implemented (see *COS Heading 52*) but as currently framed the result would be that professional fees would become ineligible for COS recovery.

The agreed mechanism is published in the *VAT Recovery Guidance for ProCure21+ Schemes* (DoH 2011) and only includes arrangements where there is no single (or composite) supply of design and construction services (there must be a separation of design from construction via the use of separate and external Primary Supply Chain Members (or PSCMs) or supply Chain Members (or SCMs). However, the "assumed path of taxable invoices" agreed would normally result in a single (or composite) supply of design & build to the recipient NHS organisation if provided outside P21+. The mechanism effectively allows the PSCP to provide a project management service to co-ordinate separate supplies of design and construction by various different providers to the NHS organisation and thus allow COS recovery.

10 LAND AND PROPERTY

10.1 Introduction

The supply of land and property is one of the most complex areas of the tax because of the underlying complexity of property law (see *VAT Notice 742*). The tax position reflects the underlying legal position. Because of this it is always prudent to take VAT advice in relation to any property transaction in the same way that legal advice would be taken (i.e. when a lease is drafted or a sale proposed or as part of the planning process).

Under Group 1 of VAT Act 1994 Schedule 9 the grant of any interest in or right over land or of any licence to occupy land is exempt (see below). With the exception of residential property where an option to tax is exercised by the taxpayer this supply becomes standard-rated.

The main supplies of land and property as a business activity are:
- lease of office or commercial accommodation (exempt);
- licence to occupy office or commercial accommodation (exempt);
- sales of land or property (exempt); and
- supplies of residential accommodation (exempt).

Therefore, where a taxpayer rents out or leases property or grants a licence to occupy for a consideration there will be an exempt supply. This means that none of the VAT incurred on costs attributable to the exempt supply of land or property is recoverable either as input tax or COS and in relation to land or property these sums can be significant.

10.1.1 The Legal Context

While the UK remains a Member State of the EU, VAT is ultimately governed by EU law (the *Principal VAT Directive 2006/112/EC*) though all Member States enact their own legislation interpreting the Directive (known as indirect effect). Where there is a conflict UK law is subordinate to EU law (although UK taxpayers are entitled to rely on domestic law until it is changed). In the UK the primary legislation is the Value Added Tax Act 1994 although there are various other Statutory Instruments and Regulations (notably the *VAT Regulations 1995 SI 1995/2518*) collectively known as secondary legislation. In addition, some HMRC publications have the force of law and amendments are regularly made via the annual Finance Acts (changes to secondary legislation can be made at any time).

The main sources of VAT law relating to land and property are:

The VAT Act 1994:

Schedule 9 Group 1 – Exempt Supplies

Schedule 8 Groups 5 & 6 – Zero-Rated Supplies

Schedule 7A Groups 2, 3, 6 & 7 – Reduced-Rate Supplies

Schedule 10 – Buildings and Land

10.1.2   Exempt Supplies

The grant of any interest in or right over land, any licence to occupy land or a personal right (in Scotland) is exempt, including sales of land or buildings, the leasing or letting of land or buildings or the sub-leasing or sub-letting of land or buildings.

An interest in land includes a legal interest, a beneficial interest, rights of entry, easements, wayleaves and profits à prendre (although these can also be standard-rated or zero-rated). A licence to occupy means a written or oral agreement for the leasing or letting of immoveable property but falling short of a formal lease for an agreed duration in return for payment the right to occupy a defined area (and exclude others from enjoying that right). The definitions of an interest in or right over land and licence to occupy are important because if a supply falls outside of these it will necessarily be standard-rated irrespective of any option to tax.

An example of a licence to occupy is the provision of office accommodation in return for a monthly rent with the right to use shared areas such as reception, lifts, tea points and rest rooms. The predominant supply is the right to occupy defined office accommodation and exclude others. The fact that the licensee may have to share other parts of the building does not affect the occupational rights granted by the licence. This means that the supply is exempt unless an option to tax is exercised.

Another example is a specified area of office space less than a complete floor or room, such as a bank of desks in return for a periodic licence fee. A licence to occupy land can be granted in respect of parts of rooms and floors and consequently can exist within an open plan office area. The important point here is that there has to be an identifiable area of land that the licensee has an exclusive right to occupy during the period of the licence or the times specified in the licence (occupation does not have to be continuous).

Other examples include specified areas of storage space within a building, such as a room, cupboard or marked area for which someone is granted exclusive use or a catering concession where the caterer is granted a licence to occupy a specific kitchen and restaurant area, or the right to run a landfill site to an operator from a specified area of land, or the hiring of a hall or other accommodation for meetings, parties, etc (including use of kitchen area, lighting, furniture, etc). Most supplies of hiring out such accommodation will constitute a licence to occupy land. Access to kitchens, toilets, car parking etc is incidental to the predominant supply of land. However, if other services, such as catering, are provided the supply is likely to be a standard rated supply of services.

10.1.3 Standard-Rated Supplies

The grant of any interest in or right over land, any licence to occupy land or a personal right (in Scotland) is standard-rated where an option to tax has been granted (but the option to tax is disapplied in relation to residential or charitable use) including sales of land or buildings, the leasing or letting of land or buildings or the sub-leasing or sub-letting of land or buildings.

The grant or assignment of the freehold interest in a non-qualifying building (i.e. a commercial building) which has not been completed, a new building which is not to be used as qualifying building after the grant (completed less than three years before the grant) or civil engineering works (e.g. roads, tunnels and bridges) which have not been completed or a new civil engineering work is standard-rated (completed less than three years before the grant). Other standard-rated supplies of property include hotel, holiday (and similar) accommodation, recreational caravans and camping pitches, parking facilities, storage facilities, and gaming and fishing rights, boxes and seats at sporting events or theatres etc, and sports facilities, except where there is a series of at least 10 bookings (exempt).

Hotel and holiday accommodation includes accommodation in a hotel, inn, boarding house or similar establishment (including short-term lets and serviced apartments) and includes furnished sleeping accommodation. Where guests stay for a continuous period of four weeks or more a reduced rate applies. Also includes chalets, cottages, huts etc, seasonal caravan and tent pitches (i.e. non-residential) but not rented residential accommodation in a caravan or mobile home (exempt). Parking facilities include the grant or assignment of facilities for parking a vehicle, the letting or licensing of garages, the letting, licensing or provision of taxi ranks, bicycle storage, rights to park vehicles, purpose-built car parks and the sale of new or partly competed garages etc.

10.1.4 Zero-Rated Supplies

The first grant of a major interest in a qualifying building (residential or for charitable non-business use) by a person constructing the building is zero-rated. The first grant of a major interest in a protected building which has been substantially reconstructed by a person reconstructing the building is zero-rated. A qualifying building is one which is designed as a dwelling or a number of dwellings or intended for use for a relevant charitable purpose (at least 95% non-business by concession) or intended for a relevant residential purpose (the main residence of at least 90% of the residents). The first grant includes the first sale or long lease but excludes any second or subsequent long lease or any sale after leasing it on a long lease. In England, Wales and Northern Ireland a major interest means the fee simple or a tenancy for a term certain exceeding 21 years and in Scotland the interest of the owner or a lessee under a lease for a period of not less than 20 years. In England and Wales the fee simple means the freehold and in Scotland the fee simple means the interest of the owner.

10.1.5 Non-Business Activities

Non-business activities are activities outside the scope of VAT which are not carried on for a business purpose including charitable activities and the statutory duties of GDs. From 1 January 2011 these are included in the £250,000 value for the purposes of the Capital Goods Scheme.

10.1.6 Accounting for VAT

Output tax is due on taxable supplies of land or property. Input tax is allowable on the direct and indirect costs attributable to taxable supplies of land or property.

There are three levels of input tax recovery related to supplies of land or property:

(1) direct recovery on directly attributable input tax – such as VAT incurred on construction, demolition, site clearance, professional fees, peripheral works, maintenance costs, utilities or any other cost directly attributable to the taxable supply etc.;

(2) indirect recovery on sectorised costs such as the administration of estates and facilities or leased accommodation. Further calculations will be necessary to determine this proportion, but typically it would be based on a floorspace analysis and ratio. This percentage is then applied to the sectorised costs and that proportion of the VAT incurred is allowable input tax; and

(3) residual recovery on general overheads. In this context the residual input tax entitlement arises as a proportion of VAT incurred on general non-attributable overheads for the organisation as a whole. Any one-off sales or purchases of land or property should be excluded as incidental. Therefore, the residual input tax entitlement will normally only arise in relation to ongoing supplies of land or property such as leased accommodation (any VAT incurred on costs which has been taken into account above should be excluded).

Input tax entitlement arises in relation to taxable supplies made or intended to be made irrespective of the type of supply. The amount of input tax allowable will depend on the proportion of the VAT incurred which relates or will relate to taxable supplies. Further calculations will be necessary to determine this proportion in each project, but typically it would be based on a floorspace analysis and ratio (excluding the common areas of buildings which are non-attributable). From 1 January 2011 any capital project with a net value in excess of £250,000 and including a business element (taxable or exempt) falls within the Capital Goods Scheme.

10.2 Sales of Land & Buildings

Except in relation to the sale of the freehold a commercial building or civil engineering work which is less than three years old (standard-rated) when an NHS organisation sells land or buildings there will normally be an exempt supply. If the option to tax is exercised the supply is standard-rated. If standard-rated, output tax would be chargeable on the full value of the supply (and any Stamp Duty Land Tax payable on the transaction would be charged on the gross value). But an option to tax is normally advisable for the supplier because it gives rise to full input tax entitlement and all of the VAT incurred on costs attributable to the taxable supply of land or property is recoverable. Conversely, if the supply is not taxed and remains exempt none of the VAT incurred on costs attributable to the exempt supply of land or property is recoverable either as input tax or COS. In relation to sales of land or property the amount of input tax can be significant.

For example, the VAT on demolition and site clearance costs would be recoverable as input tax where an option to tax is exercised (and these costs are not eligible for COS recovery). VAT on legal fees and other professional fees is not recoverable as COS in relation to an exempt supply even where the ultimate purpose of the transaction is the non-business activity of the NHS. The rule in relation to input tax or COS recovery is that for direct attribution there must be a direct and immediate link to the supply or activity. Therefore, VAT incurred where there is a direct and immediate link to an exempt supply will not be allowable input tax or eligible for COS recovery, but if the transaction is taxed all of the VAT incurred is allowable input tax.

10.3 Option to Tax

The option to tax is a provision which allows a taxable person to tax certain supplies of land, buildings or property which would otherwise be exempt (land includes any buildings or structures permanently affixed). Because these supplies are now taxable this creates an entitlement to claim credit for allowable input tax attributable to taxable supplies.

The effect of the option to tax is that VAT must be charged on all future supplies related to the opted property by the person opting unless blocked by an anti-avoidance provision or the option has been revoked. The option remains effective even where the person opting deregisters due to a fall in turnover but then has to re-register. If at any time a grant is made in relation to the land or property by the person opting (or a relevant associate) when the option to tax has effect, then the supply is standard-rated. Grant includes an assignment or surrender and the supply made by the person to whom an interest is surrendered when there is a reverse surrender.

The option to tax applies to the person making the option in relation to specified land, buildings or property. The person opting does not have to own the opted land, buildings or property and only supplies made by the person opting are affected (i.e. the option to tax does not transfer).

For example:
- a person who purchases a building where an option to tax has been exercised by the purchaser is not obliged to opt to tax or charge output tax on any subsequent lets or disposal;
- a person who sub-lets a property may opt to tax their sub-let even where they are not charged VAT on the principal supply;
- but in practice an option will follow an option to reclaim input tax.

The option applies:
- in relation to a building it applies to the whole of the building and all land within its curtilage;
- to land under and immediately around the building (including forecourts and yards);
- but not to a separate car park;
- in relation to land it covers all land and any buildings or civil engineering works on the land.

From 1 June 2008 if a building is demolished or destroyed any option still applies to the land and to any future building constructed on the land and if a new building is constructed on opted land it is covered by the option unless HMRC are notified that the building is to be excluded from the option. Real Estate Elections were introduced in 2008 as a formal decision to opt to tax all future property acquisitions. Each property is treated as separately opted (and therefore may be separately revoked). The person opting is treated as having exercised the option on the day the acquisition was made in relation to any relevant interest in land or property.

There are two stages in opting to tax:
(1) making the decision to opt to tax; and

(2) notifying HMRC of the decision to opt to tax.

A written record should be kept of the decision to opt and HMRC should be notified within 30 days of the option taking effect. HMRC permission is required where there have been previous exempt supplies (and notification is thus not required). Automatic permission is granted where the only input tax to be reclaimed is incurred after the option takes effect and relates to general maintenance and overheads otherwise written permission is required from HMRC. HMRC must be satisfied that there will be a fair and reasonable attribution of input tax to taxable supplies.

If notification is late HMRC has discretion to accept belated notifications although they cannot grant retrospection and will generally accept these where there is evidence that a genuine decision was taken to opt to tax but it has not been notified in time. They may refuse a belated notification if acceptance would produce an unfair result or in relation to an avoidance scheme. The option to tax is disapplied in relation to residential property, or in relation to non-business activities or a relevant charitable purpose (but not charity offices), or in relation to grants made to relevant housing associations in relation to residential property and in relation to DIY housebuilders. Finally, there are limited circumstances in which an option to tax can be revoked. It can be revoked by the taxpayer in a six month cooling off period or automatically where no interest has been held in the land or property for six years or by the taxpayer where more than 20 years have elapsed since the option first took effect.

(see *VAT Notice 742A*)

10.4 Capital Goods Scheme

The Capital Goods Scheme is a form of extended partial exemption. From 1 January 2011 the Capital Goods Scheme includes non-business activities, and ships and aircraft and applies to land where the owner incurs VAT bearing capital expenditure of £250,000 or over on its acquisition, or a building or part of a building where the owner incurs VAT bearing capital expenditure of £250,000 or over on its acquisition, construction, refurbishment, fitting out, alteration or extension, or a civil engineering work or part of a civil engineering work where the owner incurs VAT bearing capital expenditure of £250,000 or over on its acquisition, construction, refurbishment, fitting out, alteration or extension.

The purpose of the scheme is to separate higher value projects from the general business/non-business and partial exemption calculations to achieve a more accurate attribution of input tax to taxable supplies. Only the proportion of the input tax attributable to taxable supplies can be reclaimed. An apportionment to determine the proportion of exempt supplies, taxable supplies (and non-business activities) is necessary. The scheme does not apply if assets are just acquired for resale, or there is expenditure on assets acquired just for resale, or assets are acquired (or there is expenditure on assets) that are only used for non-business purposes.

The £250,000 includes all of the costs in making the building ready including professional and managerial costs. VAT incurred after the first interval can be incorporated into the calculation. If VAT is incurred before the first interval a calculation is required to work out the overall initial percentage which can be claimed against which the percentage of taxable use in any subsequent interval can be measured.

The adjustment period for land, buildings or civil engineering works is 10 successive (annual) intervals. From 1 January 2011 the first interval commences on the day on which the owner first uses the capital item and ends on the day before the start of the next partial exemption tax year and thereafter at annual intervals. Subsequent intervals follow annually at the end of the partial exemption tax year. These are included in the second VAT period after the interval ends (which is the VAT period after the partial exemption annual adjustment).

The calculation is based on the annual variation from the baseline percentage of taxable use. The baseline percentage is the taxable percentage at the end of the first interval. At each (annual) interval thereafter the taxable percentage is calculated and if there is a variation from the baseline there is an adjustment. The final adjustment is made in the normal way in the 10th interval and no further adjustments are required. If there is a change of use after the final adjustment it is disregarded.

If there is a transfer of a going concern the purchaser is treated as the owner of the capital item and is also treated as having done everything done by the seller. In the case of a VAT Group the representative member is treated as the owner and as having everything done by a group member in respect of the asset. If a capital item is disposed of before the end of the adjustment period, the interval in which it is disposed of is treated as the final interval. If it is disposed of before the end of the adjustment period HMRC may apply the disposal test. If the total input tax exceeds the output tax due on the disposal, then it may be necessary to adjust the amount of input tax recovered in relation to the capital item.

(see *VAT Notice 706/1/2*)

10.5 Anti-Avoidance Provisions

Some businesses whose supplies are wholly or partly exempt are not entitled to recover all of the input tax they incur on the purchase of land or buildings, or on major construction projects. As a result, some of these organisations entered into arrangements designed either to increase the amount of input tax they could claim, or to spread the VAT cost of the purchase or construction over a number of years. To counter this, an anti-avoidance test was introduced. The test is applied each time a grant is made and if caught, the option to tax will not have effect (it will be 'disapplied') in respect of the supplies that arise from that particular grant. The anti-avoidance test may also impact on the VAT treatment of a transfer of a going concern (TOGC) of a property.

If an interest is granted in a building or land and the person that is to be in occupation makes predominantly taxable supplies and is able to receive credit for the majority of input tax they incur the anti-avoidance measure is unlikely to apply. An option to tax may, however, be disapplied if any of the following situations arise:

- a business is partly exempt and grants a lease in a building that it intends to occupy at a later date;
- a business is partly exempt and enters into a sale and leaseback of a property that it occupies; or
- a business constructs a building and finance is provided by a bank that also intends to be in occupation; or a business purchases a building and finance is provided by a bank that also intends to be in occupation.

Where supplies of property become exempt supplies due to the disapplication of an option to tax, this may mean that a business cannot recover input tax, or that it has to repay input tax that it has previously recovered.

10.5.1 The Anti-Avoidance Test

If at the time of the grant of land or buildings the property is, or is expected to become, a capital item for the purposes of the Capital Goods Scheme, either for the grantor, a person to whom the property is transferred or a person treated as the grantor, and it is the intention or expectation of the grantor or the person treated as the grantor or a person responsible for financing the grantor's acquisition or development, that the building will be occupied by them or a person connected with them, and the person occupying the property will be doing so other than wholly or substantially wholly for eligible purposes, then the option to tax will not have effect in respect of supplies that arise from that particular grant.

There are several key elements to the test which potentially trigger the anti-avoidance provision:

- the property must be a capital item;
- there must be occupation of the property (either by the business or a connected person); and
- there must be exempt supplies or non-business activities.

In effect, the option to tax is only blocked where the property is a capital item and it is used or occupied by a business or a connected person to make exempt supplies (for example, it does not affect supplies to an unconnected third party). Occupation wholly or substantially wholly for eligible purposes means for at least 80% taxable purposes or by an NHS organisation, GD or other public bodies for at least 80% taxable or non-business purposes. The anti-avoidance provision still applies to the NHS, GDs and other public bodies if the occupation is for the purpose of making exempt supplies but typically this means that an NHS organisation, GD or other public body is not blocked from opting to tax part of a building where it is in occupation in respect of its non-business activities as a public body.

10.5.2 Occupation

A person is in occupation of a building or land if they have a physical presence, and the right to occupy the property as if they are the owner. This means they will have actual possession and control of the land, together with the ability to exclude others from the enjoyment of such rights. From 1 March 2011 a person in occupation of the land or building is treated as if he is not in occupation if the percentage occupied does not exceed 2% where the person is (or is connected with) the grantor, or the percentage occupied does not exceed 10% where the person is (or is connected with) a development financier (but not also (or connected with) the grantor).

Normally a legal interest in or licence to occupy the land, will have been granted to them. However, occupation could also be by agreement or *de facto* and it is therefore necessary to take into account the day to day arrangements, particularly where these differ from the contractual terms. An exclusive right of occupation is not a requirement; an agreement might, for example, allow for joint occupation. It is also not necessary for a person to be utilising all of the land for all of the time for them to be considered as occupying it.

Businesses, such as insurance companies and banks, or educational institutions such as universities or further education colleges making exempt supplies, or someone who is not, and is not required to be VAT registered are examples of businesses and organisations that may occupy a property for other than eligible purposes and organisations, such as charities, which undertake non-business activities, would not generally be in occupation for eligible purposes.

10.5.3 Grantor & Grant

The grantor is the person who sells, leases, licences or lets any of the land or buildings and the grant is the act that transfers the interest in, or possession of, the land or building e.g. a freehold sale of land or a building, the leasing or licensing of land or a building, or the assignment or surrender of that lease or licence. The word 'grant' refers to the act that transfers the interest in, or possession of, the land or building. Examples are a freehold sale of land or a building, the leasing or licensing of land or a building, or the assignment or surrender of that lease or licence. The grantor is the person who sells, leases, licences or lets any of the land or buildings. The test should be applied to each grant made.

10.5.4 Development Financier

A person is deemed to have been responsible for financing an acquisition or development if two key conditions are met: at the time the finance is provided, or the agreement to provide the finance is entered into, the person providing the finance must intend or expect that he or the grantor, or somebody connected to either of them, will occupy the particular property for other than eligible purposes and the funds must be for the purpose of financing the purchase, construction or refurbishment of that property. If either of these conditions is not met, a person will not be deemed to be responsible for providing finance, even if he has provided the funds to meet part or all of the cost of the acquisition or development.

10.5.5 Connected Persons

The test in Corporation Tax Act 2010 s.1122 applies to determine whether persons are connected. The following persons are treated as connected:

- husband, wife or civil partner; relatives and their husbands, wives or civil partners;
- husband's, wife's or civil partner's relatives and their husbands, wives or civil partners;
- in a partnership, the partners and their husbands, wives, civil partners and relatives;
- a controlled company either by an individual or with any of the persons listed above, or
- for a settlor the trustees of a settlement, or of which a person who is still alive and who is connected is a settlor. Relative means a brother,

sister, ancestor or lineal descendant. It does not include nephews, nieces, uncles and aunts.

A company is connected with another company if the same person has control of both, or a person has control of one and persons connected with him (or he and persons connected with him) have control of the other, or if a group of two or more persons have control of each company, and the groups either consist of the same persons or could be regarded as consisting of the same persons by treating (in one or more cases) a member of either group as replaced by a person with whom he is connected. For the purposes of the option to tax a company is not treated as 'connected' to another company as a result of both being under the control of: the Crown; a Minister of the Crown; a GD; or, a Northern Ireland GD.

(see *Notice 742A*)

10.6 Construction Services

The liability of construction services depends on the type of building works undertaken and the status of the person constructing the building i.e. whether the building is commercial, residential or charitable and whether the person constructing the building or carrying out the works is a developer, a main contractor or a subcontractor.

For the purposes of reduced-rating or zero-rating a qualifying building is a building which is designed as a dwelling or a number of dwellings or is intended for use solely for a relevant charitable purpose (95% non-business use by concession) or intended for use solely for a relevant residential purpose (the sole or main residence of at least 90% of its residents). A non-qualifying building is a building which is not designed as a qualifying building i.e. a commercial, non-residential building. All supplies of construction services which are not subject to the reduced-rate or zero-rated are standard-rated including all works on non-qualifying buildings (i.e. commercial buildings such as offices, factories or warehouses) or where any work requires a certificate of intended use for VAT purposes a subcontractor must standard-rate their services (including buildings to be used for a relevant charitable purpose or a relevant residential purpose and conversion services supplied to relevant housing associations). Subcontractors' services, goods and building materials and related professional services are also standard-rated in relation to non-qualifying buildings.

10.6.1 Residential Accommodation

Zero-rating applies to services supplied in the course of construction of a new dwelling or dwellings (and which relate to the construction). This also includes building materials and certain electrical goods incorporated into a building by a builder who is also supplying the zero-rated services, garages where these are attached to a dwelling and constructed at the same time, civil engineering works in relation to serviced plots where these are closely connected to the construction of qualifying buildings and where the construction of the qualifying buildings will follow on closely after the completion of the works. The zero-rating also applies to articles ordinarily incorporated by builders in that type of building but not electrical and gas appliances except ventilation and air cooling systems, burglar or fire alarms, waste disposal units or compactors (in blocks of flats), lifts or hoists, but not free standing appliances or free-standing furniture.

Specifically standard-rated in relation to new dwellings are the separate supply of architectural, surveying or consultancy or supervisory services, the hire of goods on their own e.g. plant and machinery without an operator, scaffolding without erection/dismantling.

10.6.2   Relevant Residential Purpose
Zero-rating also applies to construction of new buildings for a relevant residential purpose. Zero-rating does not apply until the customer has given the builder a certificate of intended use. Subcontractors' services are standard-rated because for zero-rating to apply the supply must be to the person who intends to use the building and subcontractors' services are supplied to a main contractor or other intermediary rather than the person who intends to use the building.

A relevant residential purpose includes residential accommodation for students or children, a residence which is the sole or main residence of at least 90% of its residents such as a home or other institution providing residential accommodation for children or personal care for persons in need, a hospice, a monastery, nunnery or similar establishment but excluding use as a hospital, prison or similar institution, and excluding use as a hotel, inn or similar establishment.

Apportionment applies to partly residential buildings and generally supplies of services to the qualifying part are zero-rated, supplies of services to the non-qualifying part are standard-rated. In general, the zero-rating only applies to the part which is a dwelling or is residential (except communal areas in residential flats).

10.6.3   Relevant Charitable Purpose
Zero-rating also applies to construction of new buildings for a relevant charitable purpose, a building which is used by a charity for at least 95% for non-business purposes. Zero-rating does not apply until the customer has given the builder a certificate of intended use. Subcontractors' services

are standard-rated because for zero-rating the supply must be to the person who intends to use the building and subcontractors' services are supplied to a main contractor or other intermediary rather than the person who intends to use the building. A relevant charitable purpose includes use by as a charity otherwise than in the course or furtherance of a business such as places of worship, school buildings where no fee is charged, grant-funded research buildings, village or community halls, scout or guide huts, annexes which are capable of functioning independently from the main building and where the main access is not via the existing building. Apportionment applies to partly charitable buildings and generally supplies of services to the qualifying part are zero-rated, supplies of services to the non-qualifying part are standard-rated.

10.6.4 Protected Buildings

A protected building is a listed building or a scheduled monument and which is or will be a qualifying building after reconstruction. Until 1 October 2012 the supply of services in the course of an approved alteration was zero-rated but from 1 October 2012 the supply of services in the course of alteration or reconstruction is standard-rated. Zero-rating continued to apply until 30 September 2015 under transitional rules which apply to the first grant of a major interest in a substantially reconstructed protected building where 60% of the work (by cost) relates to approved alterations: if those approved alterations are within the scope of a relevant consent applied for before 21 March 2012; or of a written contract entered into before 21 March 2012; or if 10% of the substantial reconstruction (measured by cost) was completed prior to 21 March 2012.

10.6.5 Civil Engineering Works

Construction services related to civil engineering works (e.g. roads, bridges and tunnels) are standard-rated including subcontractors' services, goods and building materials and related professional services except where these relate to qualifying buildings (e.g. utilities or road works as part of a residential development) or residential caravan parks (zero-rated).

10.6.6 Residential Conversions

Services supplied to housing associations (RSLs) in the course of conversion are zero-rated in relation to a non-residential building or part thereof converted into a residential building designed as a dwelling or dwellings or intended for use for a relevant residential purpose. The zero-rating includes including building materials and certain electrical goods but not related professional services or the hire of goods or the services of subcontractors.

Qualifying services supplied in the course of a qualifying conversion are reduced-rate. A qualifying conversion is the conversion of a single household to multiple occupancy or relevant residential purpose, multiple occupancy into single household or relevant residential purpose, relevant residential purpose into single household or multiple occupancy or any other building to single household, multiple occupancy or relevant residential purpose.

Qualifying services include carrying out work to the fabric of the building, carrying out work within the immediate site of the building related to utilities, drainage or waste disposal etc, including all repair and maintenance, decoration or improvement. Subcontractors' services are reduced-rate except in relation to a relevant residential purpose (standard-rated). The reduced-rate applies to articles ordinarily incorporated by builders in that type of building but not electrical and gas appliances except ventilation and air cooling systems, burglar or fire alarms, waste disposal units or compactors (in blocks of flats), lifts or hoists.

Specifically standard-rated in relation to qualifying conversions are the separate supply of architectural, surveying or consultancy or supervisory services, the hire of goods on their own e.g. plant and machinery without an operator, scaffolding without erection/dismantling.

10.6.7 Other Reduced-Rate Supplies

The reduced-rate applies to the renovation or alteration of a single household dwelling that has not been lived in for two years or more, a multiple occupancy dwelling that has not been lived in for two years or more, or a building to be used for a relevant residential purpose that has not been lived in for two years or more. Where the property has not been empty for two years or more any renovations or alterations would be standard-rated. The reduced-rate also applies to supplies of services by installers of energy saving materials including supplies of energy saving materials such as insulation, draught stripping and solar panels and also heat pumps, wind turbines and water turbines. And to supplies to a qualifying person of heating appliances and installation services funded by a grant under a relevant scheme. A qualifying person is a person in receipt of benefits and a relevant scheme is one sponsored by a public body. And to the supply of services of installing mobility aids and the supply of mobility aids by a person installing them for use in domestic accommodation by a person aged 60 years or over.

(see *VAT Notice 708*)

11 INTERNATIONAL VAT

11.1 Place of Taxation

The VAT liability of international transactions depends on whether the supply is one of goods or services and whether it is within the EU (the term EC is still in use in relation to VAT e.g. EC Sales List or intra-EC transactions) or outside (and if within the EU whether the place of taxation is the UK)). The concept of import and export now only applies to non-EU transactions i.e. imports from outside the EU and exports outside the EU. Within the EU Single Market movements of goods are described as acquisitions (or arrivals) by the purchasing business and removals (or dispatches) by the selling business. There are significant differences in the rules depending on whether the supply is one of goods or services and there are general rules and special rules to determine where the supply is taxed and thus how VAT is accounted for. As a general principle VAT is only due in one Member State where the place of taxation is within the EU.

11.1.1 The Single Market

The VAT territory of the EU is made up of 28 Member States (which can be checked online or in VAT Notice 725). States such as Liechtenstein, Vatican City, Andorra and San Marino are not within the EU for VAT purposes. From a UK perspective the Isle of Man is within the EU VAT Territory but Gibraltar and the Channel Islands are not. GDs should be aware of which territories are included, or excluded, from a Member State because movements of goods between the UK and any of the above countries, or their included territories, are treated as intra-EC supplies for VAT purposes, whereas movements of goods between the UK and any of the excluded territories are treated as imported or exported goods for VAT purposes.

The EU VAT Territory currently consists of:
Austria
Belgium
Bulgaria
Croatia
Cyprus
Czech Republic
Denmark, except the Faroe Islands and Greenland
Estonia
Finland
France, including Monaco
Germany, except Busingen and the Isle of Heligoland

Greece

Hungary

The Republic of Ireland

Italy, except the communes of Livigno and Campione d'Italia and the Italian waters of Lake Lugano

Latvia

Lithuania

Luxembourg

Malta

Netherlands

Poland

Portugal, including the Azores and Madeira

Romania

Slovakia

Slovenia

Spain, including the Balearic Islands but excluding the Canary Islands, Ceuta and Melilla

Sweden

United Kingdom, including the Isle of Man

How VAT is accounted for on intra-EC supplies depends on whether the recipient of the supply is registered for VAT in the Member State of acquisition. Also, for these purposes movements of goods between Member States within the same legal entity (often referred to as a transfers of own goods) are treated as supplies. Special rules apply in the case of natural gas and electricity, along with heat and cooling (also heat and cooling).

An EC Sales List (ESL) is required if supplies of goods or services are made to taxable persons in other Member States. If Box 8 of the VAT Return is completed HMRC will automatically send an ESL to complete. The system for collecting statistics on the trade in goods between Member States is known as Intrastat. All businesses carrying out trade with other Member States (including NHS organisations) must declare the totals of their sales and acquisitions on their VAT Return. Businesses whose EU trade exceeds a legally set threshold have to complete additional statistical information called Supplementary Declarations. Statistics are compiled from the Supplementary Declarations and information supplied on the VAT Return.

While the UK remains a Member State of the EU it is within the EU VAT Territory and the Single Market.

(see *VAT Notice 725*)

11.2 Acquisitions & Removals

Where goods are removed from one Member State and acquired in another the general rule is that output tax is not chargeable by the removing taxable person to an acquiring taxable person. The acquiring taxable person accounts for VAT at the rate in force in the Member State of acquisition. In practice in the UK this means that the VAT on acquisitions is accounted for in Box 2 of the VAT Return and if allowable input tax, also in Box 4. If not allowable input tax the effect is to rebalance the acquisition in relation to partial exemption and non-business activities by excluding the VAT claim in Box 4.

For example, if an NHS organisation purchases goods or equipment from another Member State the VAT which would have been chargeable if purchased in the UK is added (in Box 2) to the output tax (Box 1) of the NHS organisation's VAT Return and forms part of the total in Box 3. If the goods or equipment relates to the non-business activities of the NHS organisation no allowable input tax entitlement would arise and no VAT would be claimed in Box 4 resulting in the same outcome as if the goods or equipment had been purchased in the UK.

(see *VAT Notice 725*)

11.2.1 Acquisitions

An acquisition in the UK occurs where:

*   there is an intra-EC movement of goods to the UK
*   the goods are received here by a VAT registered trader, and
*   the supplier is registered for VAT in the Member State of departure
*   in which case the recipient is required to account for VAT on the goods acquired in the UK.

An NHS organisation must account for any tax due on the VAT Return for the period in which the tax point occurs and it may treat this as input tax on the same VAT Return subject to the normal rules.

The time of acquisition is the earlier of either:

*   the 15th day of the month following the one in which the goods were sent, or
*   the date the supplier issued their invoice

Acquisitions are liable at the same rate as domestic supplies of identical goods in the UK. So, for example, no tax is due on acquisitions of goods which are currently zero-rated in the UK. Part or full payment for an intra-EC supply of goods does not create a tax point for the acquisition. The VAT on an acquisition is always due in the Member State where the goods are received. However, there is a fallback provision that applies where the

VAT registration number quoted to the supplier to secure zero-rating has been issued in a different Member State. In that event the acquisition tax must be accounted for in the Member State of registration, but the customer also remains liable to account for acquisition VAT in the Member State to which the goods have been sent.

(see *VAT Notice 725*)

11.2.2   Removals

The normal VAT treatment of goods supplied between taxable persons in different Member States is that the removal in the Member State of dispatch is zero-rated, and VAT is due on the acquisition of the goods in the Member State of arrival and is accounted for by the recipient on their VAT Return at the rate in force in that Member State (Box 2 of the UK VAT Return). Goods sent to the Isle of Man from the UK are treated as domestic supplies for VAT purposes therefore VAT must be charged at the appropriate UK rate in the normal way. But goods sent to the Channel Islands or Gibraltar are treated as exports from the EU for VAT purposes (the EU VAT Territory includes the Isle of Man but not the Channel Islands or Gibraltar).

The tax point for a supply of goods to a taxable person in another Member State is the earlier of either the 15th day of the month following the one in which it sends the goods to a business customer (or a business customer takes them away), or the date it issues a VAT invoice for the supply. Businesses should use the tax point as the reference date for including the supplies on the VAT Return, EC Sales Lists and, normally, the Intrastat Supplementary Declarations. The receipt of a payment in these circumstances does not create a tax point for the intra-EC supply. However, a business must issue a VAT invoice to a business customer for the amount paid to it and the date of issue of the VAT invoice will be the tax point. Where a business issues a series of invoices relating to the same supply of goods, the time limit for obtaining valid evidence of removal begins from the date of the final invoice.

(see *VAT Notice 725*)

11.2.3   Zero-Rating

The Principal VAT Directive allows Member States to exempt certain supplies subject to conditions laid down for the purpose of ensuring the correct application of such exemptions (zero-rating) and preventing any evasion, avoidance or abuse. The UK uses the term 'zero-rating' rather than 'exemption' used in EU law to avoid confusion with the use of exemption elsewhere in UK law. A supply from the UK to a customer in another Member State is zero-rated where a business obtains and shows on a VAT sales invoice the recipient's EC VAT registration number, including the 2-letter country prefix code, and the goods are sent or transported out of the UK to a destination in another Member State, and a business obtains and retains valid commercial evidence that the goods have been removed from the UK within the time limits.

A business cannot zero-rate a sale, even if the goods are subsequently removed to another Member State, if it supplies the goods to a UK VAT registered recipient (unless that recipient is also registered for VAT in another Member State – in such cases they must provide their EC VAT registration number and the goods must be removed to another Member State), delivers to, or allow the goods to be collected by, a UK recipient at a UK address, or allows the goods to be used in the UK in the period between supply and removal, except where specifically authorised to do so. The time limits for removing the goods and obtaining valid evidence of removal will begin from the time of supply. For goods removed to another Member State the time limits are three months (including supplies of goods involved in groupage or consolidation prior to removal), or six months for supplies of goods involved in processing or incorporation prior to removal.

HMRC advise that when a taxpayer makes a supply of goods to a taxable person in another Member State, but has to deliver them to a third party in the UK which is also making a taxable supply of goods or services to that recipient, a taxpayer can zero-rate the supply provided:

- it obtains and show on the VAT sales invoice the customer's EC VAT registration number, including the 2-letter country prefix code
- the goods are only being delivered and not supplied to the third person in the UK
- no use is made of the goods other than for processing or incorporation into other goods for removal, and
- it obtains and keeps valid commercial evidence that the goods have been removed from the UK within the time limits

and the records show:

- the name, address and VAT number of the customer in the EC
- the invoice number and date
- the description, quantity and value of the goods
- the name and address of the third person in the UK to whom the goods were delivered
- the date by which the goods must be removed
- proof of removal obtained from the person responsible for transporting the goods out of the UK, and
- the date the goods were actually removed from the UK.

The records must be able to show that the goods supplied have been processed or incorporated into the goods removed from the UK.

In cases where the third party is not in the UK but in another Member State, the same conditions will generally apply to allow a taxpayer to zero-rate the supply. If a taxpayer cannot obtain and show a valid EC VAT registration number on its sales invoice it must charge and account for output tax in the UK at the appropriate UK rate. If the goods are not removed or a taxpayer does not have the evidence of removal within the time limits it must account for VAT. No VAT is due on goods which would normally be zero-rated when supplied in the UK.

HMRC also advise that taxpayers should carry out normal commercial checks such as bank and trade credit worthiness references before it starts making supplies to an EU customer. As part of these checks it should ask the customer to supply their EC VAT registration number. If they do not supply the EC VAT registration number then the taxpayer is obliged to charge UK VAT on any supplies of goods. If it is supplying services and its customer cannot supply an EC VAT registration number then it must make sure there is sufficient evidence to show that the supply is to a business in order to zero-rate the supply. Businesses should check the validity of the EC VAT registration number using the Europa Website. All Member States share these arrangements and businesses in other Member States can verify a UK VAT registration number in the same way.

http://europa.eu/youreurope/business/vat-customs/check-number-vies/

(see *VAT Notice 725*)

11.2.4 Evidence of Removal
HMRC require evidence that a supply has taken place and the goods have been removed from the UK and recommend that a combination of the following documents are retained:
- the customer's order (including customer's name, VAT number and delivery address for the goods)
- inter-company correspondence
- copy sales invoice (including a description of the goods, an invoice number and customer's EC VAT number etc)
- advice note
- packing list
- commercial transport document(s) from the carrier responsible for removing the goods from the UK, for example an International Consignment Note (CMR) fully completed by the consignor, the haulier and signed by receiving consignee
- details of insurance or freight charges

- bank statements as evidence of payment
- receipted copy of the consignment note as evidence of receipt of goods abroad, and
- any other documents relevant to the removal of the goods in question which it would normally obtain in the course of its intra-EC business.

Photocopy certificates of shipment or other transport documents are not normally acceptable as evidence of removal unless authenticated with an original stamp and dated by an authorised official of the issuing office.

The documents a business uses as proof of removal must clearly identify the following:
- the supplier
- the consignor (where different from the supplier)
- the customer
- the goods
- an accurate value
- the mode of transport and route of movement of the goods, and
- the EC destination.

If a taxable person in another Member State is arranging removal of the goods from the UK directly it can be difficult for a UK taxpayer as the supplier to obtain adequate proof of removal as the carrier is contracted to the recipient in the other Member State. Before zero-rating the supply, the taxpayer must ascertain what evidence of removal of the goods from the UK will be provided. Evidence must show that the goods it supplied have left the UK. Copies of transport documents alone will not be sufficient. Information held must identify the date and route of the movement of goods and the mode of transport involved.

A business must make sure that the proof of removal is:
- retained for six years, and
- made readily available so that any VAT assurance officer is able to substantiate the zero-rating of removals

A taxpayer, as the supplier of the goods, or the customer can appoint a freight forwarder, shipping company, airline or other person to handle its intra-EC supplies and produce the necessary evidence of removal. However, it remains legally responsible for ensuring that the conditions for zero-rating supplies of goods to other Member States are met. This includes obtaining and holding evidence of removal of the goods from the UK.

If a taxpayer uses a freight forwarder, consignments (often coming from several consignors) may be aggregated into one load, known as groupage or consolidation cargo. The freight forwarder must keep copies of the original bill of lading, sea-waybill or air-waybill, and all consignments in the load must be shown on the container or vehicle manifest. The taxpayer will be issued with a certificate of shipment by the freight forwarder, often supported by an authenticated photocopy of the original bill of lading, a sea-waybill or a house air-waybill. Where such consignments are being removed, the forwarder may be shown as the consignor in the shipping documents.

(a) Certificate of shipment

Certificates of shipment are usually produced by packers and consolidators involved in road, rail and sea groupage consignments when they themselves receive only a single authenticated transport document from the carrier. It is an important document, which should be sent as soon as the goods have been removed from the UK. The certificate of shipment must be an original and authenticated by an official of the issuing company unless it is computer produced, on a once-only basis, as a by-product of the issuing company's accounting system. A properly completed certificate of shipment will help businesses to meet the evidential requirements.

(b) What information must be shown?

Although the certificate of shipment can be in any format, it must be an original and will usually contain the following information:

- the name and address of the issuing company
- a unique reference number or issuer's file reference
- the name of the supplier of the goods (and VAT number if known)
- the place, port or airport of loading
- the place, port or airport of shipment
- the name of the ship or the aircraft flight prefix and number
- the date of sailing or flight
- the customer's name
- the destination of the goods
- a full description of the goods removed to another Member State (including quantity, weight and value)
- the number of packages
- the supplier's invoice number and date if known
- the bill of lading or air-waybill number (if applicable)
- the identifying number of the vehicle, container or railway wagon

Goods sent by post may be zero-rated if they are sent directly to a taxable person in another Member State, and the business holds the necessary evidence of posting.

(see *VAT Notice 725*)

11.3 Imports & Exports

11.3.1 Imports

VAT is charged and payable on the importation of goods into the UK from outside the EU but payable directly as part of the importation process and not as output tax in the VAT Return. It can, however, if allowable, be recovered as input tax in Box 4 of the VAT Return. Again, if not allowable input tax the effect is to rebalance the position in relation to partial exemption and non-business activities by excluding the input tax claim in Box 4.

There are various reliefs on the import VAT charge including on:

- zero-rated goods under Schedule 8 VAT Act 1994 (see **Appendix 8 – Zero-Rated supplies**)
- goods to be used for examination, analysis or test purposes;
- biological or chemical substances or animals for laboratory use in a relevant establishment;
- human blood and tissue products; and
- medical equipment funded by charities.

(see *VAT Notice 702*)

11.3.2 Exports

Goods which are supplied outside the EU are held to be consumed outside the EU and therefore not taxed within the EU and are zero-rated. An exporter is a person who, for VAT purposes either supplies or owns goods and exports or arranges for them to be exported to a destination outside the EU, or supplies goods to an overseas person, who arranges for the goods to be exported to a destination outside the EU. A direct export occurs when the supplier sends goods to a destination outside the EU and it is responsible either for arranging the transport itself or appointing a freight agent. An indirect export occurs when an overseas customer or their agent collects or arranges for the collection of the goods from a supplier within the UK and then takes them outside the EU.

A taxpayer must meet certain conditions before it can zero-rate supplies of goods for export including in relation to evidence (either official or commercial) it must hold to prove entitlement to zero-rating, the time limits in which the goods must be exported from the EU and the time limits in which it must obtain evidence of export to support zero-rating and only exports that comply with these conditions are eligible for zero-rating. The time limit for direct and indirect exports of goods (and obtaining evidence of export) is three months i.e. the goods must be exported within three months of the supply or VAT must be charged and for goods involved in processing or incorporation prior to export (and obtaining evidence of export) the time limit is six months or VAT must be charged.

The evidence to be retained as proof of export (whether official or commercial or supporting) must clearly identify:

- the supplier
- the consignor (where different from the supplier)
- the customer
- the goods
- an accurate value
- the export destination, and
- the mode of transport and route of the export movement.

HMRC accept that if the overseas customer arranges the export of the goods from the UK it can be difficult for a UK business as the supplier to obtain adequate proof of export as the carrier is contracted to the overseas customer. Before zero-rating the supply, a taxpayer must ascertain what evidence of export of the goods from the UK will be provided. The evidence must show that the goods supplied have left the UK. HMRC advise that if the evidence of export does not show that the goods have left the EU within the appropriate time limits, or is found upon examination to be unsatisfactory, the supplier will become liable for payment of the VAT.

Evidence of export may include the following:

- a written order from your customer which shows their name and address, and the address where the goods are to be delivered
- copy sales invoice showing the invoice number, customer's name and a description of the goods
- delivery address for the goods
- date of departure of goods from your premises and from the EC
- name and address of the haulier collecting the goods; registration number of the vehicle collecting the goods and the name and signature of the driver
- where the goods are to be taken out of the EC by an alternative haulier or vehicle, the name and address of that haulier, the registration number of the vehicle and a signature for the goods
- route, for example, Channel Tunnel, port of exit
- copy of travel tickets, and
- name of ferry or shipping company and date of sailing or airway number and airport.

Export documentation must be kept for six years and made readily available to any visiting VAT Officer. If the correct export evidence is not obtained within the appropriate time limits, then the goods supplied become subject to VAT.

(see *VAT Notice 703*)

11.4 Place of Supply of Services

For VAT purposes, the place of supply of services is the place where a service is treated as being supplied. This is the place where it is liable to VAT (if any). There are general and special rules to determine where services are supplied. Where the place of supply of services is in a Member State that supply is subject to the VAT rules of that Member State and not those of any other country. If the Member State is not the UK, the supply is outside the scope of UK VAT. Where the place of supply of services is outside the EU, that supply is made outside the EU and is therefore not liable to VAT in any Member State (although local taxes may apply). Such a supply is outside the scope of both UK and EU VAT. If the place of supply of services is the UK, a business must charge UK VAT and account for it regardless of where the customer belongs. If the place of supply of is another Member State, the taxpayer or the customer may be liable to account for any VAT due to the tax authorities of that Member State (reverse charge).

11.4.1 Place of Belonging

UK law refers to 'belonging' whereas EU law refers to 'establishment' but these two terms have the same meaning for VAT purposes. For certain types of supply the place where a supplier or customer belongs determines where services are supplied and which of them accounts for any VAT due. The place of supply of land-related services is where the land is located. The place of supply of 'where performed' services is generally the place of performance. Therefore, the place of belonging of either the supplier or the customer does not affect the place of supply of these services.

A taxpayer belongs in the UK for the purposes of either making or receiving supplies of services when any of the following apply:
- it has a business establishment or some other fixed establishment in the UK and none elsewhere;
- it has a business establishment in the UK and fixed establishments in other countries, but the UK establishment is most directly connected with making or receiving the supplies in question;
- it has a fixed establishment in the UK and a business establishment and/or fixed establishments overseas, but the UK establishment is most directly connected with making or receiving the supplies in question; or

- it has no business or fixed establishment anywhere, but the usual place of residence is the UK.

The business establishment is the principal place of business and is usually the head office, headquarters or 'seat' from which the business is run. There can be only one such place which may be an office, showroom or factory.

(see *VAT Notice 741A*)

11.4.2 General Rules

From 1 January 2010 there are two general rules for the place of supply of services, one for business to business (B2B) and one for business to consumer (B2C) supplies. There are also special place of supply rules for certain services. The B2B general rule for supplies of services is that the supply is made where the customer belongs. The B2C general rule for supplies of services is that the supply is made where the supplier belongs. For place of supply of services purposes 'B2B supplies' means supplies to businesses whose activities are wholly of a business nature. It also includes supplies to entities which have both business and non-business activities such as charities, NHS organisations and GDs. For place of supply of services purposes 'B2C supplies' means supplies to a private individual, a charity, a public or other body which has no business activities or a 'person' who receives a supply of services wholly for private purposes.

(see *VAT Notice 741A*)

11.4.3 The Reverse Charge

The reverse charge on the supply of services arises where the place of supply of services from a non-UK supplier is deemed to be the UK and the effect is to put the UK taxable person in the same position as if they had received the supply from a UK supplier. If the place of supply is the UK the output tax due on the supply is accounted for in the UK recipient taxable person's VAT Return in Box 1 and if allowable input tax, also in Box 4. If not allowable input tax the effect is to rebalance the position in relation to partial exemption and non-business activities by excluding the input tax claim in Box 4. The reverse charge does not apply to zero-rated or exempt supplies received (the place of supply is the UK and therefore the liability is that of the UK).

The key to the reverse charge is the place of supply. The general rule following significant changes effective from 1 January 2010 is that the place of supply for business to business supplies (which includes NHS organisations) is the place where the recipient taxable person is established (previously it was where the supplier was established). The place of supply is the only place the supply can be taxed. If outside the UK but within the

EU the supply is outside the scope of UK VAT but will be taxed in the other Member State, and if outside the EU it cannot be liable to VAT in any Member State. For example, if an NHS organisation provided general rule services to a business based in another Member State then the output tax would be due in the other Member State not in the UK. The supply would be outside the scope of UK VAT but any VAT incurred by the NHS organisation in making the supply would be allowable input tax under VAT Act 1994 s.26. Conversely, if an NHS organisation was the recipient of the supply the output tax would be due in the UK and accounted for in Box 1 of the VAT Return and if allowable input tax, also in Box 4 (the net value of a reverse charge supply is accounted for in boxes 6 and 7).

(see *VAT Notice 741A*)

11.4.4 Services Relating To Land

Services related to land are not subject to the general rules on the place of supply of services. The place of supply of services related to land is where the land itself is located irrespective of where it or the customer belongs.

Land includes all forms of land and property: growing crops, buildings, walls, fences, civil engineering works or other structures fixed permanently to the land or seabed. It also covers plant, machinery or equipment which is an installation or edifice in its own right, for example, a refinery or fixed oil/gas production platform. Machinery installed in buildings other than as a fixture is normally not regarded as 'land' but as 'goods'.

HMRC give the following examples of land-related services:
- the supply of hotel accommodation;
- the provision of a site for a stand at an exhibition where the exhibitor obtains the right to a defined area of the exhibition hall;
- services supplied in the course of construction, conversion, enlargement, reconstruction, alteration, demolition, repair or maintenance (including painting and decorating) of any building or civil engineering work;
- the supply of plant or machinery, together with an operator, for work on a construction site;
- services of estate agents, auctioneers, architects, solicitors, surveyors, engineers and similar professional people relating to land, buildings or civil engineering works. This includes the management, conveyancing, survey or valuation of property by a solicitor, surveyor or loss adjuster;
- services connected with oil/gas/mineral exploration or exploitation relating to specific sites of land or the seabed;

- the surveying (such as seismic, geological or geomagnetic) of land or seabed, including associated data processing services to collate the required information;
- legal services such as conveyancing or dealing with applications for planning permission;
- packages of property management services which may include rent collection, arranging repairs and the maintenance of financial accounts; and
- the supply of warehouse space.

This place of supply rule applies only to services which relate directly to specific sites or specified land or property. It does not apply if a supply of services has only an indirect connection with land, or if the land-related service is only an incidental component of a more comprehensive supply of services.

HMRC give the following examples of services which are not land-related
- repair and maintenance of machinery which is not installed as a fixture
- the hiring out of civil engineering plant on its own, which is the letting on hire of goods;
- the secondment of staff to a building site, which is a supply of staff;
- the legal administration of a deceased person's estate which happens to include property. These are lawyers' services;
- advice or information relating to land prices or property markets because they do not relate to specific sites;
- feasibility studies assessing the potential of particular businesses or business potential in a geographic area. Such services do not relate to a specific property or site; and
- services of an accountant in simply calculating a tax return from figures provided by a client, even where those figures relate to rental income.

If a taxable person registered in the UK is a recipient of these services in relation to land situated in the UK it may be required to account for the reverse charge if the supplier belongs outside the UK. If a supplier does not belong in the UK, and the customer is not registered for UK VAT, the supplier is responsible for accounting for any UK VAT due on the supply. If not already registered in the UK, there may be a liability to register as a Non-Established Taxable Person. Equally, if a taxable person registered in the UK supplies services relating to land in another Member State it may be liable to register for VAT in that Member State.

11.4.5 Services Supplied Where Performed

The place of supply of events or performance is where the event or performance takes place:

- services of sportspersons appearing in exhibition matches, races or other forms of competition;
- provision of race-prepared cars including the hire of the car and support services to ensure optimum maintenance and operation of the car throughout a series of races;
- scientific services of technicians carrying out tests or experiments in order to obtain data;
- services of an actor or singer, whether or not in front of a live audience
- services relating to conferences or meetings, services of an oral interpreter at an event, such as a meeting;
- the right to participate in an exhibition or the provision of an undefined site for a stand at an exhibition;
- services relating to a specific exhibition including carpenters and electricians erecting and fitting out stands at exhibition venues; and
- educational and training services although such services may be exempt when supplied in the UK.

(see *VAT Notice 741A*)

VAT AND THE NHS

12 MISCELLANEOUS

12.1 NHS VAT Concessions

There are several HMRC concessions currently extant in NHS VAT:

- partial exemption calculations can be completed on a retrospective annual basis rather than in each VAT Return;
- the NHS Divisional Registrations have been created on concessionary basis (see **2.2 Divisional Registrations**);
- Capital expenditure under £5,000 can be treated as repairs and maintenance for COS purposes (see **9.2 COS Capital**);
- a nursing agency can exempt the supply of nursing staff (normally standard-rated);
- drugs or pharmaceuticals supplied by a pharmacist within a hospital or nursing home can be zero-rated (see **6.6 Pharmacy Supplies**);
- supplies of relevant goods to charities can be zero-rated (see **2.8 Charities, Social Enterprises and RSLs**);
- the supply of goods to disabled persons resident in charitable institutions and other institutions by a charity can be zero-rated (see **2.8 Charities, Social Enterprises and RSLs**); and
- resuscitation training models supplied to charities and other eligible bodies for use in first aid training can be zero-rated.

Concessions are extra-statutory but HMRC is bound by the terms of a concession while it is in operation.

12.2 Supplies to Employees

Supplies by an employer to an employee for a consideration are subject to VAT in the normal way and if standard-rated, output tax is due e.g. the supply of catering to staff or car parking. Prior to *Astra Zeneca UK Ltd (CJEU C-40/09)* salary sacrificed by employees (as opposed to salary deductions) was regarded as outside the scope of VAT (and therefore no output tax was due) but from 1 January 2012 the amount of salary sacrificed is regarded as consideration for a business supply.

HMRC issued the following transitional guidance in relation to existing arrangements:

For salary sacrifice agreements that were signed or otherwise agreed by the parties on or before 27 July 2011 and which extend beyond 31 December 2011, HMRC will allow amounts of salary foregone in return for taxable benefits to continue to be free of VAT until:

(1) The date that a fixed term agreement expires or the fixed number of salary sacrifice payments specified within the agreement are completed (if the agreement expires before 1 January 2012, any agreement

subsequently entered into should follow the VAT treatment described in section 3 below); or

(2) the date of an employee's annual salary/benefits review. HMRC will regard any salary sacrifice arrangements put in place after that date as a new agreement for VAT purposes which should follow the treatment described in section 3 below. This will be the case even if the employee continues to receive the same taxable benefits as before the review; or

(3) the date of any other review or renegotiation that leads to a change in the provision of benefits under a salary sacrifice agreement or to a change in an employment contract.

Following one of the above events VAT will be due on any taxable benefits provided on or after 1 January 2012 by way of salary sacrifice.

(*Revenue & Customs Brief 36/11*)

Therefore, if the salary sacrifice agreement was entered into on or before 27 July 2011 and extends beyond 31 December 2011 there will be no change in treatment unless one of the events listed above occurs. If the agreement was entered into after 27 July 2011 then from 1 January 2012 output tax should be accounted for on any supply subject to VAT. Where the liability of the supply to the employee via salary sacrifice is zero-rated or exempt no output tax liability arises. The main change in treatment following *Astra Zeneca UK Ltd (CJEU C-40/09)* relates to leased cars as employee benefits.

12.3 Car Leasing

Until 1 January 2012 HMRC operated a simplified approach to leased cars in the NHS:

(1) where cars were leased by an NHS organisation and an employee made a contribution via salary deduction; and,

(2) where an employee made a contribution via salary sacrifice.

HMRC took the view that the 50% input tax block arising from the Value Added Tax (Cars) Order 1992 SI 1992/3122 and the Value Added Tax (Input tax) Order 1992 SI 1992/3222 did not apply in the NHS (although the 1992 Orders "de-supply" cars as a business activity, Car Leasing (including to employees) was a deemed business activity under the Treasury Directions – see **Appendix 4**). The effect of the Orders in mainstream VAT is that only 50% of input tax can be claimed in relation to a leased car but no output tax liability arises because the input tax has been blocked.

Thus, in the view of HMRC, salary deductions gave rise to an output tax charge to the NHS employee based on the private use of the vehicle (the VAT Fraction applied to the amount of the salary deduction) with 100% recovery proportionately as input tax and under *COS Heading 26*. By contrast, salary sacrifice was treated as outside the scope of VAT and therefore all of the VAT incurred could be recovered under COS Heading 26 (providing the lease included repair and maintenance) but there was no output tax liability.

However, following *Astra Zeneca UK Ltd (CJEU C-40/09)* salary sacrificed by employees previously regarded as outside the scope of VAT is now regarded as consideration for a business supply and if standard-rated, output tax is due. HMRC have not issued specific guidance to clarify the position on car leasing in the NHS post-Astra Zeneca (which has the additional complication of s.41 refunds and the repeal of VAT Act 1994 s.41(2) in Finance Act 2012).

There was no change in the treatment of salary deductions.

HMRC are currently considering simplification proposals from the HFMA. It remains an area of uncertainty and subject to review by VAT Policy.

12.4 Supplies of Staff

Supplies of staff are standard-rated. Secondments within the NHS or between the NHS and GDs are outside the scope of VAT by concession (*VAT Notice 700/34*). Secondments outside the NHS or GDs are standard-rated (e.g. to Universities, charities or local authorities).

The liability changed significantly in 2005 with the Tribunal decision in *University of Glasgow (VTD 19052)* in relation to the dual role of medical staff in the University and in the NHS. Prior to that decision, it had been accepted practice that supplies of medical staff performing medical services (including agency locums and other agency medical staff) were exempt. The Tribunal concluded that although the staff supplied did perform medical services the supply itself was one of staff and therefore standard-rated. It led immediately to a Memorandum of Understanding between HMRC and the Department of Health, NHS Employers, the Universities and Colleges Employers Association, the University and Colleges Union, British Medical Association and British Dental Association clarifying joint working arrangements which HMRC accepted as outside the scope of VAT (the Memorandum only applies to staff with honorary contracts engaged in both teaching and/or research as well as the delivery of patient care).

An incidental consequence of the Tribunal decision was that locum and medical staff agencies were obliged to charge output tax on supplies of these staff which had hitherto been viewed as exempt. These services are not eligible for COS recovery and there was therefore a significant increase in costs. The negative impact was compounded by the withdrawal of the Staff Hire Concession in 2009 which meant that in most cases output tax became chargeable on the full value of the supply rather than just the agency commission. Only supplies of agency nursing staff are eligible for COS recovery and therefore output tax became chargeable on the full value of supplies of locums, PAMS, managerial, professional & technical staff, catering, domestic and estates staff none of which was (or is) recoverable as COS.

The decision in *Reed Employment (TC01069)* reopened the issue in 2011 but the HMRC view remains that the correct VAT treatment for employment businesses is that an employment business acting as an agent only has to account for VAT on its commission whereas an employment business acting as a principal has to account for VAT on the full amount charged to clients including the wages of the temporary worker and the employers' NICs (see *VAT Information Sheet 03/09*). The decision was not appealed by HMRC and because a First Tier Tribunal Decision does not create precedent, and is only binding on the parties, HMRC do not regard it as having any wider impact. For an employment business to act as an agent it must act only as intermediary in finding work for temporary workers or finding temporary workers for clients and must not pay or arrange to pay the workers. These conditions mean that most employment businesses act as a principal. Hence, in the view of HMRC, output tax is due on the full value of the supply.

The issue was raised again in 2015 in *Adecco (TC04743)* but contrary to expectations the appeal was not allowed because in the view of the First Tier Tribunal the economic reality of the transaction must be consistent with the contracts. However, given the cost to the NHS of irrecoverable VAT on supplies of staff (and the impact on other sectors such as financial institutions, charities and private healthcare providers) it is likely that further challenges to the HMRC position will arise.

Another aspect of this is the liability of supplies of deputising doctors (i.e. locums) which is exempt under Item 5 of VAT Act 1994 Schedule 9 Group 7:

5   The provision of a deputy for a person registered in the register of medical practitioners or the register of medical practitioners with limited registration.

HMRC have resisted any attempt to treat this as an exempt supply by an employment agency and the issue was decided in their favour in *Rapid Sequence Ltd (TC02826)* in 2013.

12.5 Charitable Funds

This section deals with the trust, endowment or charitable funds of NHS organisations themselves (see **2.8 Charities, Social Enterprises and RSLs** for more information on charitable reliefs generally). HMRC takes the view that where a charitable trust is associated with an NHS organisation as sole beneficiary (and where the trustee is the body corporate discharging its responsibilities through its Board Members) then for the purposes of VAT any supplies between the associated charitable trust and the NHS organisation are disregarded for VAT purposes.

This means:

- any service, administration or other costs arising between the NHS organisation and the charitable trust are outside the scope of VAT; and

- that where the charitable trust uses its funds to purchase eligible services under s.41 then the NHS organisation may claim any COS entitlement arising.

This does not apply to external charities even where these are closely linked to an NHS organisation e.g. a "friends of" charity. In 2015 the Department of Health announced a conversion programme for NHS charities to give them an independent status outside the terms of the NHS Act 2006. Where this is implemented the charity is likely to be viewed as external by HMRC (but this can be confirmed with the NHS Compliance Team on a case-by-case basis).

There are two main categories of qualifying goods (and associated services) which may be zero-rated when purchased from charitable funds provided that the supplier is issued with the appropriate zero-rating certificate (this can be downloaded from the HMRC website) prior to the supply being made. It may be possible to claim zero-rating retrospectively but at the discretion of the supplier. The services of repair and maintenance to qualifying goods can also be zero-rated and this is often overlooked.

12.6 Aids for the Handicapped

Under Group 12 of VAT Act 1994 Schedule 8, items for personal use by a handicapped person (defined as "chronically sick or disabled") or supplied to a charity to be made available for the personal use of a handicapped person may be zero-rated provided that they are items specifically made or adapted to suit a handicapped person's condition. Such items would include medical or surgical appliances for the relief of severe abnormality or severe injury, electrically or mechanically adjusted beds for invalids, commodes, wheelchairs, chair lifts, hoists, motor vehicles designed or permanently adapted for the carriage of a person in a wheelchair or on a stretcher plus no more than five other persons, and the parts and accessories required for use with such goods (see *VAT Notice 701/7*).

12.7 Donated Medical and Scientific Equipment

Under Group 15 of VAT Act 1994 Schedule 8, the purchase (or letting or hire) by an eligible body (including the NHS) of items of medical and scientific equipment using charitable or donated funds (e.g. from another external charity including the National Lottery) may be zero-rated provided that they are used solely for medical research, training, diagnosis or treatment. In addition to medical and scientific equipment this category (relevant goods) also includes computer, video, sterilising, laboratory or refrigeration equipment plus parts or accessories, ambulances and motor vehicles designed or adapted for the carriage of handicapped persons. The repair and maintenance of relevant goods also qualifies for zero-rating provided the supply is paid for from charitable or donated funds (see *VAT Notice 701/6*).

Items which are considered to be medical and scientific equipment include such items as:

- anaesthetic apparatus, resuscitation equipment, refrigeration equipment and physiotherapy apparatus;
- surgical gloves, microscopes including electron microscopes, bandages and dressings, stethoscopes and surgical equipment;
- patient stretchers and trolleys, net suspension beds, medical waterbeds and other specialised beds, renal haemodialysis units, x-ray equipment and x-ray films;
- centrifuges, drip poles, clinical thermometers, sphygmomanometers, graduated medicine measures, laboratory glassware and plasticware;
- first aid boxes and medical kits (which may contain some ineligible items provided they are supplied as a single unit); and
- computers including peripheral units and tapes or disks specially designed for computer use.

It is advisable to maximise benefit by using charitable or donated funds for qualifying expenditure i.e. it is not an efficient use of funds to make purchases which do not qualify for zero-rating with charitable or donated funds while purchasing goods or services which do qualify with non-charitable or non-donated funds (eligibility for COS recovery should also be taken into account).

12.8 Fleming Appeals

Following *Fleming (HL 2008)* the three-year cap (now four-year cap) on retrospective claims was temporarily lifted to allow a further transitional period (*Finance Act 2008 s.121*) until 31 March 2009. This meant that any claims for overdeclared output tax or underdeclared input tax caught by the cap could be resubmitted or reactivated. In the NHS some 800 plus claims totalling £150m were submitted in three main areas: input tax on drugs supplied as part of private healthcare before 1997 following *Bupa/Wellington (BVC 251)*; output tax overpaid on cold takeaway food following *Compass Contract Services UK (CA 2006)*; and residual or other input tax claims on business activities where these had not been made at the time or had been otherwise caught by the cap.

HMRC rejected retrospection to 1973 on the basis that succession rights to VAT repayments had not transferred through the various restructures and changes of legal entity in the NHS. This was the first time this issue had been raised and was inconsistent with established practice in relation to mergers and demergers as well as being inconsistent with the general presumption in property law that rights are transferred unless specifically excluded. After maintaining this position from the outset HMRC finally conceded the issue of entitlement in 2016.

The claims related to input tax on drugs supplied as part of private healthcare failed in 2013 with *Nuffield Heath (TC02697)*.

HMRC accepted the output tax on cold takeaway food claims in principle (*Compass Contract Services UK (CA 2006)*) but subject to the succession rights issue in terms of retrospection. Partial repayments plus simple interest under VAT Act 1994 s.78 have been made and the majority of claims are now in the process of negotiated settlements.

The other input tax claims on residual business activities or capital expenditure are still resisted by HMRC and are proceeding through the First Tier and Upper Tribunals. Two of these have been decided in favour of HMRC (*NHS Greater Glasgow (TC/2011/08215)* and *NHS Lothian (UKUT 0264)*) albeit the Tribunal concluded in both cases that input tax must be due to the NHS as a finding in fact but the appeals failed because it had been impossible to prove specific quantified amounts of input tax to be repaid (even to a reasonable approximation).

12.9 Public Sector Exemption

The EU commissioned a report into the operation of VAT in the public sector across the EU and in OECD countries outside the EU which was published in March 2011 (*VAT in the Public Sector and Exemptions in the Public Interest* (EC TAXUD/2009/DE/316) (2011)). Four EU countries (including the UK) operate a public compensation scheme in relation to healthcare (i.e. refunds under s.41 in the UK) and eight in total have some form of public compensation scheme (i.e. refunds under s.33 in the UK). The EU report found that the differential treatment between public and private sector activities caused a distortion of competition contrary to EU

Law and considered various options to eliminate this distortion which it found reduced economic efficiency and welfare (because the compensation schemes are not tax and fall outside the terms of the Principal VAT Directive it would be impossible to standardise them under the tax harmonisation provisions).

The EU completed a consultation exercise and decided to take no further action but, in any case, when the UK leaves the EU the European Commission will have no locus.

12.10 Conclusion

NHS VAT is going through a period of significant change and revision. The structural and organisation changes in the NHS introduced by the Health and Social Care Act 2012 took effect in 2013 with the abolition of PCTs and the creation of Clinical Commissioning Groups (CCGs) and are still in the process of transition.

At the same time, it is HMRC policy to align public sector VAT guidance for GDs and the NHS with the objective of having a single policy applicable to all s.41 bodies. These have historically been separate and the trend appears to be towards restricting the NHS in line with the policy on GDs which, previously, has been much more subject to the discretion of the Treasury.

In parallel (and somewhat paradoxically), there is another HMRC policy to bring NHS VAT into the mainstream with the application of normal VAT rules and provisions such as penalties and assessments. While this is appropriate in a compliance context there is an inevitable conflict with the s.41 special legal regime which HMRC have not yet resolved.

The result is that the already complex technical scenario in NHS VAT is likely to become even more complex in the future.

APPENDIX 1: VAT Act 1994, Section 41

Part III - Application of Act in particular cases

41 Application to the Crown

(1) This Act shall apply in relation to taxable supplies by the Crown as it applies in relation to taxable supplies by taxable persons.

[(2) Where the supply by a Government department of any goods or services does not amount to the carrying on of a business but it appears to the Treasury that similar goods or services are or might be supplied by taxable persons in the course or furtherance of any business, then, if and to the extent that the Treasury so direct, the supply of those goods or services by that department shall be treated for the purposes of this Act as a supply in the course or furtherance of any business carried on by it.] (Repealed in Finance Act 2012)

(3) Where VAT is chargeable on the supply of goods or services to a Government department, on the acquisition of any goods by a Government department from another Member State or on the importation of any goods by a Government department from a place outside the Member States and the supply, acquisition or importation is not for the purpose—

(a) of any business carried on by the department, or

(b) of a supply by the department which, by virtue of section 41A, is treated as a supply in the course or furtherance of a business, then, if and to the extent that the Treasury so direct and subject to subsection (4) below, the Commissioners shall, on a claim made by the department at such time and in such form and manner as the Commissioners may determine, refund to it the amount of the VAT so chargeable.

(4) The Commissioners may make the refunding of any amount due under subsection (3) above conditional upon compliance by the claimant with requirements with respect to the keeping, preservation and production of records relating to the supply, acquisition or importation in question.

(5) For the purposes of this section goods or services obtained by one Government department from another Government department shall be treated, if and to the extent that the Treasury so direct, as supplied by that other department and similarly as regards goods or services obtained by or from the Crown Estate Commissioners.

(6) In this section "Government department" includes a Northern Ireland department, a Northern Ireland health and social services body, any body of persons exercising functions on behalf of a Minister of the Crown, including a health service body as defined in section 60(7) of the [1990 c. 19.] National Health Service and Community Care Act 1990, and any part of a Government department (as defined in the foregoing) designated for the purposes of this subsection by a direction of the Treasury.

(7) For the purposes of subsection (6) above, a National Health Service trust established under Part I of the [1990 c. 19.] National Health Service and Community Care Act 1990 or the [1978 c. 29.] National Health Service (Scotland) Act 1978 shall be regarded as a body of persons exercising functions on behalf of a Minister of the Crown.

(8) In subsection (6) "a Northern Ireland health and social services body" means—

    (a) a health and social services body as defined in Article 7(6) of the [S.I.1991/194.] Health and Personal Social Services (Northern Ireland) Order 1991; and

    (b) a Health and Social Services trust established under that Order.

41A supply of goods or services by public bodies

(1) This section applies where goods or services are supplied by a body mentioned in Article 13(1) of the VAT Directive (status of public bodies as taxable persons) in the course of activities or transactions in which it is engaged as a public authority.

(2) If the supply is in respect of an activity listed in Annex I to the VAT Directive (activities in respect of which public bodies are to be taxable persons), it is to be treated for the purposes of this Act as a supply in the course or furtherance of a business unless it is on such a small scale as to be negligible.

(3) If the supply is not in respect of such an activity, it is to be treated for the purposes of this Act as a supply in the course or furtherance of a business if (and only if) not charging VAT on the supply would lead to a significant distortion of competition.

(4) In this section "the VAT Directive" means Council Directive 2006/112/EC on the common system of value added tax.

(s.41A inserted in Finance Act 2012)

APPENDIX 2: Treasury (Contracting-Out) Directions

Friday 10 January 2003 Treasury Value Added Tax

The Treasury direction dated 2nd December 2002 under section 41(3) of the Value Added Tax Act 1994 as to the refund to Government departments of tax charged on the supply of goods or services or on the acquisition or importation of goods by them otherwise than for the purpose of any business carried on by them or on a supply in the course or furtherance of a business.

The Treasury, in exercise of the powers conferred on them by section 41(3) of the Value Added Tax Act 1994, hereby direct as follows:

1. This direction shall come into operation on 2nd December 2002.

2. Subject as provided in paragraph 3, a Government department listed as belonging to a category of departments listed in List 1 of this direction may claim and be paid a refund of the tax charged on:
    (a) the supply to it of any services of a description in List 2;
    (b) the supply to it of leased accommodation for more than 21 years as part of the supply to it of any services of a description in List 2; or
    (c) the supply to it or acquisition from another Member State of importation from outside the Member States by it of goods closely related to the supply to it of any services of a description in List 2.

3. A tax refund as described in paragraph 2 will only be paid if:
    (a) either the supply of those services or goods is not for the purpose of:
        (i) any business carried on by the department; or
        (ii) any supply by the department which, by virtue of directions made under section 41(2) and (5) of the Value Added Tax Act 1994,
    is treated as a supply in the course or furtherance of a business; and
    (b) the department complies with the requirements of the Commissioners of Customs and Excise both as to the time, form and manner of making the claim and also on the keeping, preservation and production of records relating to the supply, acquisition or importation in question.

4. The Treasury direction dated 7th August 2000 is hereby revoked. Philip Woolas & Jim Fitzpatrick, Two of the Lords Commissioners of Her Majesty's Treasury. (1401/49)

APPENDIX 3: Treasury (Taxing) Directions under Section 41(2),(5) and (6) of the Value Added Tax Act 1994

Business activities of Government Departments

Treasury Directions dated 29 October 2008 under section 41(2), (5) and (6) of the Value Added Tax Act 1994 (c.23) as to the supply of goods or services by Government departments.

The Treasury, in exercise of the powers conferred on them by section 41(2), (5) and (6) of the Value Added Tax Act 1994, hereby direct as follows:

1. These Directions shall come into force on 29 October 2008.

2. In these Directions—

    "the Act" means the Value Added Tax Act 1994; "Government department" has the same meaning as in section 41(6) of the Act and includes part of a Government department designated for the purposes of that section by paragraph (3) below.

    "List 1" and "List 2" mean Lists 1 and 2 respectively in these Directions.

3. Where an entry in List 1 mentions a part of a Government department, that part is hereby designated for the purposes of section 41(6) of the Act.

4. A supply by a Government department which is mentioned in List 1 of any goods or services of a description in List 2 shall be treated for the purposes of the Act as a supply in the course or furtherance of a business carried on by that department.

5. The Treasury Directions made under section 41 (2), (5) and (6) of the Value Added Tax Act 1994 on 23 May 2002 are revoked.

D Watts

T Cunningham

Two of the Lords Commissioners of Her Majesty's Treasury

(s.41(2) repealed in Finance Act 2012 – s.41A inserted)

APPENDIX 4: Treasury (Contracting-Out) Directions - List of Eligible Services (December 2002)

1. Accounting, invoicing and related services
2. Administration of the following: Career development loans, Certificates of Experience, Government support payments to the Railway Industry Pension Funds, Grants and awards, Services supplied under the Companies Acts and the Patent and Trademarks Acts, Teachers' Superannuation Scheme, Vehicle Excise Duty refunds, Winter fuel payment scheme, Inherited State Earnings Related Pension Scheme, Student Loan Scheme, Fast Track Teaching Programme
3. Administration and collection of toll charges
4. Aerial photographic surveys and aerial surveillance
5. Agricultural services of the kind normally carried out by the Farming and Rural Conservation Agency
6. Alteration, repair and maintenance of road schemes, except (a) any works carried out pursuant to an agreement made under section 278 of the Highways Act 1980, or (b) works involving construction on land not already used for road schemes.
7. Broadcast monitoring services
8. Cartographic services
9. Cash in transit services
10. Catering
11. Ceremonial services
12. Childcare services
13. Collection, delivery and distribution services
14. Computer Services supplied to the specification of the recipient, including the provision of a fully managed and serviced computer infrastructure
15. Conference and exhibition services
16. Debt collection
17. Departmental staff records and payroll systems including administration and payment of pensions
18. Employment advisory services as directed by the Race Relations Act 1976
19. Engineering and related process services
20. Environmental protection services of the kind normally carried out for the Department of the Environment, Food and Rural Affairs
21. Estate management services
22. Export intelligence services

23. Filming, audio-visual and production services
24. Health promotion activities
25. Hire of reprographic equipment including repair and maintenance
26. Hire of vehicles including repair and maintenance
27. Insolvency services
28. Interpretation and translation services
29. Issue of documents to, and control of, bingo halls and off-course bookmakers
30. Issue of documents under Wireless and Telegraphy Act
31. Laboratory services
32. Laundry services
33. Library services
34. Maintenance and care of livestock and fauna in connection with the Royal Parks
35. Maintenance, non-structural repair and cleaning of buildings
36. Maintenance and repair of civil engineering works
37. Maintenance, repair and cleaning of equipment, plant, vehicles and vessels
38. Maintenance and repair of statues, monuments and works of art
39. Medical and social surveys
40. Messenger, portering and reception services
41. Nursing services
42. Office removals
43. Operation and maintenance of static test facilities, engineering and support services and test range industrial support and security/safety services including those acquired for the purposes of research and development
44. Operation and maintenance of stores depots
45. Operation of hospitals, health care establishments and health care facilities and the provision of any related services
46. Operation of prisons, detention centres and remand centres, including medical services
47. Passenger transport services
48. Pest control services
49. Photographic, reprographic, graphics and design services
50. Preparation and despatch of forms
51. Press cutting services
52. Professional services, including those of any manager, adviser, expert, specialist or consultant
53. Provision under a PFI agreement of accommodation for office or other governmental use, together with management or other services in connection with that accommodation

54. Publicity services
55. Purchasing and procurement services
56. Radio services
57. Recruitment and relocation of staff and other related services
58. Research, testing, inspection, certification and approval work for the Health and Safety Executive
59. Scientific work of the kind normally carried out for the Department of the Environment, Food and Rural Affairs and the Food Standards Agency
60. Security Services
61. Services of printing, copying, reproducing or mailing any documents or publications, including typesetting services
62. Share Registry Survey
63. Storage, distribution and goods disposal services
64. Surveying, certification and registration in connection with ships and relevant record-keeping and verification, issue of certification, cards, discharge books and campaign medals to seamen
65. Training, tuition or education
66. Transport research of the kind normally carried out for the Department for Transport
67. Travel services, excluding hotel accommodation and fares
68. Travel and transport surveys, including traffic census counts
69. Typing, secretarial, telephonist and clerical services including agency staff
70. Waste disposal services
71. Welfare services
72. Careers guidance, mentoring and counselling to help people into work as part of the New Deal and ONE service
73. Services relating to Action Teams for Jobs and Employment Zones
74. Original research undertaken in order to gain knowledge and understanding
75. Inspection of woodland sites for approval of felling licence applications and of timber imports/imports using timber packing to prevent entry of foreign tree pests and diseases

APPENDIX 5: Treasury (Taxing) Directions - List of Business Activities (October 2008)

BUSINESS ACTIVITIES - GOODS AND SERVICES

1. Accommodation, including property acquisition and disposal and any related services
2. Administration services
3. Admission to premises and to events, e.g. entertainments, air displays etc.
4. Advertising or publicity services
5. Archives
6. Attendance of staff at court or any similar place
7. Bankruptcies and insolvency services
8. Broadcasting services
9. Catering, including supplies from vending machines
10. Car leasing
11. Community tradeable emissions allowances in return for payment pursuant to section 16 of the Finance Act 2007 where such allowances could also be obtained from the private sector
12. Computer services or goods
13. Concessions for catering or other services
14. Conferences, exhibitions and any related facilities or services
15. Construction, alteration, demolition, repair or maintenance work, civil engineering work, any related services or goods
16. Contract or procurement services
17. Copying or supply of any reproductions or of any documents
18. Copyright, patents or licences to manufacture
19. Delivery or distribution services
20. Drainage work
21. Electronic transfer of data
22. Export of goods and related services
23. Filming, replay or recording services
24. Financial and any related services
25. Fishing licences or permits
26. Fire service assistance
27. Freight transport
28. Fuel and power
29. Government car service
30. Grant, assignment or surrender of any interest in or right over land, or of any licence to do anything in relation to land
31. Grant of a right to inspect records

32. Goods, including goods manufactured within a Government department and sold to its staff and to other customers, stores, surplus or other equipment
33. Grave maintenance
34. Grounds maintenance
35. Hairdressing
36. Heating
37. Hire of vehicles, machinery or equipment, with or without operator or crew
38. Hydrographic, cartographic and similar services
39. Information or statistical services
40. Inspection services
41. Laboratory services including analysis and testing of any substance
42. Laundry services
43. Licensing, certification, authorisation or the granting of any rights other than rights over land
44. Manufacturing, assembling and other services
45. Medical services
46. Membership subscriptions
47. Meteorological and related services
48. Mineral or prospecting rights
49. Mortuary services
50. Nursery and day-care facilities
51. Occupational health services
52. Passenger transport
53. Payroll and pension administration services
54. Pest or animal control
55. Photocopying services
56. Photographic services
57. Port, airport or harbour services and related goods
58. Postal, packing or distribution services
59. Professional services, including those of any manager, adviser, expert, specialist or consultant
60. Publications
61. Radio or communication services
62. Recruitment services
63. Research, testing, experimentation, sampling or other related laboratory services
64. Repair or maintenance of machinery, equipment or other goods
65. Searches
66. Secondment of staff where such services could also be obtained from the private sector

67. Secretarial services
68. Security services and related goods
69. Shipping services
70. Slaughter, rendering and disposal of animals
71. Social services
72. Statistical services, including the collection, preparation and processing of data
73. Storage facilities and related services
74. Telecommunications
75. Training, tuition or education and any related services or goods
76. Transfer of milk quota leases
77. Translation services
78. Tree planting and afforestation
79. Vehicle conversions
80. Vehicle servicing and maintenance
81. Verification of particulars of births, marriages or deaths
82. Waste disposal
83. Water
84. Weighbridge services

APPENDIX 6: Treasury (Taxing) Directions - List Of Eligible Departments (October 2008)

GOVERNMENT DEPARTMENTS

1. Advisory, Conciliation and Arbitration Service
2. Department of Agriculture and Rural Development
3. Army Base Repair Organisation
4. Cabinet Office
5. CADW (Welsh Historic Monuments)
6. Central Office of Information
7. Charity Commission
8. Crown Office Scotland
9. Crown Prosecution Service
10. Department of Culture, Arts and Leisure
11. Department for Culture, Media and Sport
12. Communities Scotland
13. Revenue and Customs
14. Ministry of Defence
15. Defence Aviation Repair Agency
16. Defence Science and Technology Laboratory
17. Driver and Vehicle Testing Agency for Northern Ireland
18. Department for Education and Skills
19. Department of Employment and Learning
20. Department for Enterprise, Trade and Investment
21. Department of the Environment
22. Department for Environment, Food and Rural Affairs
23. ESTYN (HM Inspectorate for Education and Training in Wales)
24. Export Credits Guarantee Department
25. Office of Fair Trading
26. Department of Finance and Personnel
27. Fire Authority for Northern Ireland
28. Fire Service College
29. Office of the First Minister and Deputy First Minister
30. Food Standards Agency
31. Foreign and Commonwealth Office
32. Forensic Science Northern Ireland
33. Forensic Science Service
34. Forestry Commission
35. Office of Gas and Electricity Markets
36. General Register Office for Scotland
37. Government Actuary's Department

38. Government Car and Dispatch Agency
39. Office of Government Commerce
40. Government Communications Bureau
41. Government Communications Centre
42. Government Communications Headquarters
43. Department of Health
44. Health Authorities (including Primary Care Groups, Local Health Groups (Wales) and Community Health Councils), Special Health Authorities, Special Health Boards (Scotland), Area Health Boards (Scotland), National Health Service Trusts, Primary Care Trusts, The Common Services Agency (Scotland), Dental Practice Board)
45. Health and Safety Executive
46. Department of Health, Social Services and Public Safety
47. Historic Scotland
48. Home Office
49. Hydrographic Office
50. Department for International Development
51. Land Registry
52. Lord Chancellor's Department
53. Meteorological Office
54. National Investment and Loans Office
55. Office for National Statistics
56. National Archives of Scotland
57. National Assembly for Wales
58. Northern Ireland Assembly
59. Northern Ireland Court Service
60. Northern Ireland Education and Library Boards
61. Northern Ireland Housing Executive
62. Northern Ireland Office
63. Office of the Ombudsman
64. OGC buying.solutions
65. Ordnance Survey
66. Ordnance Survey of Northern Ireland
67. Privy Council Office
68. Public Record Office
69. Public Record Office of Northern Ireland
70. Office for the Regulation of Electricity and Gas
71. Office of the Rail Regulator
72. Department for Regional Development
73. Registers of Scotland
74. Royal Mint
75. Royal Parks

76. Scotland Office
77. Scottish Executive
78. Scottish Parliamentary Corporate Body
79. Scottish Prison Service
80. Office of the Secretary of State for Wales
81. Security Service
82. Security Services Group
83. Serious Fraud Office
84. Department for Social Development
85. Office for Standards in Education (England)
86. Office of Telecommunications
87. Department of Trade and Industry
88. Department for Transport, Local Government and the Regions
89. Queen Elizabeth II Conference Centre
90. Treasury
91. Treasury Solicitor's Department
92. Office of Water Services
93. Department for Work and Pensions

APPENDIX 7: Reduced-Rate Supplies

The main types of reduced-rate supplies (5%) are as follows:

Children's Car Seats
Applies to the supply, acquisition or importation of children's car seats.

Contraceptive Products
Applies to supplies of any product designed for the purposes of human contraception.

Domestic Fuel or Power
Applies to domestic (residential) use or use by a charity otherwise than in the course or furtherance of business.

Energy-Saving Materials: Installation
Applies to supplies of materials by an installer and installation services.

Heating Equipment, Security Goods and Gas supplies: Grant-Funded Installation or Connection
Applies to supplies of equipment by an installer and installation services (where grant funded).

Renovation and Alteration of Dwellings
Applies to supplies of qualifying services in the course of the renovation or alteration of certain buildings (where empty for two years or more).

Residential Conversions
Applies to supplies of qualifying services in relation to certain residential conversions.

Smoking Cessation Products
Applies to supplies of pharmaceutical products designed to help people stop smoking tobacco.

Women's Sanitary Products
Applies to supplies of products designed solely for use in collecting discharge from the womb or menstrual flow.

(any supply of goods or services in the UK is standard-rated unless specifically excluded)

APPENDIX 8: Zero-Rated Supplies

The main types of zero-rated supplies (0%) are as follows:

Bank Notes
Applies to the issue of bank notes.

Books etc
Applies to books and printed matter.

Caravans and Houseboats
Applies to residential caravans and houseboats (but not the supply of holiday accommodation).

Charities
Applies to the sale or letting on hire of donated goods by charities, aids for disabled persons, advertising by charities and the supply of relevant goods for medical or veterinary use or research etc.

Clothing and Footwear
Applies to children's clothing and footwear.

Construction of Buildings etc
Applies to the construction of new dwellings or buildings for a relevant residential purpose or a relevant charitable purpose.

Drugs, Medicines, Aids for the Handicapped etc.
Applies to qualifying goods.

Exports
Applies to goods which exported from the UK or removed to another EU Member State.

Food
Applies to food and groceries (but not to confectionery, soft drinks or alcohol).

Gold
Applies to supplies of gold between central banks and the London Bullion Market.

Imports
Applies to goods which would be zero-rated if supplied in the UK.

International Services
Applies to certain international services such as training supplied to an overseas government or work on goods to be exported outside the EU.

Protected Buildings
Applies to approved alterations to listed buildings (transitional period to 30th September 2015).

Sewerage Services and Water
Applies to the services of reception, disposal or treatment of foul water or the services of emptying cesspools, septic tanks or similar.

Talking Books for the Blind and Handicapped and Wireless Sets for the Blind
Applies to apparatus supplied to charities for use by blind or disabled persons.

Transport
Applies to passenger transport e.g. by bus, rail, boat or plane (but not taxis).

(any supply of goods or services in the UK is standard-rated unless specifically excluded)

APPENDIX 9: Exempt Supplies

The main types of exempt supplies are as follows:

Betting, Gaming and Lotteries
Applies to games of chance and betting.

Burial and Cremation
Applies to burial and cremation services.

Cultural Services etc
Applies to cultural services provided by public bodies or not-for-profit eligible bodies.

Education
Applies to supplies of education (e.g. by schools, colleges and Universities).

Finance
Applies to credit, bank interest, share dealing, investments, insurance and other financial services.

Fund Raising Events by charities and other Qualifying Bodies
Applies to supplies of goods and services by a charity or endowment fund in connection with a one-off fundraising event or a number of one-off events organised for charitable purposes by a charity or endowment fund.

Health and Welfare
Applies to the provision of welfare services, i.e. services directly connected with the provision of care, treatment or instruction designed to promote the physical or mental welfare of elderly, sick, distressed or disabled persons.

Insurance
(see **Finance** above)

Investment Gold
(see **Finance** above)

Land
Applies to the supply of a right over land

Postal Services
Applies to the supply of public postal services by the Royal Mail.

Sport, Sports Competitions and Physical Education
Applies to the supply of sporting services or physical recreation facilities by a not-for-profit eligible body.

Supplies of Goods (Blocked Input Tax)

Applies to supplies of goods where input tax is non-deductible.

Subscriptions to Trade Unions, Professional and other Public Interest Bodies

Applies to the provision of membership facilities by a professional, learned or representational association.

Works of Art etc

Applies to certain disposals of works of art including to approved bodies (such as the National Gallery).

(any supply of goods or services in the UK is standard-rated unless specifically excluded)

APPENDIX 10: Glossary of Terms

Attributable	Relates to a specific supply, activity or VAT liability
BA	Business Activities
BNB	Business/Non-business
Business	Within the scope of VAT
CAP	Capital Expenditure
CCG	Clinical Commissioning Group
CCS	Commissioning Support Services
CJEU	Court of Justice of the European Union
Composite Supply	Supply with a single liability where other elements of the supply are treated as incidental to the principal supply and the liability is determined by the principal supply (aka **Single Supply**)
COS	Contracted-Out Services
Direct Attribution	Wholly and exclusively attributable to a specific supply, activity or VAT liability (100%)
DH	Department of Health
EBA	Exempt Business Activities
EC	European Community
ECJ	European Court of Justice
ECN	Error Correction Notification
EDD	Effective Date of Deregistration
EDR	Effective Date of Registration
EX	Exempt
EXI	Exempt Income
FA	Finance Act
Fully Taxable	Only making Taxable Supplies
FT	Foundation Trust
GD	Government Department
HMCE	HM Customs & Excise
HMRC	HM Revenue & Customs

HMT	HM Treasury
IT	Input Tax
Indirect Attribution	Attributable to various supplies, activities or VAT liabilities (by various %)
JV	Joint Venture
LIFT	Local Improvement Finance Trust
LIFTCO	LIFT Joint Venture Company
Non-Attributable	Cannot be attributed to any specific supply, activity or VAT liability
Non-Attributable Income	Income which cannot be attributed to any specific supply, activity or VAT liability
Non-Business	Outside the scope of VAT
Non-Business Income	Income which is attributable to Non-Business activities or is outside the scope of VAT
NB	Non-Business
NBA	Non-Business Activities
NBI	Non-Business Income
NHS	National Health Service
NHS CB	NHS Commissioning Board (Authority)
NHSE	NHS England
NHSNI	NHS Northern Ireland
NHSS	NHS Scotland
NHSW	NHS Wales
OJEU	Official Journal of the European Union
OS	Outside the Scope
OT	Output Tax
P21	ProCure21
P21+	ProCure21 Plus
Partial Attribution	Sectorised attribution to a specific supply, activity or VAT liability which is neither wholly and exclusively directly attributable nor wholly non-attributable i.e. a % of attribution can be determined on an objective basis
PESM	Special Method of Partial Exemption

PEX	Partial Exemption
PFI	Private Finance Initiative
PropCo	NHS Property Services
PVD	Principal VAT Directive
Reduced-Rate	Rate of tax chargeable @ 5%
RR	Reduced Rate
Single Supply	Supply with a single liability where other elements of the supply are treated as incidental to the principal supply and the liability is determined by the principal supply (aka **Composite Supply**)
SI	Statutory Instrument
Special Method	Partial Exemption Method which has been specifically designed and requires prior approval from HMRC
SPV	Special Purpose Vehicle (PFI)
SR	Standard Rated
Standard Method	Defined Partial Exemption method which does not require prior approval from HMRC
Standard-Rated	Rate of tax chargeable @ 20%
Taxable	Within the scope of VAT and liable to the charge to tax
TBA	Taxable Business Activities
TX	Taxable
TXI	Taxable Income
VAT	Value Added Tax
VATA	Value Added Tax Act 1994
VAT Regulations	VAT Regulations 1995 SI 1995/2518
ZR	Zero-Rated
Zero-Rated	Rate of tax chargeable @ 0%

APPENDIX 11: Definitions

Business

The meaning of business is not comprehensively defined in the VAT Act 1994 or the Principal VAT Directive despite its significance to the scope of the tax. There is a partial definition in VAT Act 1994 s.94:

S.94 Meaning of "business" etc.

(1) In this Act "business" includes any trade, profession or vocation.

(2) Without prejudice to the generality of anything else in this Act, the following are deemed to be the carrying on of a business—
   (a) the provision by a club, association or organisation (for a subscription or other consideration) of the facilities or advantages available to its members; and
   (b) the admission, for a consideration, of persons to any premises.

(4) Where a person, in the course or furtherance of a trade, profession or vocation, accepts any office, services supplied by him as the holder of that office are treated as supplied in the course or furtherance of the trade, profession or vocation.

(5) Anything done in connection with the termination or intended termination of a business is treated as being done in the course or furtherance of that business.

(6) The disposition of a business as a going concern, or of its assets or liabilities (whether or not in connection with its reorganisation or winding up), is a supply made in the course or furtherance of the business.

A series of tests (now collectively known as "the business test" was summarised in *Lord Fisher (QB 1981)*:

- is the activity a "serious undertaking earnestly pursued" or a "serious occupation not necessarily confined to commercial or profit making undertakings"?
- is the activity an occupation or function actively pursued with reasonable or recognisable continuity?
- does the activity have a certain measure of substance as measured by the quarterly or annual value of taxable supplies?
- is the activity conducted in a regular manner and on sound and recognised business principles?
- is the activity predominantly concerned with the making of taxable supplies to consumers for a consideration?
- are the taxable supplies of a kind which are commonly made by those who seek to profit by them?
- are others are carrying on the same type of activity and clearly doing so on a commercial basis?

Profit of itself is not definitive in determining whether an activity is carried on in the course or furtherance of business. Until the repeal of VAT Act 1994 s.41(2) in Finance Act 2012, NHS organisations and Government Departments were subject to the Treasury Direction on deemed Business Activities and therefore activities which may not have been carried on in the course or furtherance of business were treated as business activities in the NHS. HMRC now rely on s.4, s.94 and Article 13 of the Principal VAT Directive.

Supply

There is no specific definition of supply in the VAT Act 1994 or EU law but it includes all forms of supply but not anything done otherwise than for a consideration (e.g. services provided for no consideration). A supply must be a supply of goods or of services to fall within the scope of the tax and Treasury may, by Order, deem any transaction to be a supply of goods or of services or vice versa. Alternatively, a supply may be neither a supply of goods nor services and thus outside the scope of the tax e.g. transfer of a going concern.

A supply with various components may be either a single (or composite) supply or a multiple (or mixed) supply. This was clarified in *Card Protection Plan Ltd (CJEU C-349/96)*: regard had to be given to all of the circumstances; a supply must normally be regarded as distinct and independent; a supply should not be artificially split; and, where there are component elements consideration should be given as to whether each component supply could be regarded as a principal supply or whether merely ancillary (but a single price is not definitive).

Consideration

Consideration is not defined in the VAT Act 1994 or the Principal VAT Directive but is given the following meaning in the EC Second Directive (normally relied upon):

"everything received in return for the supply of goods or the provision of services, including incidental expenses (packing, transport, insurance etc.) that is to say not only the cash amounts charged, but also, for example, the value of goods received in exchange or, in the case of goods or services supplied by order of a public authority, the amount of compensation received"

Thus, the definition is very wide and includes barter or an exchange of services etc. Consideration does not have to be a monetary payment but it must be capable of expression in a monetary value. Also, for a payment to be a consideration within the scope of the tax there must be a direct and immediate link to the supply.

VAT Fraction

To avoid arithmetic variations, the VAT Fraction is a specified proportion (of the gross amount):

20% = 1/6 (i.e. equivalent to 20/120)

5% = 1/21 (i.e. equivalent to 5/105)

15% = 3/23 (i.e. equivalent to 15/115)

17.5% = 7/47 (i.e. equivalent to 17.5/117.5)

APPENDIX 12: References

Statutes
Principal VAT Directive 2006/112/EC

Value Added Tax Act 1994

VAT Regulations 1995 (SI 1995/2518)

Publications
VAT in the Public Sector and Exemptions in the Public Interest (EC TAXUD/2009/DE/316) (2011)

Managing Public Money (HM Treasury) (July 2013)

VAT Manuals
VATSC03100 – Basic Principles and Underlying Law: Scope of VAT

VATGPB2000 – Bodies Governed by Public Law

VATGPB3000 – Non-Business Activities

VATGPB9000 – Government Departments and Health Authorities

VAT Notices
VAT Notice 700 The VAT Guide

VAT Notice 701/2 Welfare

VAT Notice 701/5 Clubs & Associations

VAT Notice 701/16 Water and Sewerage Services)

VAT Notice 701/30 Education & Vocational Training

VAT Notice 701/40 Food Processing Services

VAT Notice 701/47 Culture

VAT Notice 701/49 Financial Services

VAT Notice 702 Imports

VAT Notice 703 Exports

VAT Notice 706/1/1 Partial Exemption

VAT Notice 706/1/2 Capital Goods Scheme

VAT Notice 708 Buildings & Construction

VAT Notice 725 The Single Market

VAT Notice 727 Retail Schemes

VAT Notice 741A Place of Supply of Services

VAT Notice 742 Land and Property

VAT Notice 742A Option to Tax

VAT Guidance

A Step by Step Guide to VAT Online Filing for Government Departments and NHS Trusts (HMRC 2010)

HMRC Guidance Notes for Government Departments 7th Edn 2012

Websites

www.hmrc.gov.uk

www.legislation.gov.uk

Public Bodies Group

HM Revenue & Customs
NHS Compliance Team
Euston Tower
286 Euston Road
London
NW1 3UL

VAT Supply Team
HM Revenue & Customs
VAT Supply Team
100 Parliament Street
London
SW1A 2BQ

INDEX

VAT guides from Spiramus

VAT and Government Departments   By Martin Kaney

A reference manual and a practical guide for those managing VAT in Government Departments, their advisers and key suppliers. Government Department VAT has recently been the subject of an HMRC consultation and review with new guidance published in 2015.

Paperback 9781907444098 **PDF** 9781904905431 176 pages **Price: £69.95**

VAT and Property - Guidance on the application of VAT to UK property transactions and the property sector   By Ann Humphrey

This book offers clear and practical guidance on the application of VAT to property transactions providing assistance to individuals, property businesses and professionals. It covers guidance on VAT and property issues including: residential, commercial, charitable and mixed-use property, housing associations, protected buildings, and caravans. VAT refund schemes, the capital goods scheme and TOGC issues are also covered. Includes detailed HMRC guidance and forms on CD-ROM

Paperback 9781904905608 **PDF** 9781904905745 280 pages **Price: £75.00**

Trading Places? VAT and Customs Treatment of Imports, Exports, Intra-EU Transactions, and Cross -border supplies of Services in the Digital Age   By Andrew Rimmer

introduces the main concepts and trade facilitation reliefs that businesses must understand if they are to trade internationally with the least intervention and disruption from the Tax Authorities. The book highlights the means of importing goods and arriving at the Customs value on which import duty and import VAT are computed. It also provides commentary on export procedures and the VAT treatment of intra-EU trading, including potential fiscal barriers to exploiting non-UK markets.

This second edition introduces the myriad rules concerning intangible services and the taxation of downloaded digitised products. Whilst the rules can be said to be easy to follow, as ever with VAT understanding the exact nature of the service, how it is provided, and where it is consumed are all fundamental problems to be grappled with.

It also covers the Union Customs Code, which came into effect on 1 May 2016.

Paperback 9781910151327 **PDF** 9781910151334 440 pages **Price: £74.95**